CW00808746

NORTH AMERICAN

AMERICAN

INDIGENOUS WARFARE
AND RITUAL VIOLENCE

NORTH AMERICAN INDIGENOUS WARFARE and RITUAL VIOLENCE

Edited by Richard J. Chacon and Rubén G. Mendoza

The University of Arizona Press   Tucson

 THE UNIVERSITY OF
ARIZONA PRESS

© 2007 The Arizona Board of Regents
All rights reserved

www.uapress.arizona.edu

Library of Congress Cataloging-in-Publication Data
North American indigenous warfare and ritual violence /
edited by Richard J. Chacon and Rubén G. Mendoza.
   p. cm.
  Includes bibliographical references and index.
  ISBN 978-0-8165-2532-4 (hardcover : alk. paper)
   1. Indians of North America—Warfare. 2. Indians of North
America—Rites and ceremonies. 3. Violence—North America.
4. Social archaeology—North America. 5. North America—
Antiquities. I. Chacon, Richard J., 1959– II. Mendoza, Rubén G.
E98.W2N67 2007
970.004'97–dc22   2007011043

Frontispiece: A Cahokia-style drilled figurine showing an armored
warrior smashing the face of a victim with a club. (Conquering Warrior
pipe from the collections of the National Museum of the American
Indian, Smithsonian Institution; photo by David Heald, courtesy of the
Illinois Transportation Archaeological Research Program)

Manufactured in the United States of America on acid-free, archival-
quality paper and processed chlorine free.

16 15 14 13 12   7 6 5 4 3 2 1

CONTENTS

Acknowledgments   vii

Introduction   3
>   Richard J. Chacon and Rubén G. Mendoza

1   Traditional Native Warfare in Western Alaska   11
>   Ernest S. Burch Jr.

2   "Barbarism and Ardour of War from the Tenderest Years":
Cree-Inuit Warfare in the Hudson Bay Region   30
>   Charles A. Bishop and Victor P. Lytwyn

3 Aboriginal Warfare on the Northwest Coast: Did the Potlatch Replace Warfare? 58

   Joan A. Lovisek

4 Ethnohistoric Descriptions of Chumash Warfare 74

   John R. Johnson

5 Documenting Conflict in the Prehistoric Pueblo Southwest 114

   Polly Schaafsma

6 Cahokia and the Evidence for Late Pre-Columbian War in the North American Midcontinent 129

   Thomas E. Emerson

7 Iroquois-Huron Warfare 149

   Dean R. Snow

8 Desecrating the Sacred Ancestor Temples: Chiefly Conflict and Violence in the American Southeast 160

   David H. Dye and Adam King

9 Warfare, Population, and Food Production in Prehistoric Eastern North America 182

   George R. Milner

10 The Osteological Evidence for Indigenous Warfare in North America 202

   Patricia M. Lambert

11 Ethical Considerations and Conclusions Regarding Indigenous Warfare and Violence in North America 222

   Richard J. Chacon and Rubén G. Mendoza

References 233

About the Contributors 275

Index 279

ACKNOWLEDGMENTS

I wish to thank my good friend Rubén Mendoza for the pleasure of working together on this volume. Much appreciation goes to Don McVicker, who aided in organizing the "Problems in Paradise" symposium on Amerindian violence at the 2003 American Anthropological Association meeting in Chicago. I am most appreciative of the many scholars who entrusted me with their work in this endeavor. I am also deeply indebted to my friend and colleague David Whitely, who played an instrumental role in the genesis and implementation of both the session and this edited volume. In addition, I would like to thank the two anonymous reviewers who provided valuable critiques.

I am grateful to all the people at Winthrop University who were supportive of this project, especially the dean of the College of Arts and

Sciences, Debra Boyd, who generously provided financial assistance to defray the expenses associated with the manuscript's publication. I also wish to acknowledge Douglas Eckberg, chair of Winthrop's Department of Sociology and Anthropology, and Jonathan Marx, interim chair, for their continued backing of my research. This project benefited greatly from the diligent efforts of Douglas Short, Carrie Volk, and the entire Inter-Library Loan (ILL) staff of Winthrop University's Dacus Library, who succeeded at securing some of the most obscure documents ever published. I also received indispensable computer technical support from Campus Information Technology personnel, particularly Taylor Glass and Joseph Martin.

I wish to thank Patricio Moncayo (Pontifica Universidad Catolica de Ecuador) for years of friendship and collaboration. Also, much gratitude is extended toward Steve Nelson and his wife, Dorothy, for their gracious hospitality while I was in Ecuador. Lastly, I would like to thank my lovely wife, Yamilette Chacon, for her indefatigable support (academic, technical, and emotional). Without her assistance, this project would have never come to fruition.

Richard J. Chacon

I would like to acknowledge the many scholars and students who have informed my perspective on the question of indigenous ritual violence and conflict in the Americas. I am particularly indebted to my good friend Richard Chacon, whose diligence and determination to see through both the "Problems in Paradise" symposium and the creation of this volume proved both an inspiration and the beginning of a long-term collaboration. Moreover, I am particularly indebted to the many scholars who contributed significant new findings and research for the "Problems in Paradise" symposium. I also wish to thank the dean of the College of Arts and Sciences at Winthrop University, Debra Boyd, for her provision of a publication subvention when California State University–Monterey Bay was not in a position to fund my editorial treatment of the manuscript prior to submission to the University of Arizona Press.

At California State University–Monterey Bay, Lilly Martinez

continues to provide critical clerical and administrative support and department chair George Baldwin remains extraordinarily committed to creating a collegial and scholarly research and teaching environment for the faculty of the Social and Behavioral Sciences. Donaldo Urioste of CSU–Monterey Bay and Charlie Cambridge of Metropolitan State College of Denver provided invaluable feedback on many of the ideas presented in my chapter on Neo-Mexika revisionism, as well as offering suggestions pertaining to the introductory and concluding chapters of this volume. Eddy Hogan and the staff of the CSU–Monterey Bay Library are to be commended for their extraordinary efforts on behalf of this and related projects via Interlibrary Loan requests and other research support. I also wish to acknowledge CSU–Monterey Bay student Genetta Butler, who assisted with word processing and related typescript revisions necessary to the completion of the introductory and concluding portions of the manuscript.

Finally, I acknowledge my wife and companion, Linda Marie Mendoza, and my daughters, Natalie Dawn Marie and Maya Nicole Mendoza, for their generous understanding, ongoing support, and the many personal sacrifices made in support of my many research and writing projects.

Rubén G. Mendoza

NORTH AMERICAN

AMERICAN

INDIGENOUS WARFARE
AND RITUAL VIOLENCE

INTRODUCTION

Richard J. Chacon and Rubén G. Mendoza

The goal of this volume is to explore those uniquely human motivations and environmental variables that underlie the question of why the native peoples of North America have engaged in warfare and ritual violence since precontact times. Both American popular culture and less-than-accurate scholarly characterizations of the Amerindian past have come to dominate a contrasting body of public perceptions regarding North American indigenous warfare and ritual violence. As a result, a fundamental challenge to the status quo now threatens to topple cherished assumptions and misguided beliefs that inform the collective consciousness of many Westerners and thereby serve as the edifice on which the archetype of the Noble Savage is erected. A sort of cognitive dissonance reverberates throughout the academy and serves to deepen a philosophical divide that spans centuries of scholarship and popular lore. On one side of this divide stand those who dogmatically adhere to the endemic cultural "reality" of Amerindian warfare and ritual violence; on the other stand those revisionists who seek to co-opt the argument altogether. For those attempting an impartial, or reasonably impartial, assessment of Amerindian violence, the landscape of competing social, cultural, and nationalistic interests and agendas has become increasingly volatile and highly politicized.

To address the prevailing challenges, a distinguished group of interdisciplinary scholars came together to review the archaeological, ethnohistorical, ethnographic, and forensic evidence for indigenous armed conflict and ritual violence in North America. This volume, the result of our effort, ventures well beyond the essential questions and revisionist works that challenge the very notion that Amerindians ever engaged in significant levels of organized violence prior to the European invasions. As contributors, we individually and collectively explore those causes and consequences that underlie indigenous conflict in North America both past and present. Although warfare has been defined in a variety of ways, we adopt the definition of warfare as "socially organized armed combat between members of different territorial units (communities or aggregates of communities)" (Ember and Ember 1994a, 190). To accommodate the broader theme of conflict and violence in North America, we have chosen to supplement the aforementioned definition so as to specify, and thereby include, cultural, religious, ideological, political, and economic motivations as well.

Our collective assessment of the data clearly indicates that armed conflict and ritual violence are of considerable antiquity in North America. Warfare was ubiquitous; every major culture area of native North America reviewed herein has produced archaeological, ethnohistorical, osteological, or ethnographic evidence of armed conflict and ritual violence.

It would be unreasonable and naïve to attempt in this context to propose any given primary cause or set of variables for the evolution and persistence of warfare and ritual violence in native North America. Theoretical discussions concerned with indigenous combat and ritual violence in North America necessarily require consideration of the region's tremendous ecological and cultural diversity. Concomitantly, we acknowledge the fact that the human motivations for going to war in any given context may vary dramatically and change through time.

Rather than risk promoting a monolithic explanation for any and all forms of warfare, we collectively assess the evidence for those patterns that belie the root causes of intergroup conflict by considering the evidence for organized violence in each North American culture area on a case-by-case basis. We believe that this approach most effectively brings to the fore the causes and consequences of armed conflict and ritual violence for those case studies. Moreover, this treatment will serve as an impetus to further research centered on theory building and the quest for the essential dynamics underlying warfare and ritual violence in North America more generally.

Because armed conflict and religious violence were continent-wide phenomena, we have endeavored to be as inclusive as possible by featuring those scholarly contributions that cogently reflect current research trends from nearly all major culture areas of native North America. This consideration was at the heart of the assembling of a distinguished cohort of scholars for a recent symposium on the theme of war and ritual violence in the Americas. Relevant symposium papers solicited by invitation of the senior editor were originally presented before the 2003 annual meetings of the American Anthropological Association in Chicago, Illinois. Findings were featured within the context of an interdisciplinary symposium titled "Problems in Paradise." Our prime objective at that time was to review a spate of recent findings that challenge revisionist arguments regarding the question of human conflict and ritual violence in aboriginal America. A secondary aim was to explore evidence germane to the understanding of the fundamental dynamics underlying Amerindian warfare. Ultimately, so successful was our call for papers on this theme that the day-long symposium had to be divided into North American and Latin American sections, just as the publication of this research required two volumes. Contributors subsequently revisited the preliminary insights and observations presented within the context of the "Problems in Paradise" symposium to more thoroughly interrogate the evidence and challenge the antithetical and divisive views of the radical revisionists. The characteristic revisionist perspective on aboriginal America is exemplified by that of Russell Means and Marvin Wolf, who describe precontact indigenous warfare in idealized terms by arguing, "Before the whites came, our conflicts were brief and almost bloodless, resembling far more a professional football game than the lethal annihilations of European conquest" (1995, 16).

In chapter 1, Ernest S. Burch Jr. acknowledges that warfare was but a single, albeit particularly significant, dimension of the traditional Arctic way of life. He cites patterns of retaliation and revenge as the primary inducements to violent conflict, and he finds that neither the acquisition of territory nor the desire for Western trade goods necessarily underlay such aggression. In point of fact, Burch found that contrary to the oft-stated role of Western incursions and influence in exacerbating hostilities, traditional forms of intergroup conflict actually ended during the early contact period.

In chapter 2, Charles A. Bishop and Victor P. Lytwyn examine patterns of Lowland Cree–Inuit warfare and find that such conflict predates the arrival of European colonials. They go on to document postcontact change in the patterns and sources of warfare that have been identified in those contexts. The authors illustrate that from a Cree perspective, warfare had little to do with questions of territoriality. Bishop and Lytwyn advance the claim that access to Western trade goods inadvertently served to suppress indigenous warfare in those instances in which outsiders clearly favored exchange relationships with one group over another. The authors maintain that the prime motives for warfare entailed mutual mistrust attributable to irreconcilable ethnic differences, as well as arising from Lowland Cree misfortunes born of postcontact ecological change attributed to Inuit sorcery.

In chapter 3, Joan A. Lovisek reevaluates Helen Codere's (1950) assertion that the Northwest Coast potlatch replaced warfare; Lovisek concludes that the potlatch was rooted in a secularized reformulation of the Winter Ceremonial. Moreover, she contends that Northwest Coast warfare predates European contact and has its origins in raiding activity motivated by the quest for revenge, territorial imperatives, and prestige borne of human trophy-taking or headhunting. The author acknowledges that the Winter Ceremonial provided a ritualized venue within which the taking of human trophies was sanctioned and encouraged. Lovisek goes on to argue that the participation of Northwest Coast peoples in the Western fur trade radically transformed the scale and intensity of traditional native warfare. Accordingly, the author describes how patterns of warfare shifted from raiding based on revenge, and a desire to acquire prestige goods and status, to an extremely violent pattern of engagements arising from unequal access to foreign trade goods and the quest for war booty, revenge killings, status intensification, and slaves.

In chapter 4, John R. Johnson undertakes the examination of the documentary evidence for patterns of armed conflict and violence once prevalent among Chumash Indian coastal versus inland mountain villages of southern California. The author traces such conflict to motives born of revenge, subsistence stress and competition, and accusations of sorcery. The resulting violence sometimes entailed the mutilation of fallen enemies. Johnson's findings include revelations regarding the complexity of Chumash intertribal relations and conflict interaction, such as how the neighboring Yokuts might suffer the consequences of Chumash raiding activity yet serve as allies to the Chumash in subsequent engagements with common enemies. In addition, the author explores a correlation between postmarital residential patterns and warfare for further indications pertaining to the causes and consequences of warfare in early California.

In chapter 5, Polly Schaafsma provides a valuable overview of the visual evidence for indigenous warfare in the Pueblo Southwest. By analyzing prehistoric rock art and kiva mural images in the light of ethnohistorical and ethnographic data, she provides an ideological template for the undertaking of war. Significantly, she traces various southwestern beliefs linking warfare and fertility to Mesoamerica.

In chapter 6, Thomas E. Emerson's study of Mississippian warfare for the period AD 900–1400 concerns the archaeological recovery of disturbing evidence from mass interments of war captives and/or sacrificial victims. According to the author, recent findings reveal that pre-contact-era hostilities resulted in the massacre and mutilation of hundreds of men, women, and children. The skeletal evidence of intensive warfare is also supported by the erection of fortifications, iconographic depictions of warriors, and warfare-induced regional social and political reorganizations. Emerson argues that the emergence of complex chiefdoms or incipient states, such as Cahokia, transformed regional conflict from short-lived and relatively small scale interactions into formally organized, relatively large scale, and vastly more intensive and bellicose patterns of internecine warfare.

In chapter 7, Dean R. Snow contends that precontact Iroquoian warfare was fueled in large part by the quest for revenge. In the sixteenth century, the League of the Iroquois was established as a collective response to intratribal hostilities. In the century that followed, the Iroquois sought trade relationships with various European colonial powers to exchange furs for guns. Such trade led to an increase in raiding activity by non-League nations during the course of the seventeenth century. Snow explains that such conflict heightened the demand for war captives and human trophies. This was in turn exacerbated by population losses arising from the epidemics of the time, coupled with the desire to acquire status goods and prestige items. In the eighteenth century, a surrogate for war and intertribal or intratribal conflict materialized as status and prestige could then be enhanced by the accumulation of monetary wealth and luxury goods. The rise and consolidation of power by European colonists eventually brought an end to intertribal warfare between the American Indian tribes and nations of the region.

In chapter 8, David H. Dye and Adam King review evidence from a multidisciplinary body of findings in an effort to demonstrate that Mississippian elites of the Southeast vied with one another for power and prestige through the desecration and destruction of the ancestral shrines of rivals. These sacred locations often contained the remains of chiefly ancestors, sumptuary art and elite grave goods, and related ritual paraphernalia. These items in turn were deemed to represent the physical manifestations of a ruler's political power and authority. The desecration of one's ancestral shrine thereby served to undermine the affected leader's claims to the divine right to rule. Dye and King conclude that ethnohistorical accounts of southeastern warfare are in turn corroborated by the available archaeological and osteological findings.

In chapter 9, George R. Milner demonstrates that Eastern Woodlands war and conflict varied over time and space and was affected by the sociopolitical milieu in which it was manifest. Significantly, extant osteo-logical evidence indicates that Archaic hunter-gatherers of the region fought one another with considerable frequency. Milner contends that the first widespread use of cultigens is correlated with evidence for a several-century decline in conflict and violence in the region beginning two thousand years ago. Several lines of data indicate a dramatic resur-gence in armed conflict after that hiatus among the competing tribes and chiefdoms of the region. At the same time, the southern portion of the Eastern Woodlands was characterized by well-organized chiefdoms capable of mounting large-scale attacks. By contrast, in the northern por-tion of the Eastern Woodlands, combat was often instigated or directed by tribal headmen who conducted themselves in presumably less for-mally organized and certainly lower-intensity military engagements.

In chapter 10, Patricia M. Lambert's study of the osteological evi-dence for prehistoric violence and conflict in North America unequivo-cally illustrates that armed conflict was both ancient and widespread. Moreover, analysis of casualty counts indicates that small-scale inter-tribal raids could very well result in large numbers of casualties and extraordinarily high mortality rates. Significantly, Lambert reports that for the region as a whole, the intensity of war and conflict peaked between AD 1000 and 1400, long before the advent of European expansion in North America. Lambert contends that the continent-wide escalation of war and conflict may be correlated with the ever-changing dynam-ics of regional population density and carrying capacity, which in turn coincide with major environmental perturbations, including the onset of the medieval Wurm and Little Ice Age climatic episodes.

In chapter 11, Richard J. Chacon and Rubén G. Mendoza explore the ethical issues raised when evidence for Amerindian warfare and ritual violence is published. Conversely, we discuss those ramifications that stem from the reticence of or refusal by some scholars to report indigenous armed conflict and ritual violence. Additionally, we summa-rize key findings regarding aboriginal warfare and ritual native violence advanced by the contributors to this volume. As editors, we hope that the following chapters provide insight into and serve as a stimulus for further research on Amerindian warfare and ritual violence in North America.

1 TRADITIONAL NATIVE WARFARE IN WESTERN ALASKA

Ernest S. Burch Jr.

Early-contact-period Eskimos are typically portrayed in Western literature as having been happy, peaceful, honest, smiling people who were friendly toward strangers. Alaskan Eskimos, however, described their ancestors to me as having been quarrelsome and warlike, and they supported that general view with numerous accounts of specific raids and battles.[1] The experiences and observations of early Western observers in the region (e.g., Beechey 1831, 2:303; Kotzebue 1821, 1:211; VanStone 1977, 81; 1988, 30, 40, 91, 94) corroborate what my informants told me. The oral and documentary sources combined show that relations between and among Alaska Native societies were variously neutral, friendly, and hostile, but hostility was widespread and serious enough to keep everyone in western Alaska in a constant state of preparedness for war.

The purpose of this chapter is to present a summary of what is known about the causes, nature, and consequences of hostile intersocietal relations in the western part of Alaska during the early contact period. I define that period as being roughly 1775 to 1850, beginning and ending somewhat earlier in the south than in the north.

THE GEOGRAPHIC SETTING

The region covered by this chapter is shown in figure 1.1. It is approximately 1,000 kilometers from east to west and 1,330 kilometers from north to south. Its far northern location, indicated by the broken line showing the Arctic Circle, had a number of implications of both strategic and tactical significance. At Pt. Barrow, the northernmost point on the map, fresh water froze in late September or early October and remained frozen until late May or early June.[2] Freezeup brought boat travel to a halt, but it also turned fresh water into an extension of the land, enabling people to walk overland in just about any direction. Also at Pt. Barrow, there are about two months every year in which there is no sunlight and more than three months during which there is little or no darkness (the difference owing to refraction). Temperature and light conditions became progressively less extreme as one moved south across the region, but seasonal environmental fluctuations were everywhere more pronounced here than in most other parts of the inhabited world.

Western Alaska straddles the tundra/forest ecotone. The dotted lines in figure 1.1 show the location of the main continental tree line as well as the largest "forest islands" located beyond it. Outside the forested region, the country is covered with tundra vegetation, which generally is under fifty centimeters in height except along waterways and in protected, well-drained locations, where shrubs can reach a height of three or four meters or more. Extensive areas of tundra and muskeg also lie within the forest zone, particularly at higher elevations.

Western Alaska is characterized by diverse landscapes ranging from extensive lowlands to rugged, heavily glaciated uplands (see Spencer et

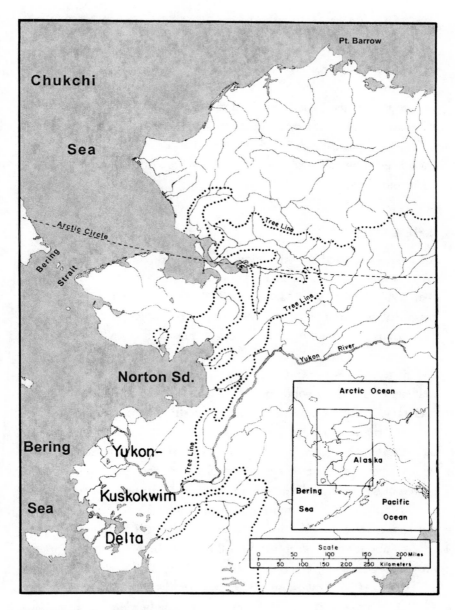

FIGURE 1.1 Western Alaska.

al. 2002 for an environmental summary). Over most of the region, rivers and streams flow through relatively well defined drainages. An exception is the Yukon-Kuskokwim (Y-K) Delta, in the southwestern sector of the study region. This is an area where the deltas of two large rivers merge. It is generally flat, poorly drained country covered by countless lakes and ponds and crossed by myriad rivers, sloughs, and creeks. It is a dynamic landscape in which watercourses change frequently during the spring snowmelt and in which villages are often flooded, leading to their relocation.

THE ETHNIC SETTING

The region covered by this study has been inhabited by Eskimo and Athapaskan speakers for at least the past two thousand years (Ackerman 1998; Clark 1981; Mason 1998, 2000; Shaw 1998), although the precise distribution of the different peoples has of course fluctuated over time. Language borders as of the beginning of the nineteenth century are shown in figure 1.2.

The map is presented simply as a general guide to the ethnic makeup of the study population during the relevant time period. Intersocietal violence was at least as common within language zones as it was between them. Furthermore, intersocietal conflict followed the same basic strategy and tactics throughout most of the region, regardless of which language group was involved, although the specifics of conflict played out somewhat differently in different environmental settings.

Bilingualism and multilingualism were common near language borders, as were the diffusion of ideas and goods. It is important when reading about war to keep in mind that violence was by no means the only form of intersocietal contact (Burch 1988, 2005; Clark 1977; Clark and Clark 1976; Townsend 1979, 164, 166; VanStone 1978, 14–15; 1979a). In a few areas, relations across language borders had been conducted on reasonably friendly terms for such a long time that, by the beginning of the study period, whether the inhabitants were Athapaskan or Eskimo was unclear (Burch et al. 1999; Osgood 1940, 29, 31, 33, 62, 63; Townsend 1979).

The inhabitants of each language zone were divided among a

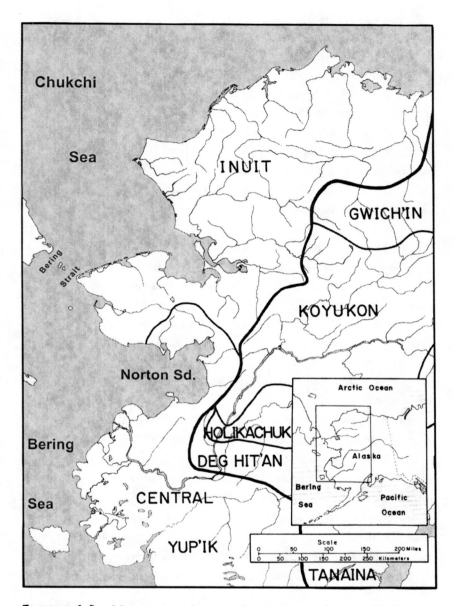

FIGURE 1.2   Major nineteenth-century linguistic areas of western Alaska.
Eskimo languages are to the left of the heavy line; Athapaskan languages are to the
right. Data from Burch 1998a; Krauss 1982; VanStone and Goddard 1981.

number of societies ranging from about 300 to perhaps 2,000 members, each of which was "segmental" (Service 1975, 70) in structure. All of the societies in the region were based on a hunter-gatherer economy.

In the northern and eastern sectors of the study region, the members of each society exercised dominion (Radcliffe-Brown 1952, 34) over a discrete estate having relatively well defined borders (Burch 1998a; 1998b, 9, 309–12; Ray 1967, 372, 376). These borders appear to have been relatively stable over periods of several generations, possibly even centuries in some instances. In the Y-K Delta, by contrast, estate borders seem to have been rather poorly defined (Fienup-Riordan n.d.; 1984, 64–65; Pratt 1984a, 46–47, 57–58). The societies in that region seem to have had well-defined heartlands in the form of one or two large winter villages, but just which society exercised dominion over what land beyond that heartland became progressively less certain as one moved away from the main village(s). The lack of clear-cut borders was probably a consequence of poor drainage definition and frequent landscape changes caused by erosion or alluviation (Pratt 1984b, 27–28).

The members of each society exercised dominion over a more or less discrete estate, but that did not mean that they had exclusive use of that estate. There were three basic contexts in which people ventured beyond their own borders (Burch 2005, 26–33). The first is what I call an easement, which gave certain people the right, based on ancient custom, to cross or use all or a portion of another society's estate at particular times and for particular purposes every year. The second is what I call license, which involved people seeking and receiving permission to use or cross another society's estate for a particular purpose on a one-time basis. The third is trespass, which included any use of foreign territory that did not meet the requirements of easements and licenses. Trespass was considered a hostile act and, if discovered, was met with force.

THE DATA

The data on which this chapter is based include (1) the observations and experiences of Western visitors to the region in the late eighteenth and early nineteenth centuries, (2) information acquired from Alaska Native historians by social scientists during the twentieth century, and (3) information generated during the investigation of historical and cemetery sites following passage of the Alaska Native Claims Settlement Act of 1971. The major compilations of the relevant data are the following: on (Alaskan) Inuit Eskimos, Burch 1974 and 2005, Ostermann and Holtved 1952 (pages 12–13, 19), Rasmussen 1933 (306–7), and Sheehan 1995 and 1997 (32–34, 43–50, 62–65); on Central Yup'ik Eskimos, Fienup-Riordan 1988 (29–50), 1989, 1990 (153–60), and 1994, Kurtz 1984, Michael ed. 1967 (281), Nelson 1899 (241, 264, 327–30), O'Leary 1995, Oswalt 1967 (185–86), VanStone 1967 (109, 118–19), 1973 (52–53), 1979b (70–72), and 1988 (30–31, 45, 91, 94); on the Deg Hit'an/Holikachuk Athapaskans, Michael 1967 (247, 292n42) and Osgood 1940 (207–10), 1958 (63–65), and 1959 (77); on the Gwich'in Athapaskans, McKennan 1933 and 1965 (36–37, 67–70), Osgood 1936 (86–90), and Slobodin 1960 (81–82); on the Koyukon Athapaskans, Clark 1974 (186–203); and on the Tanaina Athapaskans, Osgood 1937 (109–13) and Townsend 1979 (166–68).

DEFENSIVE MEASURES

Several types of defensive measures were employed. The first was constant alertness. Men went about fully armed all the time, not only when surveying the countryside in search of game but also when attending dances or other festivities in their own settlement. Charles Brower (n.d., 143, 166), who traveled widely in northwestern Alaska during the 1880s (some decades after armed hostilities had ceased) said that he did not think that he ever went "into a village day or night that someone was not outside looking to see that no strangers arrived without their knowing." If an attack was considered imminent, sentries were posted.

Defense was one of the factors taken into account in settlement location. Small settlements were often situated behind beach ridges, along the coast, or in willow thickets, inland. Larger settlements were located on points of land that could be approached on foot from only one direction during the period of open water, or near lakes where an approaching force could be easily seen approaching at all times of year.

Other defensive measures included the placement of pungi sticks around settlements, the construction of stockades or bunkers, and the

excavation of hidden tunnels through which people trapped inside buildings could escape and either flee or counterattack. On a more individual
level, men expecting an attack wore either armor made from ivory or
bone plates linked together in a vest or else a vest of fur, caribou hide, or
bird skins thick enough to impede an arrow's penetration.

Magic, primarily in the form of amulets, was employed to keep all
sorts of hostile forces at bay, including both supernatural and human
enemies. Amulets were worn all the time, however, and I have never
learned of any used exclusively in armed conflict.

WEAPONS

The same basic array of weapons seems to have been used everywhere.
Firefights were conducted with bows and arrows, which seem to have
had a maximum range of about 150 meters (Bockstoce 1988, 1:197;
Simpson (1852–54: entry for January 31, 1853; VanStone 1977, 47, 56).
Bows ranged from simple curved staves to complex recurved staves reinforced with sinew backing. Arrows were variously tipped with bone, flint,
slate, ivory, or iron and the points were tanged or barbed. Arrowheads to
be used specifically in combat were sometimes made with a deliberate
weakness so that the head would break off inside the victim's flesh. Shock
encounters were conducted with spears, clubs, and long knives.

Magic was also employed as a weapon, primarily in the form of
songs; these were used to kill wounded enemies trying to escape. Rituals led by shamans were sometimes performed prior to departing for a
raid or battle, although these seem to have been more common among
Athapaskans than among Eskimos. In some districts, shamans were
employed specifically to accompany an attacking force.

INTERSOCIETAL CONFLICT

Intersocietal armed conflict took three basic forms: (1) terrorist forays
into foreign estates by individuals or very small groups of men; (2) surprise attacks by somewhat larger parties; and (3) open battles with dozens
or (rarely) even hundreds of combatants. In the Inuit language zone, the
people distinguished conceptually between terrorists (*iññuqutat*), raiders

(*suġruich*), and soldiers (*aŋuyaich*); I do not have comparable information from the Athapaskan and Yup'ik Eskimo language areas.

I have not been able to learn the goal of terrorist forays, but the objective of surprise attacks and battles was to kill as many of the enemy as possible: men always, and usually women and children as well. Captives—usually women, sometimes children—were taken only rarely, and booty was usually limited to a few, easily transported items, such as labrets or knives. Athapaskans seem to have been more interested in booty and captives than their Eskimo neighbors were; but they, like the Eskimos, usually had to solve some major transportation problems to take home much in the way of spoils.

To the extent that new land was acquired through battle, the victors had to abandon some or all of their original estate. These societies lacked both the population and the organization required to occupy a new estate while continuing to maintain control over the old.

Given the above considerations, one may wonder what led people to go to war in the first place. Some of the general factors identified by Carol and Melvin Ember (1992, 1994a, 1994b, 1997), such as the threat of natural disasters and socialization for mistrust of foreigners, seem to have been broadly applicable in western Alaska (cf. Sheehan 1995). However, when I asked Native historians what their ancestors' actual motives for attacking the members of another society had been, they invariably responded that revenge was the primary or exclusive reason. Since these peoples had lived in roughly the same part of the world for centuries, if not millennia, they had plenty of grudges to draw upon whenever a catalyst evoked hostile sentiments.

The people of the study region lacked specialized fighting forces. Every able-bodied man and boy was expected to help defend his people against aggression and was generally expected to join any major expedition that was headed out on an attack. Leadership was provided by clan heads among Athapaskans and compound family heads among Eskimos. In the southern part of the study region, there seems to have been an institutionalized role of war leader in some districts, although I have not been able to learn how a man was selected to fill it. Just how the command function was fulfilled, particularly in open battle, is the least adequately known aspect of traditional warfare in western Alaska. This is probably because leadership, both in general and in armed confrontations, was rather weakly developed.

TERRORIST FORAYS

Terrorist forays were a special form of trespass that seem to have been limited to the northern half of the study region, although they occurred on both sides of the Athapaskan-Eskimo border. They were usually made between mid August and late September, a season when there was still a fair amount of daylight but also at least some darkness. Such expeditions involved one or a few men deliberately and secretly entering the estate of another society and stealing food, damaging boats, and making weird noises near a settlement at night, at one extreme, to committing homicide, at the other.

Just what motivated terrorists is unclear. During the study period, they may have been trying to reconnoiter enemy settlements in anticipation of making a raid, but why they caused mischief and committed murder and why they continued to operate more than a century after raiding came to a halt remain mysteries. Whatever the goal of their activities may have been, the effect was to spread fear among the people and to keep tension at a much higher level than it otherwise would have been; the terrorist forays helped keep people convinced that they were surrounded by enemies.

SURPRISE ATTACKS

Surprise attacks were of two basic types: ambushes and night-time raids. Both were reported from all parts of western Alaska.

Ambushes took place in two situations. One was when a raiding party or other large attacking force was observed approaching a settlement and ambushed on the way in. An ambush of this type required enough advance warning for the home forces to muster sufficient troops and get them into position, but it was undertaken successfully from time to time. For example, on one occasion in the Y-K Delta, a large invading force reportedly was spotted far enough from its target to give runners time to recruit reinforcements from another village (Fienup-Riordan 1988, 32–33). The invaders, traveling by boat, had to travel up a narrow stream to reach their goal, so the defenders spread out along both of its banks and hid. At a signal, the defenders started shooting, catching the invaders in a cross fire. The entire invading force was wiped out except for one man, who was sent home to tell his people what had happened.

The other context in which ambushes occurred was when people knew that their enemies would be traveling along the shore or up a river in late summer on the way home from summer trade gatherings. Since the boats employed for this purpose were usually propelled by people moving along the shore or riverbank, all the members of the attacking force had to do was hide at a particularly advantageous point and wait for their intended victims to arrive. This type of ambush was not particularly common, however, because there was usually a general truce during periods of widespread seasonal travel, and it seems not to have been broken very often.

The second type of surprise attack was the nighttime raid, which was the most common form of intersocietal violence throughout the study region. In the north, these raids were usually undertaken by forces of one to two dozen men between late September and early November, when there was plenty of darkness (but still some daylight) and the rivers and lakes were frozen (facilitating cross-country travel on foot) but still rather little snow on the ground (which would have inhibited walking and left tracks). In the Y-K Delta, by contrast, raids tended to be made in mid to late summer by raiders traveling by boat. There was at least some darkness in the delta at this season, so that an attack could be made at night; the basic approach to the target settlement, however, had to be made in daylight. Because, as a consequence, surprise was more difficult to achieve, raiding parties in this area apparently tended to be larger than they were farther north.

The general procedure of the nighttime raid was for the members of the attacking force to sneak into a settlement when its residents were asleep in their houses or enjoying some kind of festivity in the *kashim* (community hall). The objective was to catch everyone inside the buildings and block the doors. Torches and flammable material were then dropped into the buildings through the skylights. After the fire and smoke had had sufficient time to build up, the door was unblocked, and the people inside the building had the alternatives of staying inside and suffocating or burning to death, or trying to escape and being clubbed or speared to death.

If surprise was complete, and if everyone in the target settlement was trapped inside a blockaded building, a nighttime raid could be devastatingly effective. Everyone in the target settlement would be killed. In the Y-K Delta, where the men and older boys slept in the kashim, raiders sometimes contented themselves with investing it and restricting their killing to the men inside. They might rape a few women and steal a few things, then leave. Alternatively, they might kill everyone, and they frequently set many of the buildings on fire.

Surprise was not always complete, however. Invaders were often observed by someone before they could approach a settlement; the alarm was given, and defensive measures were put in motion. Sometimes the invading force was spotted some distance from a settlement and was ambushed on the way in. If the approaching force was observed early enough, runners might be sent to neighboring settlements for reinforcements, which might arrive before or during the attack. Some houses, and many kashims, had hidden escape tunnels; because the men inside always had their weapons with them, they could emerge and mount an immediate counterattack. Alternatively, the residents might flee before the invaders arrived, in which case they usually returned home to find their houses burned and their food stocks destroyed.

Raiders were also opportunistic. For example, on one occasion, a party of upper Kobuk River Koyukon reconnoitering the upper Noatak River settlement of Makpik in preparation for a night-time raid saw all of the settlement's active male inhabitants carrying their kayaks off to hunt caribou at a lake some distance away (Burch 2005, 110–11). The raiders waited until the hunters had gone, then made a daylight raid on the settlement, killing all of the elderly men and children in the camp and all of the women except two, whom they took as captives.

If a raid was a failure, the defenders attempted to annihilate the entire attacking force—save one. That one was given some food and any necessary first aid and was sent home with instructions to tell his countrymen what had happened and to warn them never to attack the victors again.

OPEN BATTLE

Open battles usually took place under one of two circumstances. The first was when defenders went out to confront an invading force before it reached any settlements. The second was when the members of two societies, or of two sets of allied societies, decided to have at each other in a decisive confrontation. Confrontations of the latter type seem to have been held at some distance from any settlement. The former was probably the more common of the two.

Open battles could take place at any time of year, in contrast to the other types of armed conflict (which tended to have seasonal emphases). Most seem to have occurred during the summer or early fall, and all of the ones I have heard about took place in tundra rather than forest settings. In the northern and eastern sectors of the study region, the members of invading forces usually traveled on foot. In the Y-K Delta and along the coast, however, they were more likely to travel by boat. On the coast, the preferred conveyance was the large open boat known as an *umiak*. Umiaks were also used in the Y-K Delta, but fleets of kayaks were more commonly employed there. As they neared the enemy force, men in all districts placed feathers in their headbands and/or painted their faces.

Opposing forces apparently approached a battlefield in columns, the men in the lead shooting arrows ahead along their line of travel to signal their hostile intent. When the two forces were within sight of one another, they redeployed into lines perhaps 200–250 meters apart. The best archers were stationed at the ends of the lines to prevent flanking movements. The formation of ranks was deliberately avoided because a man standing behind someone else could not see incoming missiles and might be struck when the person in front dodged them. A sufficient lateral separation was kept for a man to dodge incoming arrows without interfering with comparable maneuvers on the part of others in the line.

The first order of business was sizing up the enemy force. The people of western Alaska were extremely sensitive to discrepancies of scale. The members of a force that was smaller by just a few men often tried to withdraw before battle with a larger one began. This was difficult to do, however, unless the members of the superior force decided not to pursue them.

The members of each force wanted an uphill position with the sun and the wind at their backs. These variables were of course not always in harmony with one another, and wind and especially light conditions rarely remained constant over the two or three days of confrontation that might ensue. There seems to have been some knowledge of how to maneuver battle lines, but I was never able to learn what the procedures for doing this were.

The opening stage of battle consisted of the soldiers shouting imprecations at one another and shooting an occasional arrow toward the enemy line. In many accounts, an old man from one side or the other attempted to prevent the battle from occurring by walking between the lines and declaiming to all who could hear him that both forces should withdraw. I have never heard of these old men being successful in their effort.

Gradually the lines approached one another, and a firefight at maximum range began. One or two particularly agile young men then moved out ahead of the line, possibly on each side, and began performing ridiculous-looking and insulting movements intended to provoke the enemy into shooting at them. In theory, they dodged incoming arrows and picked them up, thus reducing the enemy's supply of ammunition and enhancing their own. A few young men became famous for their ability to do this successfully, but many others must have been killed, particularly by well-coordinated volleys.

This maximum-range firefight could continue for hours or even days. Firing could be halted for a period by mutual agreement to permit the troops to rest, but sentries were posted to make sure that the other side did not cheat.

As time passed, the opposing lines gradually closed to within more effective range of their weapons, and people started getting wounded or killed. When the members of one side perceived that they were beginning to gain an advantage in numbers, they began to press the attack by moving toward the enemy line, firing as they did so. The members of the weaker force then had to decide whether to stand and fight or try to escape. If they stood their ground, the converging lines gradually became disorganized and the battle turned into a general melée in which spears, clubs, and knives augmented bows and arrows. If a man tried to escape, of course, he ran the risk of being shot in the back.

If the confrontation turned into a standoff, the members of the opposing sides eventually agreed to a truce and everyone went home. If one side lost, however, all but one or two of its men were killed. These survivors were sent back to their homeland to tell their compatriots not to threaten the victors again. The bodies of the losers were either simply left where they fell or else heaped in a pile, often after being mutilated or dismembered. The victors tended their own dead with some kind of ritual but left their bodies on the field as well. However, they made every effort to treat their wounded and take them home.

DISCUSSION

It is impossible to calculate the number of incidents involving terrorists that occurred during the study period. Judging from informants' statements, at least one or two must have taken place in every estate in the northern half of the study region every year. Raids and battles, by contrast, were much fewer and easier to locate. Figure 1.3 shows the raid and battle sites whose locations have been reported. Because armed combat pretty well ceased in the late 1830s in the southern part of the region and in the late 1840s in the north, the vast majority of encounters represented by dots on the map must have occurred before those dates. Most of the dots represent armed encounters between different Eskimo societies. Some were between different Athapaskan groups or between Eskimos and Athapaskans, while a few involved Athapaskans or Eskimos on one side and English or Russians on the other. All the theoretical possibilities were realized in fact except Russians versus English.

Accounts exist of many more confrontations than these, but they have been impossible to locate spatially with the precision required for mapping even at the scale used in figure 1.3. There are also many sectors of the study region for which there are no relevant data, because early population loss caused by famine or disease led to an insurmountable loss of information. Nevertheless, a glance at this map suggests that people's fear of being attacked probably had a rational basis.

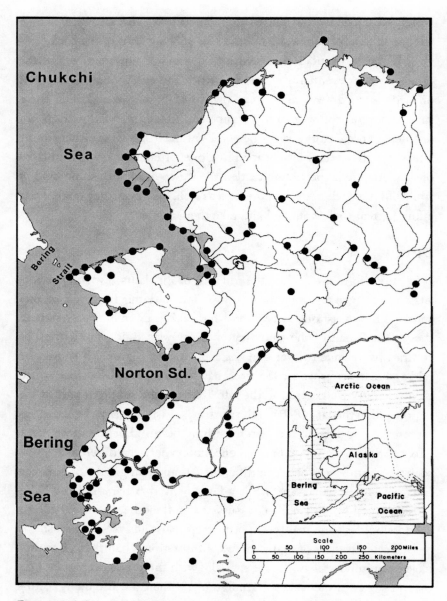

FIGURE 1.3 Reported locations of early-contact-period raids and battles in western Alaska.

CONSEQUENCES

The primary consequence of intersocietal violence in early-contact-period western Alaska was a lower population than would have been there in its absence (cf. Sheehan 1995, 189). The frequency and the lethal nature of warfare in the region virtually guaranteed this outcome. Furthermore, since victors usually tried to annihilate everyone on the losing side in the northern part of the study region, losses there must have been spread pretty much evenly over all age and both sex cohorts. In the Y-K Delta, however, the loss of adult males may have been disproportionately high because of the custom there of the men sleeping in the kashim, which was the primary target of most raids. Elsewhere, men slept in family dwellings; hence, they were more widely dispersed at night unless they were with women and children enjoying some festivity in the kashim. Ironically, warfare also contributed to the formation of intersocietal marriages because it sometimes left a number of widows or widowers who could not find suitable spouses among their own people.

Another consequence of intersocietal conflict was a new set of grudges between the societies involved. It was usually possible to ascertain who had conducted even a successful surprise attack by footprints and other evidence left at the scene. The custom of sending one or two surviving invaders home with the bad news would have eliminated any doubts on the matter.

Territorial dislocations were a fourth consequence of warfare, although the acquisition of territory seems to have been a motivating factor only rarely. The only example I know of deliberate expansion was in northwestern Alaska, where the Utuqqaġmiut (Inuit) enlarged their estate by taking over some land claimed by the Tikiġaġmiut (Inuit) (Burch 2005, 59). The real estate in question was of marginal significance to its original owners, however, and the example is not particularly instructive.

Territorial change sometimes occurred more or less by default. For example, in northwestern Alaska, after repeated raids and encroachments by Di'hạįi Gwich'in (Athapaskans), Kuukpigmiut (Inuit) gradually killed them off and drove them out over a period of years, eventually expanding into the demographic vacuum left behind (Burch 1998a, 31;

Burch and Mishler 1995). But there is no evidence that the acquisition of territory as such was a contributing factor to the violence.

Another example of territorial shift occurred in the Y-K Delta (O'Leary 1995; Oswalt 1990, 40–42). Once again, however, revenge rather than the desire for new territory initiated hostilities. The Aglur-miut (Yup'ik), who became severely beset in their own homeland, fled south to another region to survive. To remain there, they had to fight the previous inhabitants of that region. Ultimately, it was the newly arrived Russians who saved them from extinction.

CONCLUDING REMARKS

When I began the research that eventually resulted in this chapter, war-fare was the last thing I was interested in. It never even crossed my mind, since everyone knows that Eskimos, in contrast to Indians, did not engage in warfare. What I was interested in was land use, seasonal cycles, and social boundaries (Burch 1998b, 12–17). I used U.S. Geo-logical Survey topographic maps when interviewing Native historians concerning these subjects. As elders took me on vicarious tours around their homelands via the maps, they occasionally mentioned places where battles or raids had taken place or where they had played with piles of human bones on former battlefields during their childhood. Eventually it dawned on me that I was onto something interesting here, and only then did I make warfare a special focus within my larger study.

Ann Fienup-Riordan (1990, 147–53; 1994, 321–25), although investigating different subjects, evidently had a similar experience far-ther south. However, there, in contrast to my own experience, she was occasionally confronted directly by Natives who categorically denied that their ancestors had engaged in intersocietal violence. Unfortunately for the ideologues, both the early documentary sources (e.g., Nelson 1899, 327–30) and Yup'ik elders, when interviewed about historical places as part of the land claims process (Kurtz 1984; O'Leary 1995), told a different story.

If one wants to understand what life was like in Alaska during the early contact period, one must take intersocietal violence into account. Theorists might attempt to blame it on Russian, British, or American influence, but the fact of the matter is, warfare in western Alaska came to an abrupt halt shortly after Westerners arrived. Left to their own devices, Alaska Natives were no more peaceful than anyone else.

ACKNOWLEDGMENTS

My research on Alaska Native societies began in the fall of 1960. It has been supported over the years by the Department of Anthropology, University of Chicago; the Department of Biological Sciences, University of Alaska; the Alaska Historical Commission; NANA Museum of the Arctic; the U.S. National Park Service; the U.S. Minerals Management Service; the Division of Subsistence of the Alaska Department of Fish and Game; and the Canada Council (now the Social Sciences and Humanities Research Council of Canada). I thank Kenneth L. Pratt and Matthew O'Leary of the U.S. Bureau of Indian Affairs in Anchorage for guiding me through the mass of reports on historical and cemetery sites compiled by that agency; Kenneth Pratt for critical comments on an earlier draft of this chapter; and Ann Fienup-Riordan for responding informatively to my inquiries about warfare in the Y-K Delta.

NOTES

1. The methodology of my work with Alaska Native historians is discussed in Burch 1991; 1998b, 12–19; 2003, 405–13; and 2005, ix–xii, 48–52. Historical and cemetery sites were investigated in the Bering Strait, Calista, Doyon, and NANA regions by the Cooperative Park Studies Unit of the University of Alaska–Fairbanks and by the U.S. Bureau of Indian Affairs. A similar investigation was the Traditional Land Use Inventory, compiled by the North Slope Borough Commission on History, Language, and Culture.

2. The study period occurred during the later part of the so-called Little Ice Age (Fagan 2000), when the study region was significantly colder than it is now.

2 "Barbarism and Ardour of War from the Tenderest Years"
Cree-Inuit Warfare in the Hudson Bay Region

Charles A. Bishop and Victor P. Lytwyn

Currently there is a "war" between those scholars who believe that warfare prior to the Neolithic was nonexistent or relatively insignificant (Haas 1996, 2003, 2004; Reyna 1994a; Roper 1969, 2003; Sillitoe 1985) and those who see it as pervasive at all levels of societal complexity (Ember 1978; Ember and Ember 1994a; Keeley 1996; LeBlanc 1999, 2003; Otterbein 1973, 1999). Keith Otterbein has discussed the historical roots of these contradictory positions, referring to the two groups as "doves" and "hawks" (1999, 801). Despite abundant cross-cultural evidence in support of hunter-gatherer warfare (Ember 1978; Ember and Ember 1992, 1994a; Otterbein 1970, 1973, 1999), the former views persist.

Those who argue that pre-Neolithic warfare was either nonexistent or rare maintain that this is because most hunter-gatherer societies were egalitarian bands—meaning, among other things, that members are peace loving, cooperative, and sharing of their resources. Band members continually work at maintaining peace and resolving conflicts, or fission if they are unable to, making warfare virtually impossible. While individuals could fight and even kill or murder others, organized violence by members of one band directed toward those of another is thought to be either unthinkable or structurally impossible because of the egalitarian ethos and extensive kin networks linking them. Consequently, because this type of fighting involves only individuals and not groups, it is assumed to have little or no demographic or territorial effect. As Stephen Reyna states (1994a, 37–38), "My view is that regardless of how much fighting there was in bands, it was relatively harmless."[1] Where historically documented evidence for warfare among band-level societies does exist, the fighting is viewed either as a ritualized event with gamelike qualities rather than a violent encounter, or as a recent manifestation attributable to colonial influences (Leacock 1978). Moreover, archaeological evidence for warfare was either missed or ignored by many archaeologists who relied on ethnographic analogy that downplayed violence to interpret their findings (Keeley 1996, 23).

In contrast is the view that warfare among bands is both common and lethal. Otterbein, for instance, has shown that uncentralized political societies waged war quite efficiently (1970) and that "offensive external war is not significantly related to level of political centralization" (1973, 946–47). His findings differ from those cited by scholars who maintain "that primitive peoples are not warlike, in the sense that they infrequently engage in warfare" (1973, 947). Otterbein points to "mounting evidence for warfare in a number of pre-Neolithic regions," including Upper Paleolithic Europe (2003, 9). He, however, does not subscribe to the extreme position of either the hawks, who argue for a state of constant warfare, or the doves, who argue for a state of perpetual conflict resolution (1997, 252; 1999, 801). This is our view also.

Cross-cultural data that support Otterbein's position have been employed by Carol Ember and Melvin Ember (1992, 1994a), who note that just because the absolute numbers of people killed in warfare was relatively small "does not mean that the warfare in pre-industrial societies was inconsequential. In the few cases where we have detailed information on the number of people killed over time, it appears that 'primitive' warfare might have been even more lethal proportionally than modern warfare" (Ember and Ember 1994a, 189–90).

There are, nevertheless, conditions that militate against the potential for warfare among bands. Extensive bilateral kinship networks linking different groups and a relative absence of competition over subsistence and other resources makes war less likely. Raymond Kelly, for instance (2000, 46), has offered the notion of social substitutability, or lack of it, to explain why unsegmented hunter-gatherer societies, those without discrete groups, lack warfare. Where victims of violence are not members of a well-defined group whose structure is regulated by prescribed marriage rules, as in the case of descent groups, there is no social substitutability, hence no definable group seeking revenge. Kelly's argument accounts for why there is little or no warfare within relatively homogeneous societies and also suggests why warfare exists between hunter-gatherer societies that have no kinship or social ties with each other (Kelly 2000, 118–19). The latter situation is the subject of our chapter.

Both pre- and postcontact warfare existed between two distinct hunter-gatherer peoples: the Lowland Cree and Inuit of the Hudson Bay and James Bay region of subarctic Canada. Although the European presence altered the nature of warfare, tipping the balance in favor of the Cree, early references to it combined with the nature of the warfare documented in historical accounts provide convincing evidence for its roots in the precontact period. Inuit territorial ambitions probably precipitated war, but cultural, linguistic, and biological differences between these two peoples generated fear and mistrust, making rapprochement impossible. After contact, disasters experienced by the Cree because of altered ecological adjustments were blamed on Inuit sorcery and thus were a justifiable reason for raids. In contrast, the relative lack of violence among the Lowland Cree can be explained by their cultural homogeneity, maintained by complex kinship networks linking groups over a vast geographic region (Bishop 1975a; Bishop and Krech 1980; Lytwyn 2002a).

THE LOWLAND CREE AND INUIT AT THE TIME OF EUROPEAN CONTACT

The Lowland Cree are sometimes called the Swampy Cree or Home-guards by Hudson's Bay Company (HBC) fur traders, or in Cree, Mus-kekowuck Athinuwick (Lytwyn 2002a, xi). They are Algonquian-speak-ers belonging to the Western Swampy Cree dialect group (Rhodes and Todd 1981, 55). Their territory was approximately coterminous with the Hudson Bay Lowlands, a relatively flat region of muskeg and bogs bro-ken by major rivers flowing to the coast (fig. 2.1). It extended from the Nelson River in the northwest to the Nottaway River near the southern tip of James Bay, and inland from the coast for nearly 250 miles. To the northwest, the region between the Nelson and Churchill rivers was an uninhabited "no-man's land" between the warring Cree and Inuit. To the southeast, the Nottaway River region was also avoided for fear of the Iroquois who raided into that area during the second half of the seventeenth century (Nottaway being the Cree name for the Iroquois). Cree groups living farther inland were sometimes called Half-Home-guards because they rarely visited the coastal posts in winter but had kin ties with the Lowland Cree (Lytwyn 2002a, 17–18). Archaeologi-cal evidence suggests that the Cree occupied the lowlands for centuries before European contact (Julig 1982, 1988; Pilon 1987). The mid-eigh-teenth-century Lowland Cree population numbered between about 500 and 700 persons, while the inland Cree population is estimated at between 1,000 and 1,400 (Lytwyn 2002a, 24). Until the arrival of fur traders in the seventeenth century, the main subsistence occupation was hunting, fishing, and gathering of seasonally available foods. Soon after the Europeans settled at coastal trading posts, the Lowland Cree devel-oped close social and economic ties with them, supplying furs, water-fowl, fish and other game, and sometimes mates (Bishop 1972, 1975a, 1984; Lytwyn 2002a). This gave the Lowland Cree a major advantage in their wars with the Inuit. Consequently, much more is known about the Cree side of the equation than that of the Inuit.

The Inuit occupied the coasts and islands of Hudson Bay northwest and northeast of the Lowland Cree. Archaeological evidence indicates that they had migrated south along the western coast of Hudson Bay (McGhee 1984, 373) as far south as the mouth of the Churchill River region by about AD 1200. Jens Munk, the Danish explorer who wintered at Churchill in 1619–20, found evidence of square dwellings and wood chips, suggestive of an Inuit occupation, but met no people (Arima 1984, 458–59). Later, Inuit scavenged iron from Munk's abandoned campsite. In 1717, James Knight described an "abundance of Iskemays Tents Standing that it looked like a little Town; & our people as put up ye Beacon Sayth that they be very large Tents, bigg Enough to hold 50 people; And that thare Tents was made so thick with turf, Dirt & Driftwood that they believe they had Wintred thare . . . & that their Could not be less than 3 or 400 of them by their Tents & Warehouse, finding above 200 of the Latter where they had kept there Provisions, they being built with Stones & Driftwood" (Williams 1969, liii note 1).

In the 1740s, HBC trader James Isham reported that the Inuit frequently camped at Eskimo Point, near the entrance of the Churchill River, before European settlements were established "from the graves and mark's of their Dwellings, some of which are still Remaining" (Isham 1949, 180). Joseph Robson added mid-eighteenth-century details:

Churchill was much frequented by the Eskimaux before we settled there, the point on which the fort is built, being called Eskimaux-point. Upon digging for the fort many traces were discovered of their abode here, such as the pit in which they secured their provisions, pieces of stone-pots, spears, arrows, &c. This point they kept for some time after they were driven from the adjacent country, because it lies far to the open sea, they could discover the distant approaches of their enemies, and repair in time to their canoes, in the management of which they are peculiarly dextrous; but they were at length forced to go farther northward to Cape Eskimaux and Whale Cove: and are now totally dispossessed of this retreat. (Robson [1752] 1965, 64; see also Graham 1969, 226)[2]

Accounts by Knight, Isham, Robson, and Andrew Graham demonstrate that the Inuit had prehistoric settlements of turf and stone

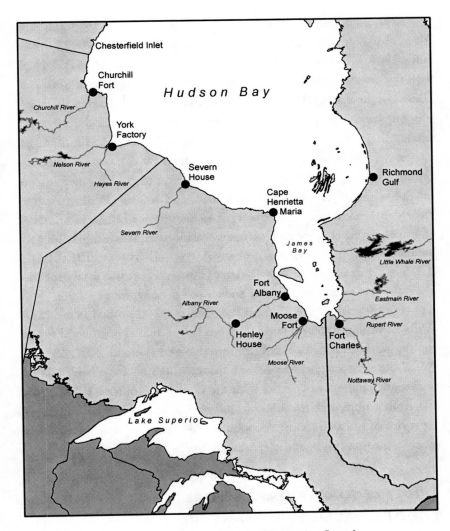

FIGURE 2.1   The Cree-Inuit area. (Map by Christopher Storie)

houses and storage pits in the vicinity of the mouth of the Churchill River. However, although Inuit wintered there as late as 1716–17 (Williams 1969, lii), they became infrequent residents after about AD 1650 with the onset of the "Little Ice Age," as winter hunting conditions near Churchill grew less attractive than those farther north (Clark 1979, 89, 96). Bowhead (black) whales are rare near Churchill, and beluga (white) whales do not winter there (Williams 1969, lvii). Warfare with the Cree also may have reduced the frequency of stays. By the late seventeenth century, visits had primarily become restricted to the summer season for the purposes of hunting seals, walrus, and whales (Williams 1969, xlvii–xlviii). As the Cree informed James Knight in 1716, large numbers of Inuit arrived only every four or five years to hunt white whales and build umiaks (Hudson's Bay Company Archives [hereafter HBCA] n.d., B.239/a/2, July 29, 1716, fol. 49). After Churchill Fort was established in 1717, the Inuit deserted the area and ceased making umiaks there.

On the east side of Hudson Bay, the Inuit had pushed as far south as the Eastmain River on James Bay but had retreated northward to the Richmond Gulf area before Europeans arrived (Fossett 2001, 63–64). As on the west side, some of these movements may have been related to climatic changes or conflict with the Cree (see Robson [1752] 1965, 63). Inuit groups on both sides of Hudson Bay spoke mutually intelligible forms of Inuit-Inupiaq (Woodbury 1984, 56), suggesting a relatively recent common origin and dispersal about the bay.

EVIDENCE FOR WARFARE BEFORE THE ARRIVAL OF EUROPEANS

The warfare between Inuit and Cree has been preserved in the oral history of the Lowland Cree as well as the early historical records. According to Lowland Cree oral history, Inuit attacks predated the arrival of Europeans. Cree elder Louis Bird described an incident that occurred near Cape Henrietta Maria:

> The name of the lake is . . . Wabagamushusagagan [milky lake] on the Cape Henrietta Maria, to remember the story about the Inuit attacking the Omushkego people. . . . The lake . . . is situated on

one of those hills that run parallel to the sea. And this was a long time before the European came into the scene. And there was no guns and other European trade goods. And this raid from the Inuit warriors attacked the group of Omushkegok people, mostly women and children and the elders, while the men were hunting . . . the Inuit descended from their hiding place and attacked the camp, killing all the elders and the children and women. And also being so excited by killing, they begun to act very strangely and very savagely which led them to cut the breast of the women who were . . . nursing the children. And . . . they throw away these glands into the water and turn the water white. And therefore the lake was called Wabagamushusagagan. (Bird 1999a, 1)

This story is reminiscent of one recounted by Nicolas Jeremie early in the eighteenth century from Fort Bourbon (York Factory and then in French hands). Jeremie observed that the Inuit "make war on all their neighbours, and when they kill or capture any of their enemies, they eat them raw and drink their blood. They even make infants at the breast drink it, so as to instil in them the barbarism and ardour of war from the tenderest years" (Jeremie 1926, 16).[3]

HBC traders were told of Inuit invasions of Cree territory near the mouth of the Severn River. For example, James Knight recounted in 1716 that the Lowland Cree "see one of them [an Inuit umiak] off Severn once which they took it by the bigness of it to be one of our ships under Sail twill they see them putt into Shore and take in a great number of there Men as was along Shore hunting Deer and Geese" (HBCA n.d., B.239/a/2, August 2, 1716, fol. 50). The reference to ships indicates that this was a postcontact Inuit visit. The Cree tried to repel this invasion. Cree oral traditions of Inuit near the mouth of the Severn River continued into the twentieth century (Cumming 1928, 117).

On the east side of the bay, John Oldmixon in the early eighteenth century reported that the Inuit "sometimes in slight Parties make incursions on the other Indians, and having knock'd 8 or 10 on the Head return in triumph" (Tyrrell 1931, 381–82). Fifty years later, William Coats stated that the Indians living along the east side of James Bay (Eastmain Cree) "have been cruelly ravaged by the Usquemows, with whom at present [they are] at peace," living "in a sort of servile friendship with them" (Barrow 1852, 61).

The rich marine resources that were seasonally available in the southern parts of Hudson and James Bay motivated Inuit war parties to raid into Cree territory. Cree elder Louis Bird explained this territoriality:

> So that is the place . . . where the Omushkego's used to go camp during the summer . . . where all these . . . sudden attacks and scrimmages took place. On the James Bay coast that's where the Inuit people used to kill the Omushkegos too because they fight for the shores of the James Bay for the seal hunting and also the geese and ducks and everything because they wanted it for them self according to the story. But of course the Omushkegos wanted it too, so it's the only section that I truthfully find it in my research where two tribes fight for land. . . . So, that's . . . the place where the two tribes actually fight for the piece of land, and that's for the fight for the seals and the fish and the waterfowl. (Bird 1999b, 1)

Early European accounts indicate that Inuit raids ceased within a few years after fur-trade posts were constructed by the HBC in the 1670s and 1680s along the coasts of Hudson Bay and James Bay. Instead, the Lowland Cree became the aggressors, often raiding deep into Inuit territory along the northern coasts of Hudson Bay. Chevalier de Troyes met four Indians in his expedition against Fort Charles near the mouth of the Rupert River in 1686, commenting that "ils venoient de faire la guerre aux Eskimos" "they came to make war with the Eskimos" (Francis and Morantz 1983, 75). Again in 1693–94, HBC trader James Knight, then at Fort Albany, recorded purchasing "an As'scomore slave boy for the use of ye factory"—paying a gun, a blanket, a kettle, one pound of tobacco, and a woman's shroud (HBCA n.d., B.3/d/2, fol. 12d). These early references and the presence of Inuit slaves among the Lowland Cree support the view that warfare predates European contact (Lytwyn 2002a, 64). In the summer of 1716, Knight (who was then at York Factory) interviewed a Cree man who reported that Cree war parties had been searching for Inuit. Knight remarked, "he has been many times in their country to War against them but they never had the luck to kill any Iskemays" (HBCA n.d., B.239/a/2, August 2, 1716, fol. 50). Other Lowland Cree described geographical details of the Hudson Bay coast far to the north of the Churchill River. They informed Knight that "the Shore is very flatt all along a foul broken ground out a great way towards the Sea and the water ebbs so farr out that they cannot see the Land in there Canoos at Low water but when they are gotten pretty ways to the Norward the Land rises very high again and the water begins to grow deep to the very Shore and that there is abundance of islands and many Iskemays" (HBCA n.d., B.239/a/2, April 29, 1716, fol. 25). Knight estimated that these people had been as far north as 64 degrees, in the vicinity of Chesterfield Inlet. This supports statements made earlier by Lowland Cree to Nicolas Jeremie who said that they had traveled along the coast north of the Churchill River to "a strait: where one can readily see across from one side to the other" (Jeremie 1926, 21).

Another source of evidence for precontact Lowland Cree–Inuit warfare concerns the complexity of the behavior associated with it. Elaborate rituals and considerable preparation prior to raids suggests that such behavior did not just arise after contact. For example, in the late seventeenth century, Bacqueville de la Potherie observed Cree rituals near the mouth of the Hayes River: "When their enemies fall into their hands they scalp them. They tear off the skin which covers the skull and they put as many marks of themselves as they have taken scalps. I saw three Ouenebigouchelinis [Lowland Cree] who had wild goose feathers attached to their caps above their ears as trophies of their victories over their enemies" (Tyrrell 1931, 233). Likewise, in the 1740s, Henry Ellis observed, "An Indian who kills an Eskemaux scalps him; then takes and rounds a Bit of Willow, sowing the Scalp to it, and hangs one or two, or more of them, if he hath them, on a Stick at the End of his Canoe, when he returns; when at Home carries it to all Feasts, there dancing with it in his Hands" (Ellis 1968, 2:46).[4]

Andrew Graham, who lived in the Hudson Bay region almost continually between 1749 and 1791, has provided additional details:

> They have many ceremonies before they set out; I shall mention a few out of many. When a set of Indians propose to make war they assemble together, and the adventurers enjoin themselves an

abstinence from drink during seven days by way of probation. He who fails in this trial is thought unfit for the arduous enterprise, and therefore rejected from amongst them. They afterwards make a choice of a leader. He is generally elected who is best beloved, and has a knowledge of the enemies' country, their manner of war, tenting etc. The headman, or general, throws away his gun and kettle, either as an oblation to the Evil Spirit, that he would be favourable to the undertaking; or else shew his valour that he dare go in quest of an enemy, with no other defence than the stick held in his hand, and destitute even of necessaries for preparing his food.

They travel with their families to the confines of their enemies' country; they then have a dance, and conjuring feast. The old men are left to provide for the women and children, while the young people pursue their journey. Their attacks are all by stratagem, surprise and ambush . . . they are the more esteemed for having circumvented the enemy with the greatest cunning, accounting it a disgrace to lose their friends in an open engagement. For this reason when they discover the habitation of the adversaries, they lurk about in the woods till night, and then set upon the poor creatures while sleeping defenceless, and imagining nothing of the enemy's approach. (Graham 1969, 172–73)

Graham said that because the Inuit generally lived on islands, before attacking, the Cree would first destroy all the Inuit boats so that none could escape. They would then kill all of the men and old women. Graham observed,

But frequently they reserve some of the young women and children, taking the former for wives, and adopting the latter as their own offspring; and ever afterwards treating them with the tenderness and affection such a relation demands. On their return from these hostile expeditions, those who have killed an enemy are painted all over with black; and when they meet their families they have a grand dance. All the scalps, having been stretched on a small willow, are exposed in triumph: and if they are near the grave of a deceased friend a scalp is hung upon it as a Requiem of his manes. . . . There is such enmity between the Indians and Esquimaux, that the former have massacred all of the latter within their power. There is a grand ceremony in which every warrior eats a bit of an Esquimaux, about the size of a nutmeg, and raw. (Graham 1969, 174)

Numerous details, some apparently omitted by Graham, associated with the preparation for war—including abstinence from food and water, dances, feasts, ritual cannibalism, treatment of scalps, body painting, and the very strategy of attack—support the view that Lowland Cree–Inuit warfare was not a simple response to the European presence.

FIREARMS AND WARFARE

Inuit raids into Cree territory ceased by the late seventeenth century, but Cree raids into Inuit territory continued until 1793. This asymmetrical pattern developed when the Lowland Cree acquired firearms from the HBC. In contrast, the Inuit did not trade at these posts, and trade in firearms to them was prohibited by company policy (Graham 1969, 236). Further, there is no evidence that the Inuit had any relations with the Cree whereby they might have acquired guns, and historical evidence indicates that they did not know how to use guns until taught by the fur traders in the late eighteenth century. In contrast, the Lowland Cree probably obtained their first guns in the early seventeenth century from the French in the St. Lawrence Valley, but a regular supply would have become available only after HBC posts were established at the coastal posts after the 1670s. About this time, the Inuit on both coasts of Hudson Bay shifted north, visiting Churchill and Eastmain rivers less frequently until these too were abandoned.

The importance of early firearms in tribal warfare has been questioned. As Brian Given states (1978, 105), "Until the development of breech-loading, and later, repeating rifles during the nineteenth century, the gun offered no practical advantage over Native weapons in terms of its utility as a projectile weapon." Muskets took valuable time to reload in the heat of battle, powder could get wet, locks could break, and guns could misfire or jam, especially if barrels were corroded. Under these conditions, in theory, one's enemy had time to regroup, shoot a volley of arrows or retaliate with hatchets, clubs, lances, and knives. Nevertheless, despite the technical disadvantages of firearms, those possessing them were usually said to have had a tactical advantage. As stated by the HBC trader Andrew Graham, the Inuit "are less given to war. We may charitably imagine this to proceed from a peaceable disposition; though perhaps it may be out of fear, for their southern neighbours, having the use of fire-arms, attack the Esquimaux to a great advantage" (Graham 1969, 236). The Inuit relied only on "the bow and arrow, and [were] not provided with arms to bring them nigher to an equality with the cowardly assailants" (Graham 1969, 174). Likewise, Joseph Robson remarked that the Inuit on the east side of the bay "used to inhabit the country on the east main between the straits and the bottom of the Bay: but they are since driven northward by the Indians, who are rendered much superior to them on account of the supply of arms and ammunition which they receive from the English" (Robson [1752] 1965, 63).

The main advantage of the gun was psychological. Certainly, guns could kill, but after the first volley, their primary use would have been as clubs. It was probably the combination of the element of surprise and the element of noise that gave the Cree the advantage. Indeed, the sound of many guns exploding simultaneously must have been a terrifying experience for unsuspecting foes. Bruce Trigger has remarked (1976, 2:629), "That the possession and use of guns conferred a military advantage on tribes has never been doubted. . . . The real power of the gun in Indian warfare appears to have been psychological; its noise and mysterious operation added to the terrors of foes and to the confidence of those who used them." Louis Bird likewise noted,

> The gun, it gives one-way for the person using it, who has acquired it, it gives him additional power because it added the fear in enemy because you have gun—gives you confidence as an attacker or, if you are in retaliating the attack, whatever you do, defending. So the gun gives you that additional confidence and also the powder gun, the sound also brings more power into your side. . . . So it, the sound gives the power to the person who use it because it's a loud noise and also it has the mystic fire-smoke. Further give a person

who attack to see that this is a, they call it a fire stick, it's, it's similar to what the dream quest visualized the thunder, the lightning and everything. (Bird 2001, 2)

Hence, the advantage that guns provided would have created a demand for them by those involved in warfare, for without guns a group would have felt defenseless against those possessing them. This explains why the Inuit abandoned their southern settlements while the Cree with guns were able to raid deep into Inuit territory, massacre the inhabitants, and drive other Inuit on both coasts of Hudson Bay ever farther northwards.

LOWLAND CREE–INUIT WARFARE IN THE EIGHTEENTH CENTURY

After Churchill Fort was established in 1717, the Inuit kept far to the north until the late eighteenth century. About this time, Lowland Cree–Inuit conflict on the west side of the bay ended. This was partly because the fur traders at Churchill Fort discouraged Lowland Cree war parties from going north to war against the Inuit. As Henry Ellis while at York Factory in 1746–47 observed, Cree-Inuit warfare had been "almost entirely lay'd aside, through the good Management of the Governors at the Factories" (Ellis 1968, 2:44). Probably a more important reason was the shift eastward of the Chipewyan to trade at Churchill Fort. The Chipewyan and related Dene-speaking peoples attacked Inuit settlements unmercifully (Hearne 1958, 73–75, 96–105). The Chipewyan presence then acted to further minimize contacts between the Inuit and Lowland Cree.

On the east coast of Hudson Bay, Lowland Cree raids on the Inuit continued until 1793. The east coast was occupied by Eastmain Cree, sometimes called Montagnais (Francis and Morantz 1983, 12), who did not oppose, and probably could not have opposed, Lowland Cree warriors traveling through their territory. The Eastmain Cree did not participate in raids on the Inuit and were themselves occasionally attacked by the Lowland Cree. For example, in the summer of 1738, warriors failing to find their intended Inuit victims attacked and killed three or four families of Eastmain Cree (HBCA n.d., B.3/a/28, July 31, 1739, fol. 4). Among the warriors were "5 Uplanders . . . that has been att ye Warrs with ye Eskemoes" (HBCA n.d., B.3/a/28, fol. 4, Thomas Bird)—these may have been Northern Ojibwa (Lytwyn 2002a, 66). On June 6, 1755, twelve canoes of mostly "home Indians" arrived at Fort Albany to go to war against the Eastmain Inuit, fifteen (ten men and five women) arriving at Little Whale River in mid July. It so frightened the Eastmain Cree that HBC trader John Potts had great difficulty convincing them to remain at the fishery. The Eastmain Cree said that it was "Common for ye Albany and Moose River Indians when they cannot find the Eusquamays they kill Our Indians, for their Scalps and Makes their country Men believe there Scalps is Eusquamays. Robinson Crouseo [an Eastmain Indian] tells me that his Brother and 3 More was kill'd by the Albany and Moose River Indians about 12 years ago and scalp'd" (HBCA n.d., B.182/a/7, fol. 43). In June 1757, Robert Temple, post-master of Fort Albany, said "a great many of our Indian hunters are gone a Usquemeaux hunting" (HBCA n.d., B.3/a/49, fol. 30). Nine canoes of warriors appeared at Whale River House "teryfying our Indians by tellng ym that if they did not See ye Eusquamays, they woud on their return kill and Scalp them, wch filld them with dread that they deserted ye fishery sooner then they would have done" (HBCA n.d., A.11/57, fol. 46). Fortunately, the warriors did not fulfill their promise, and seven canoes returned to Fort Albany on August 22 to participate in the fall goose hunt (HBCA n.d., B.3/a/50, fol. 1).

The first eighteenth-century account of warfare on the east coast of Hudson Bay was recorded by HBC trader Anthony Beale in the spring of 1707; he reported "Home Indians" departing for the "Wars against the Eskemaise" (HBCA n.d., B.3/a/2, fol. 27d and 30). Beale, like most writers, did not provide much information on these wars (Francis 1979). A typical entry is given on May 25, 1728, by Joseph Myatt: "Eight Curnoes of our home Inds fitted out from hence in order to goe to Warrs with the Esquomays, I Endeavered all I Could to oppose it, but in vain." Myatt did describe the war party's motivation: "Severall of the Home Indians being Disordered the last Winter they attribute all those things to the Malice of their Enimies" (HBCA n.d., B.3/a/16, fol. 18). As noted, HBC policy directed its officers to discourage warfare. In this case, the Cree returned on August 7 without having met any Inuit.

The men who led Lowland Cree war parties were traditional leaders of river-basin bands who possessed considerable influence. Leadership among the Lowland Cree was well developed at the time of contact and was therefore not simply a postcontact creation of the fur traders, although the fur traders also created new leaders (Lytwyn 2002a, 20–23; Morantz 1982, 495). Many traditional leadership positions descended in the male line (Bishop 1975a, 1998). These men believed themselves to be equal to the postmasters to whom they were linked by ritual, moral, and especially material obligations (Ray and Freeman 1978, 63–69). In one case, a traditional chief was able to reject the authority of a chief appointed by the HBC. When a traditional chief of the Hayes River Lowland Cree named the Old Captain refused to recognize the authority of an appointed chief for Churchill River in 1718, the Churchill HBC trader said that "if I dont use him according to his expectation that I shall find he will interpose his authority in his Nation to make a general warr with the Northern [Chipewyan] Indians" (HBCA n.d., B.42/a/1, November 5, 1718, fol. 29).

The Lowland Cree residing near the Albany River often joined those near the Moose River in raids against the Inuit. For instance, on May 29, 1730, Joseph Myatt observed, "Severall of our home Inds went from hence for Moose River to goe to Warrs against the Esquemeas." He tried to prevent them but without success. He justifiably feared that "they will Kill Some of the Norward Inds who border upon the Esquemeas" (HBCA n.d., B.3/18/a, fol. 17d). On May 29, 1735, five canoes of Albany River Lowland Cree warriors arrived at Moose Fort, and on June 2, seven canoes departed "to the Eastmain to wars with the Usqueemay." The warriors returned to Moose Fort about two months later with fourteen Inuit scalps and one girl prisoner (HBCA n.d., B.135/a/5, fol. 17d, 21). Again, on June 8, 1736, a large war party assembled at Fort Albany was led by "ye Old Captin of this River." The men of this all-male war party had left their families behind: "several of our home Indian familys came here today whose husbands are at ye warrs" (HBCA n.d., B.3/a/24, fol. 27, 31d, Joseph Adams, July 24, 1736). Seventeen canoes from the Albany River area and eight from the Moose River area embarked on this expedition, suggesting a party of approximately fifty warriors (assuming two persons per canoe). Returning warriors reported that they had killed five Inuit men and fifteen women and had taken ten Inuit children prisoners (HBCA n.d., B.135/a/6, fol. 13). The Albany River Cree took six of the Inuit children, while four remained with the Moose River Cree (HBCA n.d., B.3/a/24, August 1, 1736, fol. 32d).

One of the Inuit captives taken during the 1736 raid, "a young Eskemoe boy," was purchased by the HBC from the Cree for one pound of tobacco, one gallon of brandy, and one and a half yards of blue cloth (HBCA n.d., B.3/d/45, fol. 7d). Such purchases were often made to prevent the murder of captives. For example, on April 19, 1783, Edward Jarvis said that he had "traded an Esquimaux boy" from the Albany River Lowland Cree, paying thirty made beaver, the HBC standard of trade.[5] He justified his expenditure because the Lowland Cree had planned to kill him in retribution for the sickness and deaths caused by the smallpox epidemic in 1782–83 (HBCA n.d., B.3/a/81, fol. 24).

HBC traders often exhibited ambivalence in regard to Lowland Cree "Esquimaux hunts." Daniel Francis and Toby Morantz state, "On the one hand all the postmasters in James Bay were ordered to discourage the sorties in whatever ways they could and the masters claimed to be doing so. . . . Yet on the other hand it was common for the 'hunters' to be outfitted at the company posts with ammunition and other items they needed for the trip north" (Francis and Morantz 1983, 77). Thus, for example, when a large group of Lowland Cree assembled on June 9, 1767, at Fort Albany in preparation for war against the Inuit, postmaster Humphrey Marten observed, "25 men came dressed and Painted to the Fort, they said they were determined to go to war with the Esquemaes, on which they sung the war Song, after which about 60 more, Men, Women & Children, all home guard, came to Joyn with them in the Begging Dance, they said it was usual for the Chief to give them great Presents on such occasions that they did not happen Often; and that they expected I would do as my Predecessors had done before, as I am not willing to give Indians cause of Quarrell, I complyed" (HBCA n.d., B.3/a/59, fol. 34).

The reciprocal rights and obligations linking the fur traders and Lowland Cree may account for why the former were willing to outfit the latter despite company policy discouraging warfare. As noted, both sides depended upon each other for key resources needed for trade and survival. Nevertheless, sometimes the relatives of the warriors who remained behind also regretted these raids. For instance, when Fort Albany and Moose Fort Cree failed to return from "an Esquimaux hunt" by September 2, 1774, Humphrey Marten remarked that "almost all the other hunting Indians [were] in despair, at not hearing from their friends that went to war with the Esquimauxs" (HBCA n.d., B.3/a/66, fols. 19d, 33d). The company men missed the warriors because most were employed as goose hunters in the spring and autumn. Goose hunting was left almost entirely to the Indians, and geese were an important element in the diet of the HBC men almost from the time when the posts were established. The fall hunt that began in early September was especially important in stocking winter larders. The Fort Albany Lowland Cree killed approximately two thousand geese each fall in the mid eighteenth century (Lytwyn 2002a, 146). Hence, as Thomas Hutchins lamented in the fall of 1774, "Our Goose season turned out poorly, having ten of the best hunters about at war with the Esquimaux" (HBCA n.d., B.198/a/19, fol. 27). When three warriors returned on September 28, Hutchins exulted: "to my great joy with an account of the welfare of all the rest. Made them heartily welcome & desired them to become Goose hunters immediately" (HBCA n.d., B.3/a/68, fol. 3).

There is only one known example in the historical records in which an HBC trader may have encouraged the Lowland Cree to attack the Inuit. This occurred in 1754 at Richmond Fort after the outpost at Whale River was ransacked and the trader Matthew Warden disappeared (he was later found murdered) (see Francis and Morantz 1983, 74–75; Honigmann 1962, 8–9). The Richmond Fort traders blamed the Inuit and took captive three Inuit men who visited the post. One was released to warn his people, and the other two were thrown in chains. When the two fought back, they were shot, but before the corpses were disposed of, postmaster Richard Potts cut an ear from each body. Potts sent the ears "in a Bottle of Spirits which you Gentlemen Chiefs of Moose and Albany Forts may dispose of them to the Indian Captains of each place" (HBCA n.d., A.11/2, fols. 44–45, March 13, 1754), possibly to incite them to raid the Inuit. Whether the Cree received the ears is not known, but they would not have arrived at Fort Albany in time for the Lowland Cree to organize a raid that summer. However, in the summer of 1755, fifteen Cree warriors arrived at the Whale River post and terrorized the Eastmain Cree before continuing to Richmond Fort, where they received ammunition to attack the Inuit. The explicit reason for the raid was in revenge for the deaths of their kinsmen that winter, which they blamed on Inuit sorcery. The Lowland Cree, however, appear to have been informed about the events of the previous winter, because Potts, after a three-week absence, reported, "Came here two of ye Eusquamays Hunters and informs me they had found some of ye Eusquamays that kill'd Our Boy and plunder'd Whale River House the Indians kill'd all they found and has got 4 children for Slaves, they found Several of the things wch was Stole from Whale River House" (HBCA n.d., B.182/a/7, fol. 47d). Although the main reason for this raid was to avenge the deaths of their kinsmen, the Cree war party may also have believed that they were doing the fur traders a favor.

Cree raids after the 1770s often included "Half-Homeguards," those Cree who resided farther inland during the winter (Lytwyn 2002a, 17). In June 1791, a prominent Lowland Cree hunter named Saquot led a war party against the "Esquimaux" that included Half-Homeguards who resided up the Albany River near Henley House (HBCA n.d., B.3/a/92, fol. 27). Captain Wausakeeshick led the Henley House contingent. The following spring, John Hodgson, postmaster of Henley House, reported that Captain Wausakeeshick and his "gang" were "drinking and exulting over the scalps of the Esquimaux some of these Indians having had a hand in the murders of 4 last summer" (HBCA n.d., B.86/a/46, fol. 19, May 15, 1792). On May 27, 1793, Saquot and his "gang" left Fort Albany on another expedition against the Inuit, again being joined by the Henley House leader, Captain Wausakeeshick, and some of his followers. This was the last Cree raid against the Inuit recorded in the HBC documents.

CAUSES OF LOWLAND CREE–INUIT WARFARE

Prior to contact, the Inuit appear to have been expanding southward into Lowland Cree territory to exploit the resources along the coast of Hudson Bay southeast of the Churchill River. They also appear to have been pushing south into the territory of the Eastmain Cree. Thus, although Inuit territorial aims may have precipitated precontact warfare, ethnic differences probably were also a factor. Because the two peoples were culturally and linguistically distinct, if at first contact between them the Inuit failed to engage in the appropriate gestures of goodwill and gift giving expected of visitors because of their mistrust, they would have been viewed as hostile invaders by the Lowland Cree, and conflict would have occurred immediately. The first battle would then have given rise to periodic and continuing retaliatory revenge raids by both sides.

The initial causes of the warfare do not explain why warfare continued in the historic period. Fear and mistrust deriving from cultural differences became a primary reason for why the Lowland Cree continued to attack the Inuit. They also prevented the two peoples from being able to negotiate a peace, a situation that was exacerbated by the HBC arbitrators when they traded guns to the Cree but refused to trade guns to the Inuit. In consequence, the Inuit avoided trading at posts frequented by Cree. Moreover, because Cree cosmology did not distinguish between the natural and supernatural, misfortunes were blamed on Inuit sorcery, thus giving the Cree a justifiable reason to attack and punish those who had caused the misfortunes (Francis and Morantz 1983, 76; see also Lytwyn 2002a, 60). As stated by Henry Ellis when visiting York Factory in 1746–47, "The Indians are inclinable to War; if there is a bad season of hunting in the Winter, or anyone of their People is missing, or that they have a Sickness amongst them, they must prepare in Spring to go and seek out the Eskemaux, and make a Carnage of them; for they attribute to them the Cause of their Misfortunes: It is the Eskimaux that have killed their Friend; It Is the Eskemaux have kept the Deer away; and the Sickness is occasion'd by a Charm or Witchery of the Eskemaux" (Ellis 1968, 2:43–44). The Fort Albany postmaster, Joseph Isbister, tried to prevent the Lowland Cree from going on the 1755 raid, "but all to no purpose, they said that they must go because they are displeased with the Eskemays for the loss of their friends and some children that died this last winter (as if they were ye cause thereof) so idle are the notions of these people" (HBCA n.d., B.3/a/47, June 6, 1755, fol. 37d). To the Cree, however, sorcery was an invasion by supernatural means. Referring to earlier times, Edward Chappell in 1814 observed that the Lowland Cree believe the Esquimaux to be a nation of sorcerers. Should the season prove a bad one in procuring their furs, they say that the Esquimaux have enchanted the game; and they then set off to the northward, to punish them accordingly. Whenever they discover the tents of the supposed magicians, they remain lurking about the place until a favourable opportunity offers; when raising the dreadful war-whoop, they rush on to the attack with inconceivable fury. Every individual of the vanquished is instantly massacred, whether they make resistance, or implore mercy. The animosity between them is hereditary, bloody, and implacable. (Chappell 1817, 110)

And Andrew Graham stated, "Revenge, jealousy, animosities, death of one of the family, or even the indulgence of an human levity, are sufficient for a hostile expedition" (Graham 1969, 172).

Another motive for warfare was the prestige that warriors could gain in such raids. Although the prestige quest was not the initial cause of warfare, by the eighteenth century it had become an important secondary reason. Macho behavior is reflected in the tests of endurance that warriors had to undergo to make themselves worthy and in the acts of bravado of leaders. Also, failure to avenge the misfortunes of their kin was not a happy option, as revealed by the face-saving practice of killing and scalping innocent Eastmain Cree and then telling their relatives at home that the trophies were Inuit scalps.

Raiding was also done to take captives. Women were sometimes taken as wives, perhaps in some cases to avoid bride service obligations, and children were adopted, perhaps to fill a void following the death of a Cree child. Some captives were purchased by the HBC, often to prevent them from being killed by the Cree (Lytwyn 2002a, 61). Another reason for taking captives given by William Coats was to trade them to the Ottawa, who in turn were said to have traded them to the "Notawais," presumably the Iroquois (Barrow 1852, 56–57).

The primary motives for Cree raids in the eighteenth century derived from the fear and mistrust between the two peoples. This interpretation supports a cross-cultural study of war and peace conducted by Ember and Ember, who state, "The strongest of our socialization predictors of more war is socialization for mistrust. Theoretically, people who grow up to be mistrustful of others, and who therefore fear others, may be more likely to go to war than to negotiate or seek conciliation" (Ember and Ember 1994a, 192). Ember and Ember argue further that "mistrust is more likely a cause than a consequence of more war" (1994a, 193).

Another factor given by the Embers that predicts whether war will occur is "the threat of natural disasters, which occur rarely and unpredictably" (Ember and Ember 1994a, 195). Cree involvement in the fur trade, the means whereby they obtained guns and other necessary materials, had made them vulnerable to environmental fluctuations once they began to split their time between hunting for fur bearers and hunting for food, even though some fur animals could be eaten (Bishop 1984). Death from starvation, exposure, an accident, or illness was frequently attributed to supernatural forces controlled and manipulated by persons with special powers, that is, by conjurers (Brightman 1993; Brown and Brightman 1988). Many Cree misfortunes were blamed on Inuit malevolence, a situation that often led to revenge raids.

Apart from statements by fur traders linking misfortunes with Lowland Cree raids, the precise details in the daily journals connecting disasters and raids are often elusive. The eighteenth-century Fort Albany journals recorded eighteen years in which Cree war parties attacked Inuit on the eastern coast of Hudson Bay: 1707, 1728, 1730, 1735, 1736, 1738, 1755, 1757, 1766, 1767, 1770, 1774, 1777, 1781, 1782, 1783, 1791, and 1793.[6] It is unlikely that raids went unrecorded, because Cree warriors mustered at HBC posts to obtain necessary equipment from company stores, and the traders tried to discourage them. Evidence indicates that calamities suffered by the Cree preceded the attacks against the Inuit. For example, the first raid on the Inuit reported in the Fort Albany post journals occurred in the summer of 1707. Earlier, on March 26, Anthony Beale stated that the Cree who arrived from the north were "very poore and Hungerry and tells me that 3 or four familys of Indians that ways has perrished this Winter by Reason there was but Fuew Beasts" (HBCA n.d., B.3/a/2, March 26, 1707). The winter of 1728 was also punctuated by several calamities. On January 25, a woman who was accidentally shot by a fur trader died; on January 28, "Old Metistesou's Eldest Son Died who came in Starved"; on February 2, "2 families of home Ins came in starving having had the misfortune to bury both of their Wives"; and on March 20, another man and his family arrived starving, "his Wifes being in a very Weak and Sickly Condition" (HBCA n.d., B.3/a/16). The winter of 1735 was especially severe. On May 3, two Cree arrived from the north complaining of the great scarcity of food in general. The trader remarked, "Wee knowing of about 30 Indians of our home, Western & Northern Natives being dead this Year & yt furrs is very Scarce wth them by reason of ye Great Quantity of Snow they had this Winter they Could not hunt" (HBCA n.d., B.3/a/23). Similarly, on January 11, 1755, ten hungry Cree arrived at Fort Albany reporting that "there are no deer not Any thing in their Country to Subsist on." On January 22, six starving people came from Moose Fort. On January 30, an HBC trader who carried food to starving Cree returned with a "Tribe of Starvd Indians to ye Number of 21 Men women & childn in a low & distresed state." Deaths from starvation also occurred that winter (HBCA n.d., B.3/a/47). The winter of 1782 was another bad one. The inland post, Henley House, burned to the ground, killing three HBC traders and consuming all of its goods (HBCA n.d., B.3/a/79, January 22, 1782). Consequently, the Cree of the region—being deprived of any supplies they might have needed for hunting—were reported to have been starving. On February 5, as a last resort before coming to Fort Albany for food, some Cree were to try to catch fish. Having no luck by the 13th, those able to reach the post arrived after devouring "all their Dogs, and part of their Beaver Skins." On April 12, there was an eclipse of the sun, a natural event of supernatural significance to the Cree (HBCA n.d., B.3/a/79, April 12, 1782). Finally, there was the winter of 1792, one of the worst in memory at Fort Albany. On May 9, Edward Jarvis summed up the winter's effects after Saquot, a leading hunter, came in with only twenty made beaver in pelts: "[H]e is quite dejected and fainted away in the room such a Calamitous year I never knew or heard of to be so universal—several whole families of Indians was suspected to be starved to Death which gives me the most alarming Apprehensions for the Trade this year Albany having lost several hundreds of Mbeaver [i.e., made beaver] by the Deaths & famine of the Natives" (HBCA n.d., B.3/a/93a, May 9, 1792). There is also evidence for cannibalism (April 23 entry), a not-uncommon occurrence under conditions of extreme physical and psychological stress (Bishop 1975b). In sum, the evidence indicates an association between disasters and raids upon the Inuit although the links between the two are not always specified.

A common argument for the cause of warfare is territorial conquest generated by competition over scarce resources. This may, in part, account for the initial conflict between the Lowland Cree and Inuit, but it does not explain eighteenth-century warfare. Although the Lowland Cree suffered from periods of extreme deprivation caused by their inability to acquire food, they never occupied the areas that they raided (Francis and Morantz 1983, 76). Ecological and economic reasons account for this. The Lowland Cree preferred to be near the trading posts and easy access to the materials on which they relied to supply their subsistence needs as well as those required for warfare. During harsh winters, the fur traders frequently fed hungry people who in times of scarcity visited the post, especially in the lean, late winter months (Bishop 1984). Hence, resource stress in the eighteenth century, rather than encouraging the Lowland Cree to occupy Inuit lands, kept them near the trading post. Moreover, many of the fur bearers whose pelts they traded were unavailable farther north. Also, warriors who left their families behind while on raids probably wished to return quickly. Still another reason that would pertain to both the pre- and the postcontact period for why the Lowland Cree never took over the lands of defeated Inuit is that the subsistence technology of the former was not suitable for exploiting sea mammals. Birch-bark canoes are less well suited than umiaks and kayaks for hunting whales and seals, and the Cree lacked harpoons with detachable heads and other items adapted for survival in the open sea region. Furthermore, some Cree living near the coast did not possess canoes, because sufficient bark suitable for making them could only be found farther inland. Thus, multiple reasons explain why the Lowland Cree made no attempt to expand their territorial control northward into lands occupied by the Inuit. They nevertheless had no compunctions about attacking Dene-speakers and occupying the fur-rich lands to the northwest.[7]

One question remains, and that concerns the reasons why warfare ended.

The End of Lowland Cree–Inuit Warfare

Warfare between the Lowland Cree and Inuit ended with the last raid in 1793. Termination is best explained by the expansion inland of the HBC fur trade and establishment of interior posts to compete effectively with the North West Company. Beginning in the 1780s, Lowland Cree were hired to load and transport large quantities of goods for these new posts, some located hundreds of miles inland, during the summer season that was the traditional time for raids against the Inuit (Francis 1979, 79–80). The boats then had to be loaded with the winter furs and other country produce and conveyed back to the main posts, Fort Albany and Moose Fort. Simultaneously, new employment opportunities for Cree not working on the brigades became available at the coastal establishments, which were expanding to stock additional goods for the inland posts and to accommodate more employees in transit to new inland locales. These chores required a considerable labor force, keeping most able-bodied adult Lowland Cree males occupied for most of the summer. Moreover, enlargement of the coastal posts and construction of new inland posts made life for the Lowland Cree more secure. A greater quantity and variety of store goods became available, while new labor opportunities other than trapping or procuring geese allowed the Lowland Cree to trade for more items, which helped to alleviate hardships in the bush.

Still another reason that may explain why warfare ended involved the trade in firearms to the Inuit beginning in the mid 1770s. As Andrew Graham stated, "When I commanded Churchill Factory Anno Domini 1773, 4 and 5 I trained up four young Esquimaux to use fire-arms, and left them fully a match for our best Indians, either at an object sitting or on the wing" (Graham 1969, 236). The Cree may have been reluctant to attack people who had come to possess guns, although the "cold war" factor was probably not a primary reason why warfare ended.

Conclusions

Ample documentary and oral ethnohistorical evidence exists to support the premise that Lowland Cree–Inuit warfare predated the arrival of

Europeans. This example indicates that warfare among band-type societies cannot be dismissed or explained as simply a reaction to colonial influences, even though the latter can exacerbate an existing situation or generate a new one.

Granted, the acquisition of European weaponry by the Lowland Cree gave them a distinct advantage, both physical and psychological, in the wars that followed. Although deaths were sustained by both sides prior to contact, with the entry of Europeans in the seventeenth century, warfare took a new direction. After the Cree obtained firearms, there is no mention of a Lowland Cree ever being killed in battle with the Inuit. Moreover, the historical evidence suggests that the total number of Inuit killed over this period may have been considerable relative to overall population size; indeed, the Inuit inhabitants of some southerly settlements may have been annihilated, while fear of attack drove others to safer regions farther north.

Nevertheless, the underlying factors leading to intergroup violence was not dependent on the European presence. The precontact population expansion of the Inuit into or near Cree territory probably precipitated conflict, but fear and mistrust deriving from cultural differences cannot be ruled out as a reason for some raids. Mutual hatred continued in the historic period. Lowland Cree memory of Inuit invasions and experiences with unpredictable human disasters attributable to altered ecological and economic conditions that they blamed on Inuit sorcery often were followed by raids. Thus, there were multiple causes of warfare operating concurrently (see also Lekson 2002, 621–22), as well as shifts in the emphasis placed on specific factors and the emergence of new ones as the conditions of warfare changed after European contact.

The Lowland Cree–Inuit example is also instructive with respect to delineating reasons why wars end. Cree raids upon the Inuit ceased after the Cree became involved in occupations that kept them busy at the very time that they formerly would have been away on raids. In addition, summer employment gave them a new source of income whereby they could trade for more items that lessened hardships in the bush. Although starvation remained a threat during severe winters well into the nineteenth century, conditions were gradually improving. There thus were fewer instances of misfortune to blame on Inuit magic. By the nineteenth century, the Lowland Cree–Inuit conflict had become a thing of the past, gone but not forgotten.

Acknowledgments

We wish to thank the Hudson's Bay Company for permission to quote from their vast archives. We would also like to thank M. Estellie Smith for her helpful suggestions. She cannot, however, be held responsible for any errors or for our particular interpretations.

Notes

1. Paul Sillitoe also supports this view: "When both sides are evenly matched, a common situation, fighting with these relatively ineffective weapons—bows and arrows, spears, war clubs, battle axes, knives and swords—results in few deaths, contrary to popular opinion fed by sensational and fallacious stories, and the small number of reliably documented massacres notwithstanding. Although gruesome customs like headhunting, cannibalism and scalping accompany primitive war in some regions, the bestiality and number of casualties resulting pales into insignificance compared to the horror and carnage when industrial nations fight with their technologically awesome arsenals" (Sillitoe 1985, 890).

2. Andrew Graham states, "The Esquimaux used to live on and about that [Churchill] river, until the Company erected Prince of Wales's Fort; when the concourse of other Indians to trade, obliged the poor inhabitants to retire farther to the northward, to avoid falling victims to the enmity and superstition of their inveterate and hereditary foes (the Northern [Chipewyan] and Southern [Cree] Indians)" (Graham 1969, 226).

3. James Knight added to the negative image of the Inuit when he stated, "Them Natives to the Norward [of Churchill] are more Savage and brutelike than these [Chipewyan] and will drink blood and eat raw flesh and fish and loves it as well as some does Strong Drink" (Rich 1949, xi). Confirmation that the Inuit were not to be trusted came in 1719 when Knight, who left Churchill in two ships on a voyage of discovery to the north, never returned. The remains of the ships were discovered in 1722 by Captain John Scroggs, who reported that "every Man was killed by the Eskemoes" (Rich 1949, xlv).

4. Alanson Skinner, who conducted fieldwork in the western James Bay region in the early twentieth century, noted, "Scalping was carried on, and in the old wars against the Eskimo, it was customary for the victor to eat a piece of fat cut from the thigh of the slain enemy" (Skinner 1911, 78–79).

5. To trade with Aboriginal hunters, the HBC created a system of value measurements that were applied to both furs and trade goods. As Arthur Ray and Donald Freeman state, "This accounting system was based on a unit called the *made beaver* (MB). The MB established an equivalence between volumes of goods traded and furs taken in return in terms of the number of prime, whole beaver pelts which they represented" (Ray and Freeman 1978, 54).

6. There may have been a nineteenth year. The Eastmain Indian Robinson Crusoe stated in 1755 that his brother had been killed and scalped twelve years earlier. That would have been in 1743, the year that Henley House was built. On June 3, 1743, the Fort Albany postmaster, Joseph Isbister, set out with eight HBC employees and ten canoes of Indians to construct the new post. He arrived back on June 21. During his absence, George Spence was left in charge of Fort Albany but kept few records (HBCA n.d., B.3/a/34). It is thus possible that a Cree war party left while Isbister was absent; though Spence failed to report this incursion, Robinson Crusoe's statement suggests its occurrence. The journal records that summer are devoted primarily to the activities up the Albany River.

7. James Knight in 1716 estimated that between 5,000 and 6,000 Chipewyan had been killed since the first trading post was built at the mouth of the Hayes River, about 1682 (HBCA n.d., B.239/a/1, May 6, 1716, fol. 26d). If correct, that would mean that roughly 150 Chipewyan were killed each year. Although the numbers may be exaggerated, they clearly indicate that warfare between the Cree and Chipewyan was intense and violent.

3 ABORIGINAL WARFARE ON THE NORTHWEST COAST
DID THE POTLATCH REPLACE WARFARE?

Joan A. Lovisek

The classic work on warfare on the Northwest Coast was published in 1950 by anthropologist Helen Codere as *Fighting with Property: A Study of Kwakiutl Potlatching and Warfare, 1792–1930*. Relying on the work of Franz Boas and George Hunt, Codere concluded that warfare among the Kwakiutl was insignificant, ceremonial, and characterized by some surprise raiding, the taking of a few trophy heads, and dramatic dancing. For Codere, warfare was replaced by rivalry potlatching in 1849 as a direct result of a sudden influx of trade goods, a decline in population attributable to epidemic disease, and an increase in competition for rank following the amalgamation of four Kwakiutl groups at Fort Rupert on the northeast side of Vancouver Island. This competition replaced war with rivalry potlatching and brought peace to the Kwakiutl.

Rivalry for status accompanied by large-scale conspicuous property distributions has become synonymous with the Northwest Coast culture. Codere's thesis has not only been influential but has also been applied as a general theory applicable to the entire Northwest Coast, particularly through the work of Marcel Mauss, who would view the potlatch as a "war of property" (Bolscher 1982, 5; Bracken 1997; Cole and Chaikin 1990, 8; Donald and Mitchell 1975; Duff 1997, 81–82; Jopling 1989, 15; Mauss 1990, 37, 42; Ringel 1979, 354; Rosman and Rubel 1971; Suttles 1954, 46). Although Codere's thesis was developed in 1950, it has reappeared in the 1996 *Report of the Royal Commission on Aboriginal Peoples* to portray Northwest Coast peoples as pacifists who were able to resolve their conflicts through the potlatch, free from violence (see Scheffel 2000, 178). The analogy between war and potlatch is so pervasive that the author of the report did not consider it necessary to cite Codere, leaving the reader to assume that it is self-evident that the potlatch replaced war. This new advocacy perspective, in which the potlatch is considered as a moral alternative to war, forms part of a larger revisionism in which the positive attributes of Aboriginal culture, such as peace, have supplanted the negative, such as warfare, slavery, and human trophy-taking.

Although parts of Codere's thesis have been the subject of criticism (Drucker and Heizer 1967, 25; Ferguson 1984, 301–7; Suttles 2000, 261n27; Wike 1958, 1087–1098), there has been no systematic assessment of the validity of her thesis that warfare was insignificant or ceremonial or of how it was replaced by the potlatch. This chapter examines the validity of Codere's thesis by reexamining the data within the context of current archaeological and ethnohistorical findings on Northwest Coast warfare.

NORTHWEST COAST PEOPLES

The Aboriginal peoples[1] of the Northwest Coast are Pacific Coast maritime societies situated between Yakatat Bay in Alaska to the north and Puget Sound in the state of Washington to the south. Most groups including the Kwakiutl (also known as Kwakwaka'wakw) are in British Columbia, Canada (see fig. 3.1). Precontact, the area had a population of approximately 150,000, which was the second-largest population in aboriginal North America (Ames and Maschner 1999, 43; Boyd 1990, 136; Donald 1997, 17).

The Aboriginal population is characterized by a high degree of sedentism with multiple-family households, permanent winter villages, hereditary positions of status, marked differences in wealth, ritualized exchange, and an elaborate crest art and mythology. Although the region was rich in marine resources, it was locally subject to extreme variation in production (Ames and Maschner 1999, 114).

Despite the population size and level of social complexity, Northwest Coast Aboriginal groups have been classified by anthropologists as complex hunter-gatherers or affluent foragers, because most of their food was derived from wild rather than domesticated sources and quantities were stored. Because of the varying rules of resource ownership, no single person controlled all aspects of the food collecting and preparing process, and there was little effective political organization above that of the local group. For these reasons, Northwest Coast Aboriginal groups are not generally classified as "tribes" until after contact (Ames and Maschner 1999, 17; Matson and Coupland 1995, 238, 250–51; Walens 1981, 13).

AN ARCHAEOLOGICAL AND ETHNOHISTORICAL OVERVIEW OF WARFARE ON THE NORTHWEST COAST

The archaeology of the prehistory of the Northwest Coast has focused on the origin of social inequities in power, privilege, and wealth, of which warfare has been considered an important variable (Prince 2001; Sutherland 2001). The earliest evidence of conflict on the Northwest Coast is in the form of skeletal remains showing trauma dating to 3000 BC in the Prince Rupert Harbour area, which is in the ethnographic Tsimshian territory. The osteological evidence shows a high rate of skeletal injuries among males, a high ratio of male-to-female burials, and the presence of weapons (Moss and Erlandson 1992, 73, 74). The skeletal evidence shows trauma in the form of depressed skulls, fractures from club blows, facial and anterior tooth fractures, defensive forearm

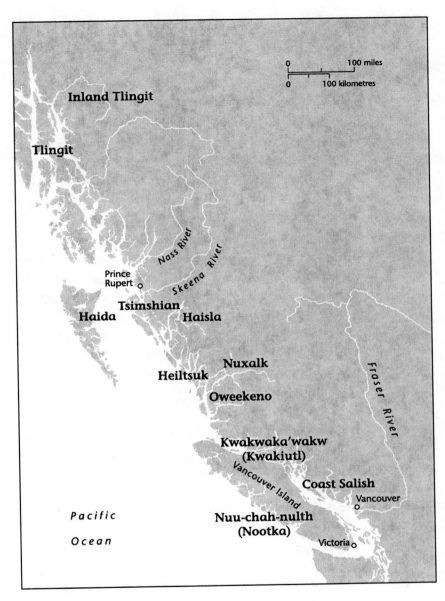

FIGURE 3.1 Northwest Coast aboriginal groups.

and outer hand injuries, and decapitation (Cybulski 1990, 58). Jerome Cybulski (1994, 76, 81) has cautioned that although skeletal trauma and warfare-related injuries are difficult to study accurately, available adult samples show an increase in trauma from 28.1 percent in the Early Stage (3500 BC to 1500 BC) to 44.9 percent in the Late Stage (AD 500 to ca. 1774). The frequency of warfare-related injuries, however, declined to 21.1 percent in the historic period, which led Kenneth Ames (2001, 10) to conclude that warfare was more prevalent prehistorically because violence caused to human remains was lowest during the early modern period (AD 1750–1850). The most lethal injuries, however, are delivered to the thorax and abdomen; these wounds do not often involve bone and do not appear as osteological evidence (Lambert 1997b, 92).

Warfare was initially more prevalent in the northern part of the Northwest Coast, where 40 percent of the individuals recovered in the Prince Rupert Harbour area were found to have fractures to the limbs and spine, and 11 percent in the Strait of Georgia (ethnographic Salish territory). Between AD 200 and 500, the evidence for warfare appears in the archaeological record as a shift in village settlement to more-defensible locales in southeastern Alaska (ethnographic Tlingit territory) and the Queen Charlotte Islands (ethnographic Haida territory), as well as a decline in population that occurred along the British Columbia mainland coast in ethnographic Coast Salish territory (Lowrey 1999, 48, 49; Maschner 1997, 285). After 5550 BP, there is archaeological evidence of economic intensification, greater dependence on salmon and other storable species, and the formation of larger groups (indicated by house and village size). Increased population was particularly indicated by larger and more frequently occurring shell middens (Moss 1993, 631).

As warfare was more prevalent in the northern portion of the Northwest Coast, the evidence of violence has been considered a major factor in the development of an elite and of slaves, which are features of northern group social and political organization (Ames and Maschner 1999; Macdonald 1989; Maschner and Reedy-Maschner 1998, 41; Moss and Erlandson 1992). Northern Coast warfare evidently spread south sometime around AD 500 (Ames and Maschner 1999, 210; Maschner 1997).

At the beginning of the Late Pacific period (AD 200/550 to ca. 775), much larger households and fortifications were constructed and there was greater use of the bow and arrow. Nathan Lowrey (1999, 52) argued that the bow and arrow, which appeared on the Northwest Coast sometime after AD 200/500 (Ames and Maschner 1999, 200), instigated the development of both defensive sites and armor. Lowrey (1999, 70) also determined that sometime after AD 400, highly effective bone points indicated increasing hostilities during the Late Pacific period.

Although Patricia Lambert (1997b, 81) has cautioned that defensive sites and structures "at best only suggest or imply the threat of violent intruders, [whereas] injuries preserved in human burials document actual events and identify the victims," nevertheless the effort and resources committed to the construction and maintenance of defensive sites, and their cultural significance as an indicator of violence (perceived or real), should not be undervalued, particularly on the Northwest Coast. The Late Pacific period (AD 200/550 to ca. AD 1775) shows major shifts in mortuary ritual, subsistence, a coastwide escalation in warfare, and demography that was accompanied by a population spike around AD 1000–1100 (Ames and Maschner 1999, 93, 95, 217–18, 256). Warfare was as pervasive in the early modern period as it was in the Late Pacific period with one notable difference—the population declined in the latter part of the Late Pacific period. Herbert Maschner (1997, 294) argued that because the population decline occurred well before contact, there was no possibility of resource or population stress in the early contact period and concluded that "conflicts must have been integral to the maintenance of Northwest Coast culture, a culture founded in the protection of status and prestige for noble leaders and their kinsmen." Herbert Maschner and K. L. Reedy-Maschner (1997, 285, 294; 1998) also concluded that in the absence of population pressure, prestige motivated warfare in the late protohistorical period and the early contact period. This would suggest that warfare may have been motivated less by competition for territory and subsistence than has been previously argued (Ferguson 1984).

When social organization is introduced as a variable to explain warfare on the Northwest Coast, the analysis again shifts to economic motivations. The prevalence of warfare on the northern part of the Northwest Coast has been positively correlated to the degree of segmentation in a group's social organization. David Riches (1979, 145–47) has hypothesized that uncertainty in resources for northern groups such as the Haida and Tlingit contributed to the formation of matrilineal descent groups. The descent group controlled production through slavery, which was a consequence of intergroup violence. Gary Coupland (1989) also identified a relationship between rank, warfare, and ecology and argued, based on stone clubs recovered from burial sites, that southern Coast Salish warfare was characterized by defensive structures while the northern ranked groups aggressively raided for food, women, slaves, and economic spoils. He concluded that war was more economically motivated for descent groups, which characterized northern social organization, than for groups in the south, where warfare would be primarily defensive. Thus, scholars of warfare on the Northwest Coast have made distinctions between economic and prestige-related motivations for warfare depending upon the weight placed on variables such as population, ecology, social organization, skeletal trauma, weapons, settlement patterns, and historical evidence.

One of the difficulties with assessing the relative importance of warfare pre- and postcontact is that the archaeological method of dating can subsume both the protohistorical and precontact data into one large period, namely, the Late Pacific period. This makes it difficult to distinguish Aboriginal patterns of warfare from those introduced by direct or indirect European contact. As indicated in the archaeological record, the early contact period was represented by numerous defensive sites.

The expansion of the maritime fur trade (centered on sea otter pelts) brought the Kwakiutl, who are located in the middle of the northern and southern warfare patterns, into the documentary record. In 1792 when Captain George Vancouver recorded the first known European contact with the Kwakiutl, he described a fortified village constructed on a rocky cliff and said it could house 300 people (Vancouver 1801, 231). The Kwakiutl actually had two basic types of fortifications: one that encapsulated the village, and another that was a separate well-stocked structure used for refuge. These defensive sites were located near trade-route junctions or in areas bordering group territories. Although Vancouver also observed fresh evidence of human trophy-taking (Vancouver 1801, 271–73, 277), we cannot determine whether the Kwakiutl were engaged in defensive, offensive, or both types of conflict at this early stage. There is some indication that interregional conflicts were restricted to the frontier between groups and in populous core areas near the center of a group's region (Maschner 1997, 274; Maschner and Reedy-Maschner 1998, 24; Prince 2001, 255, 257).

Although generalizing about the impact of the early maritime trade on the Northwest Coast is difficult because it occurred in various locations at different times, contact produced situations in which some Aboriginal groups obtained better control of the trade but in the process weakened their control of resource production (Archer 1993, 149; Inglis and Haggarty 2000). This often led to violent confrontations over the control of the trade routes, access to European trade goods, and food stores (Clayton 2000, 152, 158).

The maritime fur trade on the Northwest Coast collapsed with the decline of the sea otter population circa 1825 from overhunting, increased competition between fur traders, reduced access to the Canton market, and declining prices (Archer 1993, 159; Gibson 1992, 56). The fur trade shifted to land-based animals and land-based trading forts circa 1827–60 (Littlefield 1987, 174). Fundamental to the two fur trades was a network of Aboriginal trade routes, primarily between coastal and interior groups (Donald 1997, 223; Macdonald 1989; Mackie 1997, 123).

The type of trade goods initially exchanged suggests the importance of warfare. Muskets were introduced early in the maritime trade (ca. 1780) but were initially neither reliable nor accurate. The Kwakiutl had muskets, iron-pointed spears, clubs, large knives, and Spanish muskets prior to direct contact in 1792, having obtained them in trade from the Nootka (also known as Nuu-chah-nulth) (Gibson 1992, 8–9). The introduction of guns and the effect of these new weapons on warfare have been the subject of controversy. Wilson Duff (1997, 81) implied that the introduction of guns resulted in higher mortality and decreased population. Robert Boyd (1996, 155), however, has suggested that guns could not have had a significant impact until a continuous supply of ammunition was available, which did not occur until the establishment of land-based trading posts, circa 1827–49.

At the early stages of the maritime trade in 1793, iron, copper, and "clemons"—elk or moose skins, which were used to make "war dresses"—were in demand in all areas but particularly in the north (Beresford and

Dixon 1968, 244; Gibson 1992, 230–31), which suggests a continued importance of warfare among northern groups. The introduction of guns did reduce the use of this armor, which was directly reflected in a reduced trade for elk and moose skins (Gibson 1992, 230; Wike 1951, 21).

The combined effects of epidemics and the uneven distribution of guns may have contributed to wars of "extermination" that are frequently cited in the ethnographic accounts. However, demographic decline was local and occurred at different times. Some groups, such as the Kwakiutl, who were apparently affected very late by a smallpox epidemic, were able to militarily dominate groups such as the Coast Salish who were affected earlier (Boas and Hunt 1897, 332; Curtis 1915, 309; Galois 1994, 17; Inglis and Haggarty 2000, 101; Maschner 1997, 291). This suggests that Kwakiutl warfare was exacerbated in the early postcontact period, boosted in part by a changed demography, access to trade routes and trade goods, and the military advantage of having guns.

An important characteristic of Northwest Coast warfare was slavery. Slaves were always important to Northwest Coast cultures prior to and after contact, but the economic importance of slaves escalated after at least 1830, as warfare changed to opportunistic, individualistic predatory raiding. Slaves were ransomed for trade goods or sold to other groups for furs, which could then be exchanged for trade goods. For many groups, especially those that did not have access to fur-bearing animals, it was easier and faster to obtain trade goods by predatory raiding than by trading, trapping, or hunting animals for furs (Donald 1997, 232–33).

On October 6, 1849, for example, a Kwakiutl war party returned to Beaver Harbour near Fort Rupert with "14 skulls and about 30 prisoners." The victims were probably Bella Coola (Heiltsuk), who subsequently revenged this act in the spring of 1850 (Galois 1994, 45; Provincial Archives of British Columbia 1850; Work 1945, 61). In 1857, the Kwakiutl were reported to have dispatched several war parties to obtain slaves to sell south to the Salish (Provincial Archives of British Columbia 1857, 67).

During this post–maritime fur trade period (ca. 1830–50) of intensive predatory raiding, raiding extended over much greater distances than previous raids, which had been confined closer to home territories (Ames 2001, 3; Donald 1997). Northern groups typically had a much higher proportion of slaves (by about 30 percent) than southern groups, whose population provided most of the slaves. However, by 1850 the Kwakiutl had come to hold the highest median number of slaves, followed closely by the Northern Tlingit, Tsimshian, Northern Wakashan, and southern Coast Salish. The groups holding the largest number of slaves have been considered to be the most warlike (Donald 1997, 187).

Predatory raiding became opportunistic and individual, driven by economic motives, revenge, and prestige (Belcher 1843, 104; Donald 1997, 34, 75, 127, 231–33; Mitchell 1984, 39; Wike 1951, 99). Slaves, particularly their exchange value, contributed to shifts in Kwakiutl social ranking and innovations in political organization. Fur-trade wealth through the exchange of slaves created new leaders and increased the total number of leaders, although many would have fewer followers, sometimes including only slaves (Donald 1997, 131; Gibson 1992, 271). The killing of a slave by the Kwakiutl in 1859 or 1860, however, prompted a military response by British authorities in 1860. This act, in conjunction with mortality as a result of a smallpox epidemic in 1862, eventually ended slavery and warfare among the Kwakiutl (Donald 1997, 154; Gough 1984, 81; Jacobsen 1977, 32).

A RESPONSE TO CODERE

Codere argued that in 1849—following an influx of trade goods, particularly blankets, and depopulation from epidemics—war was stopped and replaced by the potlatch. This argument relies heavily on the assertion that there was an influx of trade goods in 1849 following an earlier depopulation attributable to mortality from disease. Both these assumptions rest on faulty evidence and a preconception of precontact pacifism. This is not supported by the historical, ethnographic, or archaeological evidence.

Cloth blankets had been sold to the Kwakiutl before 1800 (Wike 1951, 44). In 1826, the Hudson's Bay Company (HBC) started to trade with the Kwakiutl from steam vessels. The vessels were soon followed by the establishment of trading forts at Fort Langley in 1827 and Fort

McLaughlin in 1834, from which the Kwakiutl obtained trade goods (HBCA 1834; Tolmie 1963, 308). In 1835, after finding coal in Beaver Harbour near what would become Fort Rupert, the Kwakiutl started to sell it and firewood to the Hudson's Bay Company as early as 1836 in exchange for trade goods (HBCA 1849–50). In 1837 the Kwakiutl obtained 358 cloth blankets in trade and 550 in 1839 (Provincial Archives of British Columbia 1836–41). In addition to these sources of trade goods, American traders cruised the Inside Passage and traded blankets and other items with the Kwakiutl (Galois 1994, 28, 29; Tolmie 1963, 308). The historical evidence for the introduction of trade blankets seriously questions Codere's (1950, 94) estimation that before 1849 the Kwakiutl had only 320 blankets and that these were made of cedar bark and fur. The Kwakiutl had access to trade goods including blankets several decades before 1849.

In making her claims of depopulation, Codere (1950, 52) proposed that mortality wrought by epidemic—which she dates to 1837—led to depopulation, which in turn led to a shortfall of inheritors to the finite number of potlatch seats, a statement disputed by Abraham Rosman and Paula Rubel (1971, 137). The population figures that Codere relied on in arguing that the Kwakiutl population decreased from 23,566 people to 7,000 are now considered inflated and incorrect. Instead of the 23,566 figure used by Codere, the pre-epidemic Kwakiutl population (prior to 1849) was more likely 8,850 (Boyd 1999, 190).

The most likely date for Kwakiutl depopulation occurred after the smallpox epidemic of 1862. Census data for 1881, for example, indicate that the number of persons born during and after the 1862 epidemic was critically low (Boyd 1990, 147; 1999, 190; Galois 1994, 17, 44–45). Compared with the historical evidence that provides examples of warfare after 1849 (Ferguson 1984, 306; see also Codere 1950, 117), particularly in the form of predatory raiding, and evidence that Kwakiutl warfare ended by 1862, coinciding with the intervention of British gunboats and mortality resulting from a smallpox epidemic,[2] is there any residual association between warfare and the potlatch?

Codere's thesis that the potlatch replaced war was based in part on her evaluation of the type of warfare practiced by the Kwakiutl, specifically, that it was seasonal and limited to surprise ambush raids.

As described earlier in this chapter, raiding against defenseless groups for slaves or items of property was a common attribute of Northwest Coast warfare. This type of warfare has been considered more lethal and destructive than contemporary battles because it was an efficient means of inflicting damage through property destruction, acquiring plunder, and mutilating victims (Keeley 1996; LeBlanc and Rice 2001, 4, 5). Codere clearly undervalued the importance of slavery to Kwakiutl warfare and its potential significance to the emergence of the rivalry potlatch, for there is a direct association between groups that raided for slaves and those that practiced the rivalry potlatch (Donald 1997, 114; Mitchell 1984).

THE CULTURAL CONTEXT OF THE RIVALRY POTLATCH

Like other Pacific cultures, Northwest Coast groups subscribed to an ideology based on a belief in spirits of war and death, which were considered to be present during different seasons. The Kwakiutl divided the year into the profane season, marked by subsistence gathering and local group organization, and the sacred winter season, when secret societies consolidated into a winter village and celebrated the return of the spirit of war and death in a festival called the Winter Ceremonial. The Winter Ceremonial was the ritual setting for antagonism, which was often precipitated by killing an enemy (Boas and Hunt 1897, 148, 664). In fact, holding a dance ahead of the winter season could be construed by neighboring groups as an aggressive act that could lead to war (Jacobsen 1977, 33). The various secret societies that participated in the Winter Ceremonial were recognized as war parties that went into action during times of war in both summer and winter. Autumn, however, was the preferred raiding season, because it came after the production and storage of food for the winter (Boas and Hunt 1897, 418, 430, 431, 664; Codere 1950, 98–99; Goldman 1981, 148; Holm 1990, 378; Sapir 1966, 47; Walens 1981, 39–40).

All the great displays of ritual antagonism documented in the ethnographic records—such as grease feasts, the killing of slaves, the destruction of property, and the distribution of animal skins—occurred during the Winter Ceremonial (Ames and Maschner 1999, 216; Boas

1966, 105; Boas and Hunt 1897, 355; Drucker and Heizer 1967, 14n8, 126; Holm 1990; Suttles 1991, 110; Walens 1981, 84). Even the expression "fighting with property" (which, for Codere and others, became a paradigm for the potlatch) was used during the Winter Ceremonial (Boas and Hunt 1897, 580, 581; Goldman 1981, 148, 152).

The historical record indicates that predatory raiding circa 1830–50 likely contributed to an elaboration of the Winter Ceremonial characterized by the killing of slaves, aggressive property distribution, and ritual cannibalism, particularly after 1835 when an elite Kwakiutl war party attacked the Heiltsuk (Bella Coola) and acquired the rights to perform the *hamatsa*, or cannibal dance (Boas 1966, 258; Boas and Hunt 1897, 425–27, 664). War was considered the means to satiate the spirits of cannibalism, war, and death, and the Winter Ceremonial was the ritual space for the ceremonial offering of animal skins and humans (slaves and war victims).

The Winter Ceremonial of 1859–60 may have been the last one to use human sacrifice in the form of trophy heads and slaves (Lovisek 2007). After the mortality wrought by smallpox in 1862, the Winter Ceremonial changed. Sacrificing slaves was replaced with coppers,[3] which were made from the copper sheathing of European ships and first observed in use by the Kwakiutl in 1866. The Winter Ceremonial was the only ritually appropriate occasion to break or destroy a copper, an act that mimicked the destruction of a human body (Goldman 1981, 155; Walens 1981, 149). Hemlock (or cedar) wreathes replaced human trophy heads, which were thrown into a fire after calling out the name of the enemy. Arrows were then shot into the fire in a ceremony called *yi'lxoa*, which means "placing the head of an enemy on a pole" (Boas and Hunt 1897, 522; Donald 1997, 178; Jopling 1989, 71; Lord 1866, 257–59).

The Winter Ceremonial contained the important Kwakiutl military themes such as killing enemies, destroying property, ritual antagonism between rivals from different secret societies, burning houses, and the taking of trophy heads and scalps (Boas and Hunt 1897, 522, 523, 664; Drucker and Heizer 1967, 126; Goldman 1981, 170–72; Provincial Archives of British Columbia n.d.; Suttles 1991, 110). After the smallpox epidemic of 1862, death became a primary subject of ritual interest for the Winter Ceremonial. Stanley Walens (1981, 154) argued that the distribution and destruction of property during the Winter Ceremonial increased because property had to be released into the reincarnation system. The ideological rules of redistribution expressed a basic cosmological structure of keeping names and privileges moving from generation to generation within a household (Roth 2002, 126–27). The depopulation that resulted from the smallpox epidemic of 1862 likely contributed to intensive redistribution during the Winter Ceremonial because it was the primary institution concerned with death, the supernatural, and reincarnation (Grumet 1975, 305; Jopling 1989, 30, 32; Mauzé 1994, 180–81; Walens 1981).

A catastrophic decline in population often resulted in the appearance of new forms of potlatches on the Northwest Coast (Grumet 1975, 311). The separate secular rivalry potlatch among the Kwakiutl likely started to emerge from elements of the Winter Ceremonial sometime after 1862. The coppers, blankets, and other trade goods redistributed in the Winter Ceremonial by elite secret societies were subsequently co-opted by commoners who challenged the authority of the declining elite. Although the rivalry was initially between the elite and the nouveaux riche (Curtis 1915, 138; Ringel 1979, 358, 361), it expanded to various ranks of Kwakiutl society as profits derived from wages increased (ca. 1880s). This new creation, the rivalry potlatch, was the subject of Codere's thesis.

Behavior that Codere had attributed to the rivalry potlatch (such as rivalry gestures, warlike actions associated with scalp- and human trophy-taking, the breaking of coppers, and the extravagant distribution of trade blankets and other trade goods) had originated in the Winter Ceremonial. Because Codere confused the reality of warfare with the ceremonial features of the Winter Ceremonial and the rivalry gestures and redistribution in the Winter Ceremonial post-1862 with the rivalry potlatch, she mistakenly concluded that the rivalry potlatch had replaced warfare.

The last Winter Ceremonial appears to have been held in 1895 (Codere 1950, 110). Both the Winter Ceremonial and the secular rivalry potlatch coexisted until they were proscribed by the Indian Act of 1884. However, unlike the rivalry potlatch, which continued to flourish underground as a form of resistance until the 1920s (Drucker and Heizer 1967), the Winter Ceremonial died out.

By discounting the importance of warfare, particularly predatory raiding, to the Kwakiutl, Codere failed to recognize that the origin of the rivalry potlatch was the Winter Ceremonial and confused the warfare themes represented in the Winter Ceremonial with actual warfare. Although there is no relationship between the emergence of the rivalry potlatch and the decline of war, there is a relationship between the Winter Ceremonial and an increase in predatory raiding as well as between the decline of the Winter Ceremonial and an increase in the frequency of rivalry potlatches. The decline of warfare among the Kwakiutl was related solely to the combined effects of depopulation and the suppression of warfare by British authorities in 1860–62.

Interpreting Northwest Coast Warfare

Codere devalued the type of warfare practiced by the Kwakiutl because it was seasonal and limited to such tactics as surprise and ambush. This description characterized much of Northwest Coast warfare, which took the form of raids, human trophy-taking, ambushes, and surprise encounters. Regardless of whether modern observers consider this to be true warfare, one cannot deny that such intergroup violence existed before Europeans arrived on the scene. The archaeological record provides ample evidence of skeletal trauma, weapons, and the construction of defensive fortifications proving that warfare existed on the Northwest Coast thousands of years before contact. Moreover, ethnographic and historical data show that the Kwakiutl participated in the Northwest Coast warfare complex.

While Codere apparently never doubted the authenticity of Boas' informants' metaphorical statements that connected war with the aggressive distribution of property during a potlatch, she neglected to connect these statements to the Winter Ceremonial. This omission and her misunderstanding of Kwakiutl warfare led her to conclude that warfare was insignificant, dramatic, and ceremonial and that the potlatch replaced war. Contrary to Codere's (1950, 124) finding that the increased "vigour of potlatching and the extinction of warfare were related and simultaneous occurrences," however, the rivalry potlatch did not replace war.

The introduction of the maritime fur trade altered the political and population dynamics between Aboriginal groups. The land-based fur trade contributed to predatory raiding, resulting in more intensive long-distance slavery and violence, which may indicate more extensive conflict after European influence began (directly at contact and indirectly in the protohistorical period through the introduction of trade goods). As predatory raiding increased, so did the availability of trade goods, which included slaves. One of the outcomes of predatory raiding was the elaboration of the Winter Ceremonial and concomitant redistribution of property. Following the extinction of the Winter Ceremonial, the redistribution of property that had been rechannelled into the secular rivalry potlatch became the only lingering manifestation of this traditional form of warfare.

Despite her use of historical sources, Codere did not critically examine Kwakiutl warfare outside of the ethnographic and dramatic limitations of the potlatch. She thus ignored the actual social and economic basis for predatory raiding. As a result, this advocacy perspective of Kwakiutl warfare and its replacement by the rivalry potlatch is not supported by the ethnographic, archaeological, or historical data.

NOTES

1. The term "Aboriginal peoples" is used in this chapter to refer to the indigenous inhabitants of Canada.

2. It is equally tenable that depopulation alone would reduce warfare. A reduced frequency in warfare would have likely followed demographic decline regardless of the influx of trade goods.

3. Coppers are large T-shaped shieldlike pieces of copper that were sometimes painted or inscribed.

4 ETHNOHISTORIC DESCRIPTIONS OF CHUMASH WARFARE

John R. Johnson

In the popular imagination and in scholarly treatments, California Indians are frequently depicted as peaceable peoples, living in harmony with each other and the environment at the advent of European contact (e.g., Heizer and Elsasser 1980, 25; Rawls 1984, 10). This common perception is at variance with both the written record of contemporary Spanish observers and direct testimony of elderly California Indians interviewed by ethnographers during the late nineteenth and early twentieth centuries. Intervillage raids, ritualized battles, larger-scale hostilities among opposing allied groups, and even territorial conquest were all part of the spectrum of enmity relations in Native California. Yet it is true that despite the constant threat of raids from one's enemies that existed for most California groups, there does not appear to have been that formal, institutionalized warrior class that existed in many other parts of Native America, with the possible exception of the Mohave and Quechan (Yuma) along the lower Colorado River. The small-scale, localized nature of most California polities and reliance on intervillage economic exchange seem to have mitigated tendencies toward a pervasive culture of aggression and militarism.

Comparative descriptions of California intergroup hostilities have largely been based on tribal peoples who lived beyond the territory most directly impacted by the California mission system (Jorgensen 1980; Kroeber 1925; McCorkle 1978). For example, McCorkle's analysis of seventy-six cases of intergroup conflict was confined to four regions: (1) Yurok and their neighbors in northwestern California, (2) Pomoan peoples and their neighbors north of San Francisco Bay, (3) Yokuts tribes and adjacent groups in the San Joaquin Valley and southern Sierra Nevada, and (4) Yuman peoples of the lower Colorado River region. Varying forms of sociopolitical organization found in the four regions generally correlate with differing patterns of intergroup hostilities (see table 4.1). In general, the level of sociopolitical integration increased from north to south, as did the importance of unilineal corporate groups and the scale of warfare. There is, however, one major gap in this continuum—the native peoples of southern California. Clearly, additional case studies are needed to overcome the absence of data for this important region.

In my initial preparation for this study, I undertook a quick survey of some familiar cross-cultural literature to examine what had been written about warfare as practiced by a specific southern California group, the Chumash peoples of the Santa Barbara Channel region. I was disappointed to find that most comparativists excluded the Chumash area for lack of readily available data. Joseph Jorgensen, for example, noted, "The lack of information about ... the Chumash is particularly unfortunate. The Chumash are especially interesting because of their maritime, ocean-fishing economy, their proclivities for warfare (some scholars argue that they were especially militaristic, others that they were inordi-

TABLE 4.1 Features of California Indian warfare in four regions correlated with other aspects of society

Region	Regional patterns of intergroup conflict		
	Antagonists	Types of engagement	Outcome
1. Northwestern	Kin groups	Small-scale raids	Payments for deaths or injury
2. North-central	Villages or local groups	Surprise attacks, formal battles	Negotiations between chiefs, rights gained or lost to subsistence resources
3. Yokuts and southern Sierra Nevada	Tribelets or coalitions	Raids and occasional battles	Conference of chiefs, reconciliation followed by feasting
4. River Yumans	Allied federations	Raids, arranged battles, high casualties	No reconciliation between combatants, territorial conquest sometimes resulted

Region	Regional patterns of social, political, and economic organization		
	Group composition	Leadership	Economic organization
1. Northwestern	Villages of patrilateral families	Wealthy heads of families	Private ownership of food resources
2. North-central	Tribelets of several bilateral communities	Tribelet chiefs	Tribelet-owned territories
3. Yokuts and southern Sierra Nevada	Bilaterally organized tribes with multiple patrilineages (valley) and tribelets with patrilateral families (sierra)	Moiety chiefs and tribelet chiefs	Tribe- or tribelet-owned territories
4. River Yumans	Village federations	Clan chiefs, "national" war leaders	Family-owned farmlands

Sources: Forde 1931; Jorgensen 1980; Kroeber 1925; Kunkel 1962; and especially McCorkle 1978.

nately peaceful) and, perhaps, because of their development of the most complex political organization in California" (Jorgensen 1980, 2).

Even when Chumash data were included in comparative studies, the accounts cited were not especially trustworthy. Lawrence Keeley in his book *War before Civilization*, for example, uncritically accepted a third-hand account derived from sketchy oral tradition in which four hundred "Tejón Chumash"[1] warriors were supposed to have raided the Chumash coastal town of *Muwu*, with more than seventy people killed (Bowers 1897, cited in Grant 1978, 534; Keeley 1996, 194; see also Hudson et al. 1977, 99). Because this incident was recounted several generations following its occurrence and was reported by a nineteenth-century archaeologist known for his occasional exaggerations (Benson 1997), it most probably is unreliable regarding casualties and numbers of warriors involved. There are no eyewitness accounts from the earliest years of the colonial period that would corroborate military expeditions of this magnitude among Chumash peoples.

The paucity of systematically collected ethnohistoric information pertaining to aboriginal warfare practices in missionized areas has clearly hampered credible use of these data for comparative purposes. As a corrective measure, ethnohistoric descriptions of intergroup conflict in the Chumash region of southern California provide a more complete picture of the total range of variation within the California culture area.

WARFARE AND SOCIOPOLITICAL ORGANIZATION

Table 4.1 presents features of sociopolitical organization for the four other regions of California to compare and contrast these with patterns of intergroup hostilities elucidated by Thomas McCorkle (1978). In general, the scale of warfare correlated with the size of groups involved in conflicts and their level of integration. The immediate causes of intergroup conflict throughout California had to do with a fairly narrow range of factors: disputes over critical resource areas; failure to accept or give hospitality; revenge for perceived instances of witchcraft; retaliation for violent acts on one's kin or community; and fights over women or girls who were abducted (Driver 1961, 365; Laylander 2000, 173–77). Trespass into another's hunting or gathering area would provide an obvious economic motive for hostilities, but other, less obvious reasons for conflict also had ramifications for a group's subsistence regime. Certainly the death or abduction of any healthy member of a particular community was a threat to the ability of that group to support itself economically, resulting in reprisals. Broad interregional alliances extended from the Colorado River region into southern California and the American Southwest, crosscutting ecological boundaries in an east-west pattern. Adversaries in one alliance were often at odds with members of opposing alliances (White 1974).

There exist important differences and similarities between social group composition and leadership in southern California compared to other regions, thus requiring some discussion to place indigenous warfare in its larger cultural context. In general, linguistic divisions in southern California corresponded to different forms of sociopolitical organization. The higher population density of the Santa Barbara Channel led to settled towns in the Chumash region of upwards of a thousand inhabitants (Brown 1967). Postmarital residence was predominantly matrilocal, although chiefs' families were the principal exception to this rule, usually residing patrilocally. Although most towns and villages were politically independent, chiefs of certain large political centers held some form of limited authority over federations of settlements in the surrounding region (Johnson 1988).

South and southeast of the Chumash were groups speaking languages within the Takic division of the Uto-Aztecan language family. The local groups of the Gabrielino, Tataviam, Serrano, Luiseño, Cahuilla, and Cupeño were apparently based on patrilineal clans. Many of the smaller *rancherías* (villages) were single-clan communities, but there also existed larger multiclan communities, especially among the Luiseño and Gabrielino. Farther south were a succession of the linguistically related Yuman and Cochimí groups, who occupied territory extending to the mid Baja California peninsula. Like the Takic peoples, the California Yumans appear to have resided in largely patrilineal, clan-based communities with less institutionalized leadership, except for the lower Colorado River tribes already mentioned and included in table 4.1 (Forde 1931; Jorgensen 1980; Kroeber 1925; Kroeber and Fontana 1986).

GENERALIZATIONS REGARDING CHUMASH WARFARE BY EARLY OBSERVERS

The earliest descriptions of Chumash peoples come to us from explorations of the California coast during the sixteenth and seventeenth centuries (Bolton 1916; Wagner 1929). More detailed observations date to the period of the first land expedition of 1769–70 and in correspondence and reports that followed before Franciscan missionaries and Spanish soldiers actually came to live among Chumash populations (Costansó [1769–70] 1983; Crespí [1769–70] 2001; Fages [1775] 1937; Portolá [1769–70] 1983; Rivera [1774–77] 1967). Mission San Luis Obispo was established among the Northern Chumash in 1772, however, not until the Santa Bárbara presidio was founded ten years later and three missions were founded among the populous towns of the Central Chumash (Barbareño, Ventureño, Ineseño, and Purisimeño) was the most explicit information recorded pertaining to Chumash intergroup conflict. Only a few of these documents have been published.

Almost every early observer who spent any time at all among the peoples speaking Chumashan languages commented on the unsettled situation found there among native towns. The following contemporary descriptions represent a convincing sample that inter-ranchería hostilities were endemic from the time of first contact until the last of the native population had been baptized at the missions in 1822 (fig. 4.1). The surviving account of Juan Rodríguez Cabrillo's voyage of 1542–43 provides us with the earliest explicit description of California Indian intergroup conflicts, specifically those among Chumash coastal towns: "From the Pueblo de las Canoas [*Muwu* at Mugu Lagoon] to Cabo de Galera [Pt. Conception], there is a well inhabited province called 'Xexu' [*Shisholop*]. There are many different languages and they carry on great wars with each other" (Cabrillo [1542] 1929, 87).[2] Cabrillo's account later observed that there appeared to be two "provinces" (alliances of towns), rather than one, along the Santa Barbara Channel mainland coast: "The town of Çiucut [*Syuxtun*, 'Pueblo de las Sardinas' at Santa Bárbara] appears to be the head of the other towns because they came there from them when called by the chief. The town at the cape is called 'Xexo' [*Shisholop* near Pt. Conception]. From this port [*Syuxtun*] to the

Pueblo de las Canoas [*Muwu*] is another province which they call 'Xucu' [*Shuku*]" (Cabrillo [1542] 1929, 88).[3]

More than two centuries later, Pedro Fages issued similar observations about Chumash internecine strife shortly after he completed his first term as the head of colonial California's government, stating that "they are very warlike among themselves, living at almost incessant war, village against village. In each of these villages (which are very populous here, each one containing on an estimate about six hundred men capable of bearing arms) there is a captain. . . . This chief has hardly any other function than that of the military command; they always choose the most conspicuous and intrepid one in the village. The position is for life, and [the incumbent enjoys] an absolute, total independence in the government" (Fages [1775] 1937, 31–32). Fages's estimate of the number of men capable of bearing arms in each ranchería was exaggerated; nonetheless, the sizable populations of the Santa Barbara Channel worried the Spanish political leaders. Another governor of Spanish California, Felipe de Neve, worried about the supply trains between northern and southern colonial settlements being disrupted because of "the many incessant wars that are made between the twenty-one [mainland Coastal Chumash] rancherías which occupy the channel" (Neve 1782).

Insights regarding the causes of Chumash warfare may be derived from the detailed journal of the naturalist José Longinos Martínez, who traveled the length of California from Cabo San Lucas to Monterey in 1792. Speaking specifically of the Chumash, Longinos emphasized trespass into another's territory as a significant source of conflict: "If a chief merely makes an attempt to pass through another's jurisdiction, fighting and quarreling result, so great is the distrust that these nations have of one another." Speaking of California Indians generally, he stated, "Their wars are frequent and always originate over rights to seed-gathering grounds or in disputes over concubines" (Longinos [1792] 1961, 58). In these statements, Longinos specifically documents the importance of critical resource areas for California hunter-gatherers. He noted that baskets of seeds and other foodstuffs were characteristic of Chumash households but that people would suffer from hunger when their stores gave out and in winter months when inclement weather prevented coastal peoples from fishing (Longinos [1792] 1961,

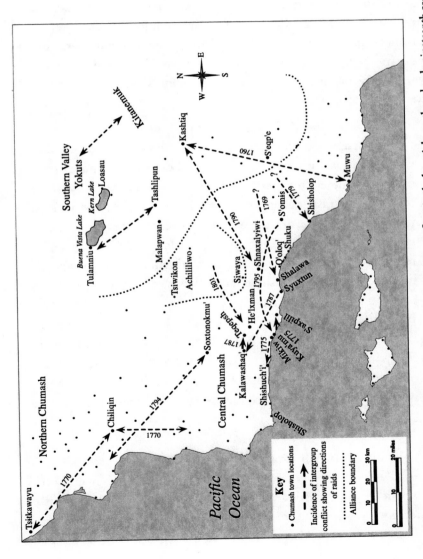

FIGURE 4.1 Documented cases of Chumash intergroup conflicts in the late eighteenth and early nineteenth centuries.

58–59). This description is consistent with the cross-cultural studies of the Embers, demonstrating that resource unpredictability, along with mistrust of others, is an important predictor of intergroup warfare (Ember and Ember 1992).

Franciscan missionaries likewise offered explanations for Chumash fighting in 1813–15 in response to a questionnaire distributed by the Crown regarding customs of the native peoples living in Spain's colonies. Particularly noteworthy are the observations penned by Fr. José Señán at San Buenaventura, who was then serving as missionary president; he had been stationed at his mission for seventeen years and was fluent in the Ventureño Chumash language. His statements reiterate some of the causes for conflict mentioned by Longinos and likewise underscore the role of traditional political leaders in warfare as described by Fages:

Reply to Question 27, Cruelty and Punishments:
   . . . although they frequently waged war and at times were somewhat harsh on their enemies, they were driven to it through the necessity of defending their wives, their right to the territory where they harvested their acorns and seeds upon which they depended for their subsistence, or also because the enemy had mentioned any one of their dead by the proper pagan name which with them is regarded as the most grievous injury and crime. Public vengeance for the curbing and punishment of excesses committed by individuals and for maintaining peace was not known among the pagan Indians. The consequence of this was that anyone who considered himself injured would himself take satisfaction and revenge. Sometimes he would enlist relatives in his cause. In some cases it was made a common cause. The chief and the whole rancheria with other friendly and allied rancherias would then plan revenge. (Señán [1815] 1976, 113–14)

Question 31, Indian Chiefs and Lifestyles:
   In paganism, every rancheria had one or more chiefs or captains whom they recognized in their battles with their enemies and with regard to invitations to their pagan feasts. Then all contributed seeds and beads which were divided among those invited. These

functions excepted, the Indians were not accustomed to recognize any chiefs. Everyone did what he pleased and lived in the widest liberty and independence. (Señán [1815] 1976, 125)

Señán further implied that raids and ambushes were the most common tactics employed:

Question 34: What famous men have they had among them notable for prowess of arms?

They had some sort of knowledge of warfare but almost always they would kill their adversaries, take vengeance on them in cold blood by coming upon them unawares or when enemies were in smaller numbers by employing cunning and malignant tricks. (Señán [1815] 1976, 139)

THE PORTOLÁ EXPEDITION, 1769–1770

The First Expedition, as it was known to the initial generation of Spanish colonists who settled in Alta California, was led by Gaspar de Portolá, who had been assigned the task of founding the first missions and presidios at San Diego and Monterey. Among the various expedition diaries, that kept by the missionary Fr. Juan Crespí is the most detailed in its descriptions of the native peoples encountered. Crespí's account and the other journals of the Portolá expedition provide the first specific instances of aggression between Chumash groups.

As the expedition traveled northward along the Santa Barbara Channel coast in August 1769, the chroniclers reported five burned towns and villages in the vicinity of Carpintería and Santa Bárbara. Two of these, Q'oloq' (near Summerland) and Shalawa (Montecito), were directly on the expedition's path. Another, apparently Mismatuk along San Roque Creek near Santa Barbara, was reported by scouts (Johnson 1986, 22).[4] On August 19, Crespí reported in the field draft of his journal,

The scouting soldiers have said that there is a ruined village close to this stream [Arroyo Burro/San Roque Creek]; for the heathens belonging to this village said that the upcountry heathens destroyed five villages when they destroyed the two we saw yesterday. They are great warriors, they say, and were about to destroy the large village [*Syuxtun*] that is behind us, but that they fought back mightily; one of their companions whom they captured was killed by them; another had his eye put out by an arrow and was given a great many wounds by them; we saw him and he was not yet entirely healed. (Crespí [1769] 2001, 419)

In his more polished version of the journal, Crespí identified the aggressors as *serranos* (mountain people).

The next mention of intergroup hostilities came after the expedition had rounded Pt. Conception and had entered territory occupied by Northern Chumash villages. Near Pismo Beach and Arroyo Grande, the expedition encountered a prominent chief and war leader the Spaniards nicknamed "El Buchón," because of a large tumor on one side of his neck:

[El Buchón] is a great man, a kind of petty king of all this country and much renowned and feared in all the surrounding parts. . . . He always goes around closely accompanied by many armed heathens, . . . because many villages give him tribute, whatever seeds they harvest or gather from the fields, [or] whether they slaughter any meat or catch fish, they take it all—or so we understood—to his village, where he receives it and then they take back whatever he tells them to. In their own fashion, he employs considerable pomp, and they bring a hide and lay it on the ground for him to sit down on. He has two brothers and two or three sons who are almost always with him, and no one sits down in front of him or his family unless ordered to. Great is the fear and awe in which he is held by the surrounding parts. . . . [El Buchón's] fame reaches as far as the [Santa Barbara] Channel and the Santa Lucia Mountains. (Crespí [1769] 2001, 475, 477, 479)

After the Portolá expedition had explored the coastal region of California as far north as San Francisco Bay, it returned to San Diego. The following spring, it again embarked on a northward journey and passed through the territory of El Buchón. Again, this leader's fearsome reputation among surrounding peoples was emphasized. While the expedition retraced its route through Purisimeño Chumash territory in what is now the northern section of Vandenberg Air Force Base, Crespí commented that El Buchón's intimidation had caused the abandonment of a ranchería they had seen occupied the previous year (Crespí [1770] 2001, 713). Subsequently the Spaniards visited and feasted with El Buchón in his own town on May 10–12, before continuing their trek. When they reached the vicinity of Cayucos, Crespí observed,

> Eight or ten heathens came to the camp, heavily painted, wearing their feather headdresses, and all of them heavily laden with their usual good-sized quivers full of arrows and their bows. Seemingly they had news of us and had come to greet us. . . . [T]heir village was the spot belonging to the San Benvenuto pinewood [Cambria Pines], which we were intending to reach by this day's march. . . . Thus in company of these fine heathens we set out along the shore. On going about a quarter-league, they became upset and refused to go on, giving us to understand that [El Buchón] with his village was coming up behind us in order to fight. . . . On going about a league, we had a message that [El Buchón] had just arrived with his village, looking for these other heathens; for they had fought with him not long before and had shot [El Buchón] in the body with two arrows. . . . Our ten heathens commenced to scatter on hearing the news verified, and shortly we saw six of [Buchón's] men going by. He was coming up behind, and they said they were on their way to fight them. The fact is that the ten then clashed with [Buchón's] six within view of us, with those on each side shooting off a good many arrows, and there is no denying they must be great warriors and very skillful. [Buchón's] six men at once turned and ran back, since no more of their people had come than the aforesaid six, whereas there were ten of the others. We continued on our way, and left them to this entertainment; no telling what may have happened to the poor wretches. There was no way we could stop their warfare, which our people attempted to do; they paid no attention, however. . . . About an hour after we had come to the pinewood here, the ten warriors we had left on the way arrived and told us they had hit [El Buchón] with an arrow;

however, we did not believe them, as we knew he had been coming with thirty or forty of his people, and these ones must have taken to flight at a quick run as soon as they had seen the situation. (Crespí [1770] 2001, 721)

This report of Northern Chumash warfare, vividly documented by Crespí, provides the only contemporary eyewitness account of actual engagement between indigenous combatants. Crespí's description is entirely consistent with the observations of Señán quoted earlier pertaining to the Central Chumash and confirms the pattern of back-and-forth feuding and surprise raids that appear to have been the predominant form of conflict found in much of Native California. The aggressors in this case were some thirty or forty warriors from El Buchón's town near Arroyo Grande (probably the ranchería of *Chiliqin*), and the defenders were the small party of eight to ten men from Cambria (probably the ranchería called *Tsitkawayu* by the Northern Chumash and "Zassalet" by the Salinan). El Buchón's raid was in reprisal for previous injuries suffered by members of his town at the hands of the Cambria group.[5] The village at Cambria was located in a boundary region between different cultural units (Northern Chumash and Salinan), and thus its conflict with El Buchón may well have been a case of *external* warfare, that is, conflict between political communities in different cultural units (Otterbein 1970). As the burned towns observed near Santa Barbara in 1769 exemplify, most Chumash intergroup fighting took the form of *internal* war, that is, conflict between political communities within the same cultural unit.

SPECIFIC CASES OF CONFLICT FROM MISSION PERIOD DOCUMENTS

Following the Portolá expedition and the founding of Mission San Carlos and the presidio of Monterey in 1770, periodic visits by Spanish observers were made to the Santa Barbara Channel region in the course of bringing people and supplies from San Diego northward. Increasingly, there were comments made by travelers regarding various characteristics of Chumash society, including brief descriptions of intergroup hostilities. With the establishment of Mission San Luis Obispo in 1772, Mission San Buenaventura in 1782, and the presidio of Santa Bárbara also in 1782, missionaries and soldiers had daily contact with native Chumash populations, resulting in a concomitant increase in observations regarding indigenous practices. In particular, the presidio soldiers were attuned to instances of violence and warfare that could potentially destabilize the region and disrupt the transportation of supplies from the missions and presidios in the south to those in the north. The mission records provide the names of Chumash towns and villages (called "rancherías"), which, combined with other ethnographic and ethnohistoric information, permit reconstruction of settlement system (see fig. 4.1).

Some of the earliest descriptions of intergroup warfare involve the two settlements known as Dos Pueblos, *Mikiw* and *Kuya'mu*, and some of their largest and closest neighbors. Two of these early accounts of fighting between Dos Pueblos and other Chumash settlements come from the diary of Fernando Rivera y Moncada, who was military governor of California between 1774 and 1777. In 1775 Rivera recorded several incidents witnessed by some Spanish travelers along the Santa Barbara Channel:

> Those gentiles [from Dos Pueblos] are troublemakers. I will relate two cases. Three or four leagues from this place [Dos Pueblos] there is a neighboring village, which is one of the largest of the [Coastal Chumash] settlements. I have counted the huts [at the latter], and including the two that serve as sweatlodges, there were more than 90. One night, [the Indians from Dos Pueblos] went out and put fire to them, and no one knows the number that they killed.
>
> Two and a half leagues to the south or southeast [from Dos Pueblos] are three very large villages [at the Goleta estuary], one of which is isolated by water that enters inland from the sea [*Helo'* on Mescalitan Island]. When I dispatched a guard to guide some families [of settlers from Mexico], they encountered [some Indians from Dos Pueblos], returning from these [Goleta towns] to their own villages. They had been fighting [and were] carrying one or more *cabelleras* [scalps], which is the skullcap with the hair that they cut from those they kill. One [of their number] had been wounded. (Rivera [1775] 1967, 135)[6]

Rivera's recounting of the first of these two incidents provides an explanation for the association of the Spanish name La Quemada, "burned [village]," with the coastal town of *Shishuch'i'*, located several canyons to the west of Dos Pueblos at the place still known as Arroyo Quemado. Alan Brown (1967, 22–23) noted that the 1769 Portolá expedition encountered a settlement of about eighty houses at Tajiguas Creek, but by 1776 that location had been abandoned and new villages established at *Shishuch'i'* at Arroyo Quemado and *Qasil* at Cañada del Refugio.

The second incident, which describes fighting between Dos Pueblos and the Goleta towns, was apparently not an isolated one. In 1782 Rivera's successor, Governor Felipe de Neve, noted that it might be wise to consider locating the Santa Bárbara presidio between Dos Pueblos and the Goleta estuary to control warfare between these two large population centers, which were "declared enemies" (Neve 1782).

Further hostilities involving Dos Pueblos included Indians from inland villages. In 1795 there was an incident in which a party of Indians from Mission San Buenaventura and some unconverted Chumash from inland villages attacked Dos Pueblos, killing two *capitanes* (Lasuén [1795] 1965, 1:363; see Brown 1967, 48). The records of the official investigation of this incident no longer are extant, but the existing summaries in the California Archives indicate that Indians from *S'omis*, inland from San Buenaventura, and from *Shnaxalyïwï*, inland from Santa Barbara, were party to the attack on Dos Pueblos (Borica 1795, 1796; Cota and Guevara 1795; Goicoechea 1795).

Another ethnohistoric description of enmity between Dos Pueblos and some inhabitants of inland villages dates to 1803 (Tapis 1803). The relevant passage has been published by Zephyrin Engelhardt (1932, 7) and has been commented upon in a number of prior studies (e.g., Brown 1967, 28; Horne 1981, 82–85; Johnson 1984; King 1982, 163–64; Lambert 1994). Engelhardt's translation follows:

Although the Gentiles [unconverted peoples], whom I found in the district about Alajulapu [Santa Ynez Valley], are not excessively numerous, it is to be noted that there is communication between these rancherías and the savages nearest to the Tulares [the San Joaquin Valley], especially the large rancherías named

Atsililihu [*Achililiwo*] and Sihuicon [*Tsiwikon*]. These *Gentiles* are of a bad disposition. They are turbulent, inclined to commit murder in a most treacherous way and from merely superstitious motives. During the month of April, 1801, a certain Lihuiasu with about six companions from the two rancherias mentioned came in the night time to set fire to Eljman [*He'lxman*], a small rancheria which lay two leagues from Tequeps [*Teqepsh*], and about six leagues from Santa Bárbara. He killed five persons and wounded two others, solely because the *Gentiles* of Eljman were relatives of Temiacucat, the chief of the Cuyamu [*Kuya'mu*] Ranchería belonging to Dos Pueblos on the seashore, whom they regarded as the author of the epidemic of the *dolor de costado*, which at that time took the lives of many Indians. (Engelhardt 1932, 7)[7]

This passage implies that there was a close relationship between Dos Pueblos and the small Santa Ynez Valley village of *He'lxman* but enmity between these and villages located farther in the interior. *Achililiwo* and *Tsiwikon* were located in the Cuyama region, and their war leader Lihuiasu is mentioned in another early reference as being from the village of *Siwaya* in the mountains behind Santa Barbara (Johnson 1984, 7).[8] It may be further noted that Lihuiasu's daughter was from *Syuxtun* (Mission Santa Bárbara Baptismal Record [hereafter MSB Bap.] 1371). This fact acquires significance because *Syuxtun* held chiefly relationships with the three uppermost villages in the Santa Ynez watershed: *Shnaxalyiwi*, *Siwaya*, and *Shniwax*.[9] A picture emerges including these three inland villages in a federation of which *Syuxtun* was the political center; the federation also was allied to the Goleta towns and opposed to Dos Pueblos and one or more of the latter's allies in the Santa Ynez Valley.

There is little other evidence regarding opposing alliances within this study area. Alexander Taylor recorded a tradition that there was a "great Council Grove of seven rancherías" in the Santa Ynez Valley and that these united to war with their neighbors (King 1982, 166). Taylor did not mention the names of the seven villages, but they may have corresponded in part to the group of intermarrying villages centered on *Soxtonokmu'*, described by Stephen Horne (1981, 78–85). Warriors from the latter village were responsible for attempting to organize an aborted rebellion against Mission San Luis Obispo in 1794 (Goicoechea 1794; King 1984, 11).

An event in 1787 may represent further evidence of intervillage hostilities in the Santa Ynez Valley, although the meager documentation prevents any certainty as to whether this particular incident resulted from an isolated, personal quarrel or was symptomatic of intergroup enmity. A band of neophytes on leave from Mission Santa Bárbara got into a fight with Indians from *Kalawashaq'*. News of this incident reached the mission and presidio with the incorrect information that the neophytes had been killed. Soldiers from the presidio sent out to investigate were barely able to keep some of the local Indians who accompanied them from wreaking vengeance on those they supposed had done the killing. It turned out that the beleaguered group of neophytes had escaped death by retreating to the village of *Teqepsh*, where they were defended from their pursuers from *Kalawashaq'* (Goicoechea 1787b).

This incident occurred less than a year after the founding of Mission Santa Bárbara, whose neophyte population was initially composed of Indians from the Santa Barbara and Goleta villages. One of those involved in the incident at *Kalawashaq'* was a young Indian of high-status background named José María. He seems to have been the son of Chief Panay of *Syuxtun* and was married to the sister of the chief of *Shalawa* at Montecito (Johnson 1986, 26). The president of the California missions, Fr. Fermín Francisco de Lasuén, described José María as "chief among the Indians at Santa Bárbara" and noted that the rumor of his death at *Kalawashaq'* caused "the greater part of the Channel" to be disposed to take up arms (Lasuén [1797] 1965, 2:18). José María's kinship connections, as recorded in the mission registers, were among the most wide-ranging noted for any individual, including relatives from the inland villages of *Soxtonokmu'*, *'Itiyaqsh*, *Teqepsh*, and *Wishap* and the coastal towns of *S'axpilil*, *Syuxtun*, and *Shalawa* (Johnson 1988). In this 1787 incident, we perhaps have indications of unfriendly relations between *Syuxtun* and *Kalawashaq'* but amicable links between the former and *Teqepsh*, although inferring this much from the available information may be pushing the evidence too far.

THE INVESTIGATION OF AN ATTACK IN 1790

A final example of intergroup hostilities involves Indians from the mountains behind Santa Barbara, who had participated in a raid against some residents of a Castac Chumash village in August 1790, resulting in three deaths. A swift reprisal led to the ambush of a party of nine soldiers from the presidio of Santa Bárbara who had unwittingly allied themselves with the enemies of those who sought revenge for the killings. The soldiers had traveled to the ranchería of *Shnaxalyiwi* in the Santa Ynez Mountains on a trip to search for a fugitive neophyte named Domingo from Mission San Buenaventura. They also had been instructed to search for a vein of silver ore that was of interest to Comandante Goicoechea of the Santa Bárbara presidio. The party was camped in the vicinity of San Emigdio Canyon and engaged in prospecting for ore when the surprise attack occurred, which resulted in the deaths of two soldiers (Jackman 1993, 14–15; Johnson 1984, 5; King 1982, 168–69). The official records of this incident are rich with details pertaining to the cooperative and competitive interactions among a sizable number of Chumash and Yokuts towns and villages and warrant more extensive treatment than the accounts of Chumash warfare cited thus far. A synopsis of the affair is contained in the letter sent to Pedro Fages, the governor of California, soon after the events had taken place:

> [Comandante Goicoechea] dispatched Sergeant José Ignacio Olivera with 8 men in search of a fugitive Indian [who was believed to be] in the ranchería of Tinoqui.[10] . . . The party left on the 24th of August—traveled five days without incident. From the ranchería of Najalayegua [*Shnaxalyiwi*], 3 Indians from these enemies of Tinoqui went along with the sergeant. On the 29th at dawn, 15 from the same rancheria joined up, then left around eleven o'clock, 4 remaining in the camp. Before that, the sergeant had ordered 5 men with 3 Indians to look over a vein of metal, a little ways off. . . . An hour after the [*Shnaxalyiwi*] Indians left, the sergeant went with a soldier to explore the surroundings of his camp [leaving two soldiers behind]. Shortly [thereafter] . . . he was attacked from the rear by more than 60 Indians, who tried to prevent his getting out

— they were not successful — fighting more than an hour on the defensive he succeeded in wounding several Indians — he could not get back to the camp [until] . . . sunset . . . — he did not find any of his companions — the camp was in ruins — the Indians threatening to attack him. . . .

They found Espinosa armed and in leather in the shelter of an oak pierced like a sieve with arrows over all his body,[11] and Carlón as if sleeping, his leather jacket folded, noting that they had carried off cloaks ponchos, 2 muskets from the deceased ones. (Goicoechea 1790b)

Sergeant Olivera described how he and another soldier had been isolated by the attack: "He was attacked from the rear by more than 60 Indians, who giving war cries and shooting arrows, tried to trap him between two lines of fire and keep him from escaping, which they were not able to do. After more than an hour of combat, always retreating in defense, he managed to wound various of them" (Goicoechea [1790a] 1978, 3).

In response to the assault, a second, larger party of twenty-eight soldiers was sent out from the Santa Bárbara presidio in September and returned with three Indian prisoners who were suspected of having a role in the affair. One of the captives had been a participant in the fighting, another was a chief of an interior Ventureño ranchería, and the third was the fugitive neophyte Domingo, for whom the first party of soldiers had been seeking before they were attacked. The transcripts of the interviews with these three prisoners are most illuminating regarding relations among the various Chumash towns. The substantive parts from these interrogations appear below:

1. Declaration of the heathen Indian called Soxollue:
   When asked which ranchería he was from, he responded the Tasicoo [*Tatsicoho*12] Ranchería. He was asked if he saw the murders of the soldiers Gabriel Espinosa and Hilario Carlón that the heathen Indians had committed right next to his ranchería, and if he took part in them. He responded that yes, he was involved and he shot two arrows at them. He was asked how many rancherías took part and how many men from each one. He responded that 8

heathens came from the Tulares ranchería called Loasi [a Yokuts village in the San Joaquin Valley]; 39 from the Castéc [*Kashtiбq*] Ranchería; three from the Cecpey [*S'eqp'e*] Ranchería, one from the Mismisaq [*Kimishax?*] Ranchería; four from the Taxilipu [*Tashlipun*] Ranchería; and only he from his Ranchería. . . . He was asked if he knew why they went to kill the soldiers if they had not done them any harm. He responded that the heathens from Loasi Ranchería told him to kill them. (Goicoechea [1790a] 1978, 34–35)

2. Declaration of the heathen Indian called Samallá, Chief of Sizá [*Sis'a*]:

He was asked why he sent messages to warn the heathens that our party was going to kill them. He responded that he did not want them to get away without the blame anymore, and that it was not he who sent the messengers to our enemies, but rather two Christians from Mission San Buenaventura. One is named [Francisco de Asís] Alisacu and is from the Rincón Ranchería [*Shuku*], and the other is called [Vital] Castacu and is from the Ranchería of the aforesaid mission [*Shisholop*].[13] It was these two who took the message to the Mopú [*Mupu*] Ranchería, and those from this ranchería to Cecpey [*S'eqp'e*] Ranchería, and from this ranchería to all of our enemies. When asked if he knew, or had heard why those heathens killed the two soldiers mentioned, he responded that he had only heard what they had told him, that the soldiers who had been guests at rancherías of their enemies wanted to go and kill them, and because of that they wanted to get them first. . . . When asked if he knew which rancherías took part in the killings of the aforementioned soldiers, he responded that the same ones that had been mentioned in the previous declaration. Everything that he said here he knows because the day after the killings took place he arrived among them to change some furs and beads for *pespiguata*[14] and he does not know nor has heard anything more than what he has said. (Goicoechea [1790a] 1978, 36–37)

3. Declaration of the Indian Domingo[15] from Mission San Buenaventura:

[When] asked . . . where he was when the heathens went on their campaign and who killed the soldiers Gabriel Espinosa and Hilario Carlón, he responded that he was in the main ranchería where the junta was held and from where the [war] party left. He was asked who the party was directed against or where they were going. He responded that they were directed against the heathens of Najalayegua [*Shnaxalyɨwɨ*] Ranchería who had killed two of their heathen men and one heathen woman three days earlier. When asked if they had any warning that soldiers were around there, he responded that they had not had any warning that they were there. He was asked why, if they only had a quarrel with those from Najalayegua, they did not go to that ranchería but instead followed the soldiers. He responded that they were going to go against that ranchería but that on the way they had found the tracks of the soldiers. The others showed that they were reluctant to follow our tracks because they were afraid, but a Tulareño [Yokuts] chief [from Loasi] determined that they should follow them, because a long time before, soldiers had passed by there, and without cause killed some heathens (it is supposed these were probably some deserters). Continuing on ahead they found one of the soldiers asleep, and the other occupied in sewing his shoe, and they began to shoot at the horse that was tethered and then at the soldiers.

When asked if he knew all of the heathens who participated in the killings and their rancherías, he responded that he does know them and their rancherías. . . . The rancherías are the same as had been said [in the earlier declarations], with the additions of Mitunami [the Chumash name for *Tulamniu*, a Yokuts ranchería at Buena Vista Lake] where one heathen came from, and Matapuan [*Malapwan*] Ranchería where Tucuchana, the one who orders the sorties and campaigns, comes from. . . . [Domingo] only stayed among those people because of the love that he had for his mother who is there, but that he did not go on any sortie, nor did he go on any campaign. He was asked if he knew who had given the notice that there was a party of soldiers who were going to kill them. He responded that he was present when the heathen from Mopú [*Mupu*] Ranchería arrived, having been sent by his chief, who told him—the one who is testifying [Domingo]—that the Christians Francisco [Alisacu] and Bital [Castacu] from Mission San Buenaventura took them the notice of the cited chief of *Mupu*, and that this is the truth so far as he knows. (Goicoechea [1790a] 1978, 38–40)

In a letter sent soon after the prisoners had been brought to the presidio, Comandante Goicoechea wrote that the original junta (war council) had taken place at *Malapwan*, the ranchería of Tucachana, a "warlike Indian" who was said to be a "companion of Tinoqui." According to Goicoechea, Tucachana's goal was to kill the chief of Najalayegua [*Shnaxalyiwi*], who was blamed for the deaths that had occurred at the ranchería of Tinoqui[16] (Goicoechea [1790a] 1978, 22).

The assault in which two soldiers were killed provides us with the most revealing look at the system of alliances that existed over a broad swath of Central Chumash territory during the early mission period. The detailed knowledge regarding which rancherías were opposed to each other sheds light on earlier incidents (see table 4.2), especially some raids back and forth between mountain rancherías behind Santa Bárbara and San Buenaventura briefly mentioned in contemporary correspondence (Goicoechea 1787a). It is even possible that the murder of a "Chief Chico" of *Shalawa* in 1785 was related to the raids of 1787–90 between *Shnaxalyiwi* and interior Ventureño rancherías, because it was said that the perpetrators blamed Chief Chico for the death of a chief of *Shnaxalyiwi*, who was son of the old chief of *Syuxtun*[17] (Goicoechea 1785; see also Brown 1967, 48). Extending further back in time, these continuing events may well have been reverberations from the ferocious battles of 1769 that led to mountain Indians burning five coastal towns with concomitant casualties, as reported by members of the Portolá expedition.[18]

ORAL TRADITIONS

Besides the contemporary accounts that provide us with primary data on Chumash warfare, there exist less direct but nonetheless revealing

TABLE 4.2 Documented cases of Chumash intergroup conflict, 1769–1801

Year	Aggressors and probable affiliations	Defenders and probable affiliations
1769	Mountain Indians	Coastal towns: *Q'oloq', Shalawa, Syuxtun, Mismatuk, Xana'yan*, and one unidentified ranchería
1770	Chief Buchón (of *Chiliqin*?)	Ranchería in vicinity of *S'axpilil* (Graciosa Vieja)
1770?	War party from *Tsitkawayu*	Chief Buchón's town (*Chiliqin*?)
1770	30–40 men from *Chiliqin*	8–10 men from *Tsitkawayu*
1775?	Dos Pueblos (*Mikiw* and *Kuya'mu*)	*Shishuch'i'*, town of 90 houses (population estimated at 400 in 1769)
1775?	Dos Pueblos (*Mikiw* and *Kuya'mu*)	Inhabitants of one or more Goleta towns (probably *S'axpilil*, but possibly *Heliyik* or *Helo'*)
1779	Unspecified neighboring rancherías	Entire populace of *Shisholop* (Ventura) (population estimated at 300–400 in 1769)
1785	Chief's men from *Syuxtun*	Chief Chico of *Shalawa*
1787?	Unnamed mountain ranchería behind San Buenaventura	Mountain ranchería behind Santa Bárbara
1787	Unnamed mountain ranchería behind Santa Bárbara	Mountain ranchería behind San Buenaventura
1787	Pursuers from *Kalawashaq'*	Party of Santa Bárbara Indians led by a young chief from *Syuxtun*, who sought refuge in *Teqepsh*
1790	Group of unknown size from *Shnaxalyiwi*	People apparently affiliated with the "ranchería of Tinoqui" (*Kashtiq*?)
1790	At least 58 men from *Kashtiq* and 7 other interior Chumash and Yokuts rancherías	Party of 9 soldiers and an Indian interpreter, accompanied by 18 men from *Shnaxalyiwi* and *Siwaya*
1794	17 men from *Soxtonokmu'* and other mountain rancherías	One of two districts in which the Mission Indians of San Luis Obispo were divided
1795	8 or more men from *S'omis, Shnaxalyiwi*, and San Buenaventura	Dos Pueblos (*Mikiw* and *Kuya'mu*) or some inhabitants from there
1801	War leader Lihuiasu (of *Siwaya*) with 6 others from *Tsiwikon* and *Achililiwo*	Inhabitants of *He'lxman* (population estimated at 40), who were friends or relatives of Chief Temiacucat of *Kuya'mu*

Note: See figure 4.1 for Chumash town locations.

Result	Source
5 towns destroyed	Crespí [1769] 2001
1 village abandoned	Crespí [1770] 2001
Chief Buchón wounded in two places	Crespí [1770] 2001
Chief Buchón wounded?, no reported casualties	Crespí [1770] 2001
Town burned, people killed, ranchería relocated	Rivera [1775] 1967
1 or more people killed and scalped, 1 attacker wounded	Rivera [1775] 1967
Town temporarily abandoned	Neve 1782
Chief Chico slain	Goicoechea 1785
13 people killed	Goicoechea 1787a
4 women and 1 man killed	Goicoechea 1787a
No reported casualties	Goicoechea 1787b; Lasuén [1797] 1965
2 men and 1 woman killed	Goicoechea [1790a] 1978
2 soldiers killed, several attackers wounded	Goicoechea [1790a] 1978, 1790b
Attack aborted, 4 men taken as prisoners to the presidio	Goicoechea 1794
2 chiefs killed, others wounded	Cota and Guevara 1795; Borica 1795, 1796; Goicoechea 1795
5 killed, 2 wounded, village burned	Tapis 1803

means of examining the topic. In particular, Chumash oral traditions can be combined with evidence gleaned from the examination and analysis of mission registers of baptisms, marriages, and burials. These sources complement and further elaborate on the inferences obtained from the descriptions contained in letters, journals, and reports. The ethnographic records reveal the attitudes and perspectives expressed by Chumash Indians, albeit one or two generations removed from those who actually participated in a society still engaged in intervillage hostilities (see fig. 4.2). The mission register data allow for the oral historical accounts to be placed in their likely chronological context and are supplemented by ancillary comments in burial records pertaining to causes of death for those who died violently while on leave from the mission in distant rancherías.

In his classic work on Chumash oral literature, Thomas Blackburn's inferences from myths that involve intergroup fighting are entirely consistent with observations derived from early Spanish accounts but include a few additional details, such as the use of smoke signals and arranged battles:

> While warfare is not a particularly strong thematic element in the narratives, there is an occasional allusion to it, and it seems to constitute an acceptable if infrequent factor in the life of the First People. Usually warfare seems to involve only a portion of the population of two feuding villages, although sometimes people from a number of widely scattered villages can become embroiled in the conflict, apparently as a consequence of the formation of military alliances. Smoke signals are used to transmit information about the forthcoming battle, and the principal weapon is the bow and arrow. The time and place of battle is decided by mutual agreement beforehand. The fighting continues until one side surrenders or withdraws from the field. (Blackburn 1975, 53–54; references to narrative numbers omitted)

In addition to myths that involved tales of war, there exist handed-down oral traditions pertaining to intergroup battles. The best known of these, cited above, refers to a battle between a sizable war party from the Tejón region (evidently referring to Castac Chumash rancherías) that

FIGURE 4.2 Rafael Solares, chief of the Santa Inés Indians, posing in ceremonial dress with bow and arrow. One tradition, recorded by J. P. Harrington, included the wearing of the tsux (ceremonial headdress), such as that shown here, by some warriors as part of their ritual preparation for impending battle. (Photographed by the French anthropologist Léon de Cessac, 1878; courtesy of the Musée de l'Homme, Paris.)

attacked the important coastal town of *Muwu*. The reason given for the hostilities was that a woman from Tejón had been put to death because she had been unfaithful to her husband from *Muwu*. The earliest source for this account was Juan Estevan Pico, a native Ventureño Chumash speaker (Bowers 1897; Hudson et al. 1977, 99n7). As mentioned earlier, the number of Tejón warriors said to be involved (400) and the number of casualties (more than 70) are likely to be greatly exaggerated. Nonetheless, a quite similar version without the inflated figures was narrated by Ventureño consultant Fernando Librado *Kitsepawit* to John Harrington (Hudson et al. 1977, 13–14), and there are certainly elements to this tradition that ring true. Hostilities between rancherías of the interior mountains and those toward the coast were frequently mentioned in the mission period, and at least one long-distance marriage between the Castac region and *Muwu* has been documented in mission records.[19]

The battle between the Castac Chumash and *Muwu* can even be given an approximate date. According to Librado's recounting of this tradition, the war between the Castac Chumash and *Muwu* led to the exodus of families from the coastal town and occurred during the time of a remembered chief named *Halashu*. Elsewhere Librado commented that *Halashu*'s two sons, *Kwaiyin* and *Wataitset'*, succeeded their father in turn as the last two chiefs of *Muwu* (Hudson et al. 1977, 102n36). *Wataitset'* is a historically known individual. He was baptized at Mission San Buenaventura as Mariano Guatahichet, *capitán* of Mugu (*Muwu*), when he was forty-five years old in 1802 (Johnson 1999b, 264–68). Thus the traditionally reported hostilities between towns in the Castac and *Muwu* regions most likely dates to the 1760s or 1770s and may even be related to a 1779 event that temporarily caused the abandonment of another large coastal town, known as La Assumpta (*Shisholop*), located up the coast from *Muwu* (Neve 1782; see table 4.2).

Another Chumash oral tradition pertains to conflicts between the Castac-Emigdiano Chumash and neighboring Yokuts tribes. Luisa Ygnacio, Barbareño consultant to John Harrington, related this version:

The Indians of the Tular [Valley Yokuts] and San Emigdio [*Tashli-pun*] were great enemies owing to the petty jealousy of their chiefs.

Once a chief of the Tular and a boy from the Tular went to the San Emigdio ranchería. The Tular people had warned this chief not to go, but the chief said that the San Emigdio people were friends and would not hurt him.

But at San Emigdio the chief was taken into a house and given pespibata (the dry form) [narcotic made from tobacco and lime], according to custom; that evening, he was suddenly killed by a man of San Emigdio named *'Usht'ó* while the Tular capitán was drunk with pespibata. His scalp was then taken and his neck cut. Later Luisa added that his hands and feet were cut off at the wrists [and ankles]. The boy who came with the captain had stayed at the door and had seen the whole thing. He had been told to go out to the *tokoy* 'playground', but did not mind. The boy ran back to the Tular and they could not overtake him. He told all of the news. The people of the Tejón, especially the Captain's mother, cried loudly. The San Emigdio people had intended to report that a bear had killed the captain, but were foiled by the boy. That was the cause of war.

They used to have many wars over there and all due to the jealousies of the chiefs and to other jealousies. (Harrington's notes, cited in King 1982, 182–83)

As was the case with the reported battle between *Muwu* and the Castac Chumash, certain elements of Luisa Ygnacio's story are supported by documentary evidence. The chief of *Tashlipun*, baptized in 1818 with a number of others from San Emigdio and Cuyama regions at Mission Santa Bárbara, was named Uichojo and is quite likely to be the individual remembered as *'Usht'ó* in Luisa Ygnacio's account.[20] Luisa Ygnacio's source almost certainly was José "Venadero" *Silinaxuwit*, an elderly Indian who had been baptized from *Siwaya* in the mountains behind Santa Barbara in 1812.[21] *Silinaxuwit* lived near Luisa Ygnacio's family for many years and was a close friend of her father and first cousin of her mother-in-law. She reported that "José Venadero [*Silinaxuwit*] ... always liked to take trips to the Tejón country" (Harrington 1914). José Venadero's wife, Dominga, was baptized with the group headed by Chief Uichojo of *Tashlipun* in 1818.[22]

The practice of dismembering an enemy's body, as recounted in Luisa Ygnacio's story, receives documentary support from another case attributed to the southern San Joaquin Valley/Tejón region as documented in a burial entry at Mission San Buenaventura: "Clodoaldo Yotchohuó [a native of Cashtéc (*Kashtiq*)], having been killed at the hands of very distant heathens. . . . His bodily remains, they say, were cast about the open country, following the customs of the heathens, who do not give the honor of burial to the dead, especially for outsiders whom they look upon as enemies" (MBV Bur. 2236, January 14, 1819).

Catarino Montes, who was born and raised at the Tejón ranchería in Kern County, reported another oral tradition regarding enmity between the Tulamni Yokuts and the people of *Tashlipun*. Montes's mother once told him that many Tulamni people had once died because the people at *Tashlipun* had poisoned the waters of San Emigdio Creek that flowed into the Buena Vista Lake (Montes 1997). This attribution of poisoning by one's enemies harkens back to accounts from the mission period in which epidemics, such as the "dolor de costado" of 1801, were blamed on supernatural poisonings.

The final oral historical account to be cited here has been frequently mentioned in studies pertaining to Chumash intergroup conflict (e.g., King 1982, 166; Lambert 1994, 58–59) and was specifically cited by Alfred Kroeber in his assessment that "the Chumash were "an unwarlike people" (Kroeber 1925, 556). The source for this account was Justo Gonzales, a native speaker of Barbareño Chumash, who had been born about 1823 (Johnson 1988, 235; Yates 1887). He is reported to have inherited the mantle of chieftainship of *Mikiw* (one of the two neighboring towns called "Dos Pueblos") in ceremonies held in the Chumash region as late as 1869 (Hudson et al. 1977, 93). In 1887, Justo provided a description of a battle that he said took place about 1833 (Yates 1887):

When Justo was a small boy he had witnessed some fighting at the Estero, about one mile [east] from the city of Santa Barbara, between the Indians of El Rincon (a point 15 miles distant) and those who lived where Santa Barbara is located.

Their method was to open a battle by tossing up a lot of feathers.

One Indian would leave his companions, advance toward his enemies and shoot a number of arrows, which were generally dodged
by the opposing forces. When the Indian got tired he retreated or
fell back, and another would advance.

The fighting did not result in much loss to the participants. In
the instance referred to the Santa Barbara Indians lost one of their
number; the Rincon part, two.

He stated that the arrows were sometimes poisoned.

When a declaration of war was made a messenger was dispatched by the aggrieved party, who repaired to the tribe with
whom they desired to open war, with a polite invitation to meet at
a certain place and on a stated day.

On the day agreed upon the opposing parties, painted and
equipped for the fight, repaired to the proposed battle ground
and opened fire by throwing handfuls of fine feathers into the air,
accompanying the action by certain peculiar sounds and a repetition of ya, ya, ya, ya, ya, ya, ya, ya, increasing the rapidity of enun-
ciation until it culminated in the exclamation *Wau-Kap-pée!!!*

In these battles, very few were killed; but the fighting was continued for some time after the loss of a man by either party.

When either side was satisfied they built a fire, which signi-
fied that their opponents were valiant warriors, and that they were
satisfied and wished to bury the hatchet for the present. (Yates
1891, 374)

Justo's account is unique among the ethnohistorical accounts of
Chumash warfare in his description of rituals associated with battles.
Although arranged battles and individualized contests in front of the
assembled warriors are certainly not unusual in aboriginal California
(McCorkle 1978) and are hinted at in Chumash myths (Blackburn
1975), there are some reasons to question certain portions of this rec-
ollection. In 1833 there were no independent Chumash towns still
occupied in coastal areas, only communities affiliated with the missions.
Thus, it appears unlikely that there was any Chumash community at
El Rincón, where the native town of *Shuku* had been abandoned some
thirty years earlier. Furthermore, there are no contemporary Spanish

accounts describing fighting among Chumash groups during the 1830s, despite a substantial documentary record, and no deaths from hostile action are recorded in burial registers for either Mission Santa Bárbara or San Buenaventura. There were several struggles for political hegemony in Mexican California, however, that led to armed confrontations in the vicinity of Santa Bárbara in 1830 and San Buenaventura in 1838 (Bancroft 1886, 76–81, 550–56). Conceivably, some skirmish among Chumash Indians connected with one of these conflicts may have taken place, and this would have been what Justo witnessed. Justo spoke little or no English, and his recorder Lorenzo Yates, working through an interpreter, may have confounded a description of a fight witnessed by Justo as a boy with oral traditions about battle rituals passed down from his elders.

THE DEMOGRAPHIC CONSEQUENCES OF INTERGROUP CONFLICT

One final source of ethnohistoric information bearing on the topic of Chumash warfare has to do with the consequences of repeated raids on the demographic structure of the native population. The mission registers recording the baptisms, marriages, and deaths provide a primary record of vital statistics pertaining to population changes among the indigenous peoples of the Californias from the San Francisco Bay region southward to Cabo San Lucas (Cook and Borah 1979; Jackson 1994; Johnson 1989, 1999a; Milliken 1995; Walker and Johnson 2003). Over a fifty-year period, from the time of the founding of Mission San Luis Obispo in 1772 until the last elderly people from inland and island rancherías were baptized at Mission Santa Bárbara in 1822, virtually the entire population of the region inhabited by people speaking Chumashan languages was resettled in mission communities. Taking the estimated ages of people at the times of their baptisms and extrapolating back to what would have been their ages at the time of initial Spanish settlement provides a picture of the demographic structure of the native population just prior to the dramatic impacts caused by introduced European diseases (Walker and Johnson 1992, 1994). Figure 4.3 presents the population pyramid in 1782 at the time of the founding

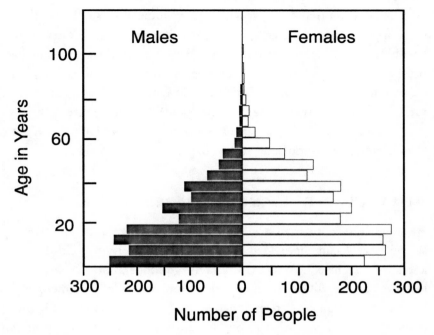

FIGURE 4.3 A reconstructed pyramid for the Chumash population in 1782 based on mission register data from Santa Bárbara, La Purísima, and Santa Inés. The number of women baptized who were twenty years old or older was nearly twice that of men, reflecting a higher mortality among men, attributable in large part to warfare.

of the Santa Bárbara presidio for Chumash Indians baptized at three missions: Santa Bárbara, Santa Inés, and La Purísima. This year marks the advent of intensive Chumash-Spanish interaction in the main part of the Santa Barbara Channel that resulted in continuous opportunities for disease transmission.

A normal population pyramid for indigenous groups unaffected by the ravages of epidemic disease is very broad at the base and tapering to a point with advancing age. The ratio between the sexes remains approximately equal, except for increasingly more women than men in older cohorts. The reconstructed Chumash population pyramid, however, is dramatically skewed, exhibiting more women than men past the age of twenty (approaching a 2:1 ratio). Although higher mortality among males in part may be due to high-risk subsistence pursuits (e.g., men lost at sea during fishing trips or while crossing the Santa Barbara Channel on trading voyages), the continuing effects of intervillage strife appears to be the most likely explanation for the great disproportion between numbers of adult men and women who were eventually baptized. When particular subgroupings within the Chumash region are examined, the speakers of the Central Chumash languages (Ventureño, Barbareño, Ineseño, and Purisimeño) exhibit the greatest disparity (Johnson 1999a). These are the groups among which most of the ethnohistoric descriptions of warfare originated (see table 4.2).

ALLIANCE POLITICS AND WARFARE

Although direct statements are lacking, some information from mission period documents allows us to indirectly ascertain political alliances from reported instances of intervillage cooperation in contrast to instances of intervillage strife. Reports on amicable relations among villages are less frequently encountered among mission period documents than are descriptions of intergroup hostilities, which naturally were of more concern to the missionaries and soldiers. Only four instances of peaceful intergroup cooperation mentioning specific towns within the Central Chumash region were encountered in the course of research. These may be briefly enumerated:

1. Chief Yanonali of *Syuxtun* (Santa Barbara) was well received when he visited the Goleta villages (Fages 1783).
2. The son of the "old chief" of *Syuxtun* was chief of the mountain village of *Shnaxalyɨwɨ* (Goicoechea 1785).
3. Chief Yanonali interceded on behalf of the Carpintería Indians after the latter had killed a bull from the mission's herd (Goicoechea 1786).
4. Many Indians from two of the largest Santa Ynez Valley villages, *Teqepsh* and *Kalawashaq'*, participated in a fiesta at one of the Goleta villages (Goicoechea 1798).

The first three of these statements accord well with independent information regarding the chief of *Syuxtun*, Yanonali, who was said to have held some form of hegemony over thirteen neighboring villages. Other indirect evidence regarding amicable relations among villages may be found in the patterns of consanguineal and affinal family links revealed in mission register data, which show there to be "clusters" of towns that tended to intermarry within themselves more often than to towns in other clusters. These towns, more closely related to each other by marriage, would undoubtedly have been likely to support each other should enemies attack anyone among their residents. Furthermore, these intermarrying clusters often crosscut environmental zones, linking coastal towns to inland rancherías, thus facilitating economic exchange within the group (Johnson 1988, chap. 9; King 1976).

FEDERATIONS AND MARRIAGE PRACTICES

The systematic recounting of all of the known ethnohistoric accounts of Chumash warfare and its effects provides us with a great deal of insight into the practice of armed conflict as it existed in south-central California at the time of initial colonial settlement. Overall, the descriptions do not differ too much from those summarized for northern and central California (see table 4.1), and at times the warfare even approached the frequency and scale of fighting documented for the Colorado River Yumans, albeit with not the same degree of militarism embedded in myth and ideology (Forde 1931; Kroeber and Fontana 1986). Inter-ranchería conflict was universally described as a frequent occurrence among Chumash peoples, and the types of engagement most often appear to have been surprise attacks or opportunistic ambushes. Small-scale conflicts between kin groups were motivated by revenge or were responses to perceived insults; however, hostilities involving whole towns or alliances of warriors from several towns were documented in a number of instances.

It is tempting to view Chumash warfare only in cultural ecological terms. Most ethnohistoric observances occurred among towns occupied by peoples speaking Central Chumash languages. These groups had higher population densities, and thus resource stress would have occurred during times of climate-induced scarcity. Indeed, unpredictable droughts and irregular, severe El Niño events certainly resulted in times of hardship in the Chumash region (Arnold 2001, 26–31; Johnson 2000; Kennett and Kennett 2000; Larson, Johnson, and Michaelsen 1994; Larson, Michaelsen, and Walker 1989). Such subsistence stress in turn would have resulted in the temptation to trespass into another group's hunting, gathering, or fishing territories, and indeed trespass is one of the causes for fighting described in ethnohistoric sources (Landberg 1965, 30; Longinos [1792] 1961; Señán [1815] 1976, 113–14). Such responses are entirely expected in light of cross-cultural studies that have shown that uncertain food supplies, when combined with mistrust of others, is a significant predictor of war (Ember and Ember 1992). The system of alliances among local polities in different ecological regions, cemented through intermarriage, was an effective way not only to facilitate economic exchange to overcome resource shortages but also to protect one's group from certain hostile neighbors.

From the perspective of Chumash peoples, however, warfare was an ongoing, ever-present reality, not attributed only to ecological events. Sudden raids leading to deaths of community members and burning of whole towns and villages were periodic actions, leading to retaliation in turn. Witchcraft by one's enemies was considered the cause of unexplained deaths, prompting revenge killings. Economic motives were not often the perceived cause for instigating hostilities, therefore. It would appear significant that in several instances, the chiefs of opposing groups were the targets of war parties. Just as has been documented for the Colorado River Yumans, Spanish sources tell us that successful Chumash war leaders would be recruited into positions of chieftainship. This observation does not necessarily conflict with the inheritance of rank in Chumash society, because in a number of instances, father and son were each recognized as a "capitán" in mission records. The patrilocal residence pattern commonly observed for Chumash chiefs extended to their sons and grandsons and contrasted with the matrilocality that predominated in the rest of society (Johnson 1988). The families of Chumash political leaders thus constituted fraternal interest groups in the midst of a society that otherwise might be considered to have adapted—through marriage of males into their wife's residence group—to break down such special interest groups for common defense against an external threat (e.g., Divale 1984).

Although we cannot now recover all of the details, the chronological sequence of many of the known incidents presented in table 4.2 leads us to suspect that hostilities between particular federations of allied rancherías may have persisted over several decades, just as has been documented among River Yumans (Kroeber and Fontana 1986, 107). In particular, certain interior Ventureño rancherías seem to have been at war with those of the inland mountains behind Santa Barbara, and acts of aggression appear to have spilled over into coastal regions at times. Within the coastal region, there were documented conflicts involving Dos Pueblos (*Mikiw* and *Kuya'mu*) with their coastal neighbors to the east and west in the mid 1770s. The repercussions from these hostilities may have extended over several decades, because the chiefs of Dos Pueblos and their allies were the targets of raids from enemies living in the inland mountains behind Santa Barbara and Ventura as late as 1795 and 1801. The extent to which conflicts between a powerful Obispeño chief, El Buchón, and peoples living to the south and north of him may fit into a longer-term pattern of warfare cannot be determined based on extant information. The death of this feared leader sometime after he was witnessed in battle in 1770 and the establishment two years later of Mission San Luis Obispo may have helped to quell hostilities in that region.

The system of alliances that came into being to defend against raids of opposing rancherías appears to have led to the emergence of some form of federated groups. These federations tended to crosscut ecological boundaries in a coastal-inland direction. Although most comparativists would class the type of warfare present among Chumash peoples as internal war, the development of enmity between any two groups of allied towns might as well be considered to have replicated the conditions of external war (Otterbein 1994). Some scholars of warfare have been argued that matrilocal residence functions to reduce strife within a society by breaking down bonds of fraternal interest groups, thus uniting males to face external threats (Divale 1984; Ember 1975). Indeed, marriage patterns among Chumash towns can be shown empirically to have been stronger within groups that were allied economically and politically (Johnson 1988, chap. 9), thus creating the conditions for strengthening cooperation within federated rancherías opposed to other groups.

The significance of different residence patterns practiced by chiefs' families in contrast to the rest of Chumash society is not entirely clear but may be related to differing needs and motivations of elites and commoners. The political leadership formed fraternal interest groups to protect themselves and perpetuate their hereditary rank, whereas the general populace best ensured their own survival because most men, residing in their wife's community, did not form such interest groups. Matrilocal residence reduces competitive urges within the local group and aids in forming alliances that would be economically and militarily advantageous.

The study of Chumash warfare and its societal implications raises many questions that beg for further comparative research within the California region and beyond. If matrilocal residence is a favored outcome in societies that engage in external war (Divale 1984; Ember 1975), then how were the Chumash different from their patrilocal neighbors in the rest of central and southern California? Fortunately, empirical data are now being assembled from the records of a number of other California missions that will allow such comparisons to be made among indigenous groups and our interpretations challenged or refined. Because of the richness of its ethnohistoric record, the region occupied by California's indigenous peoples offers unusual opportunities for studying the articulation of marriage and family patterns with forms of political leadership, economic interaction, and intergroup conflict, resulting in a more accurate description of these societies and a deeper understanding of human behavior.

NOTES

1. There actually is no such group as the "Tejón Chumash"; probably the reference is to the Castac Chumash (originally called "Emigdiano" by Kroeber [1925]), who lived in a series of rancherías in the San Emigdio Mountains. The adjacent Tejón region originally belonged to the Kitanemuk, who spoke a dialect of the Serrano, a Uto-Aztecan language. The Castac Chumash (or Castequeño) derive their name from one of their principal villages, *Kashtiq* at Castac Lake, and spoke a quite distinctive dialect of the Chumashan Ventureño language (Klar et al. 1999).

2. See figure 4.1 for the locations of Chumash towns. Harrington ([1924] 1986) and Kroeber (1925, 553) interpret "Xexu" as derived from *Shisholop*, the

name for the important native settlement near Pt. Conception (see also King 1975).

3. The Spanish explorers seem to have misunderstood the town names *Xexo* (also spelled *Xexu*) and *Xucu* as labels for larger federations of Chumash coastal settlements. The extant account of the voyage of Juan Rodríguez Cabrillo was compiled and condensed from at least three journals, now lost, including Cabrillo's original log (Kelsey 1986; Wagner 1929). Some allowance must be made for miscopying and the communication problems that would have existed between the Spanish explorers and Chumash peoples. Nonetheless, many of the town names are recognizable as those being occupied two and half centuries later, demonstrating the remarkable longevity and stability of indigenous settlements in the Santa Barbara Channel region.

4. The town and village names on figure 4.1 and mentioned in this chapter appear in linguistic orthography adapted for English-speakers, thus *sh* = *š*, *ch* = *č*, *ts* = *c*, etc. Native speakers interviewed in the late nineteenth and early twentieth centuries attested to the correct pronunciation of many of these town names (see especially Harrington [1924] 1986; Pico [1884] 1999), and others have been reconstructed by linguists based on careful analysis of versions recorded in the mission records (McLendon and Johnson 1999). Proper names recorded in phonetic/linguistic form are italicized to distinguish them from nonlinguistic spellings such as the Spanish-language spellings of the missionaries.

5. The linguistic affiliation of the people who inhabited the Cambria region is somewhat uncertain, whether Northern Chumash, Salinan, or even a third, mysterious language called "Playano" by the early missionaries (Milliken and Johnson 2005).

6. This early description of taking scalps as trophies is very explicit; however, no skeletal evidence for this practice has yet been detected in the course of examining extant collections of crania from prehistoric cemeteries in the Chumash region (Phillip Walker, pers. comm. 2004).

7. Cook (1976, 18–19) has identified the "dolor de costado" epidemic as pneumonia and/or diphtheria. It was one of several pandemics taking the lives of many California Indians during the mission period (Archibald 1978, 157; Cook 1976, 17–19; King 1984, 15–20; Walker and Johnson 1992, 1994).

8. My identification of Lihuiasu differs from that offered by Horne (1981, 82). Horne identified Lihuiasu from Atsililihu as being a man baptized in 1805

as Francisco Solano Uauisu from *Sxaliwilimu'* (MLP Bap. 2231). The names are not dissimilar, and *Sxaliwilimu'* was also a village in the Cuyama area, but a closer fit is provided by matching Lihuiasu with Rafael Liguiasu from Achililiguo, baptized in 1804 at Mission Santa Bárbara (MSB Bap. 3000).

9. Besides the chief of *Shnaxalyiwi* being a son of a chief of *Syuxtun*, cited in a later note, these family connections included Chief Yanonali's aunt living at *Siwaya* (MSB Bap. 1668) and Chief Lihuisanaiset from *Shniwax* serving as a chief of *Syuxtun* (Johnson 1984). One of the latter's children was born at *Shnaxalyiwi* and baptized at *Siwaya* (MSB Bap. 2595).

10. The identity of the ranchería of Tinoqui is unclear, because no Indian was ever baptized at the missions from a town or village having this name. Tinoqui appears likely to have been the name of the capitán of a ranchería in the San Emigdio Mountains or Tejón region, rather than the name of the village. A Kitanemuk Indian by this name was baptized at Mission San Fernando in 1819 (Mission San Fernando Baptisimal Records [hereafter MSF Bap.] 2385) and later served as a chief at the Tejón Indian Reservation in the 1860s and 1870s (Johnson 1997, 262). This man, Vicente Francisco Tinoqui, was too young to be the Tinoqui mentioned in 1790, but it would be consistent with what is known about native naming practices for him to have been named for that chief. Alternatively, Tinoqui may be a village name on upper Piru Creek, which was called the "Tinoco" in early ethnohistoric records (Johnson 1978).

11. Goicoechea's report in the Archivo General de la Nación differs from the California Archives summary in reporting that "they found Espinosa naked, hung from an oak tree, his whole body riddled with arrows" (Goicoechea [1790a] 1978, 5).

12. *Tatsicoho* is not shown on figure 4.1. Based on place-name information collected by J. P. Harrington, this ranchería appears to have been located in the vicinity of *Kashtiq* (Harrington [1924] 1986; King 1975). Only one individual was ever listed from this ranchería in mission records.

13. The information provided here permits the identification of these two neophytes in the Mission San Buenaventura baptismal register. Francisco de Asís Alisacu was baptized from *Shuku* at the age of 29 in 1784 (MBV Bap. Bk. 1:56), and Vital Castacu was baptized from *Shisholop* at the age of 40 in 1788 (MBV Bap. Bk. 1:359).

14. *Pespiguata* (more often spelled *pespibata*) was made from the dried

leaves of wild tobacco (*Nicotiana attenuata*) mixed with lime and used by southern California Indians as a narcotic and stimulant (Timbrook 1987).

15. Only one individual named Domingo was baptized at Mission San Buenaventura prior to 1790. This was Domingo José Suquip, the first Chumash convert at that mission, who was about ten years old at the time of his baptism on December 28, 1782. He was from the ranchería of Alaleygue (*'Alalhew*), more frequently spelled "Alalehue," which was described at the time of his baptism as being "in the nearest mountains" (MBV Bap. Bk. 1:2). This ranchería was located somewhere between *Mupu* and *S'eqp'e*, two of the towns mentioned in the 1790 investigation, according to a letter written by Fr. José Señán in 1804 (Señan [1804] 1962, 14).

16. Tinoqui may have been the chief of *Kashtiq*, because the largest numbers among the warriors were from that town.

17. Although one might suspect that this "old chief" was Yanonali (Brown 1967, 48), the evidence is far from clear. Yanonali's baptismal entry (MSB Bap. 1147) reveals that he would have been about 48 years old in 1785, perhaps not old enough to be described as the "old chief" of *Syuxtun*. Another chief of *Syuxtun*, named Panay, who apparently was never converted, was mentioned as father of a child baptized in 1790 (Johnson 1986, 26). If Panay was older than Yanonali, then he could have been the "old chief" mentioned as the father of the chief of *Shnaxalyiwi*.

18. Duggan (2000) comes to a similar conclusion. She suspects that there may well have been a relationship between the 1769 raids by mountain Indians that led to the destruction of coastal towns, including *Shalawa*, and later enmity between *Shalawa* and *Shnaxalyiwi* that led to the deaths of their respective chiefs (Duggan 2000, 34).

19. The San Buenaventura baptismal register for 1803 includes an entry for an infant born to a mother from *Muwu* and a father from "Mastéc" (MBV Bap. Bk. 1:1721). "Mastéc" is apparently a reference to "Castéc" (*Kashtiq*) in the *Muwu* dialect.

20. MSB Bap. 4030.

21. MSB Bap. 3535. José Venadero *Silinaxu'wit* died at an advanced age. His name last appears in the 1870 federal census, and he was noted as living in Santa Barbara's Indian community at La Cieneguita. According to oral tradition, he took one last trip into the mountains but never returned. When his tracks were followed, they changed into those of a bear (Blackburn 1975, 265).

22. MSB Bap. 4052.

5 DOCUMENTING CONFLICT IN THE PREHISTORIC PUEBLO SOUTHWEST

Polly Schaafsma

It has been said that the absence of warfare should be surprising, not its presence (LeBlanc 1999, 150). Examination of various components of the prehistoric record has led to agreement among archaeologists that there is ample evidence to thwart the long-standing stereotype of the "peaceful Pueblos" proposed by Ruth Benedict (1934). Evidence of prehistoric violence has often been noted and described in the course of archaeological studies in the American Southwest and its peripheries. Early citations of indications of hostilities, sporadic and largely descriptive, are summarized by Jonathan Haas and Winifred Creamer (1997, 235–40). These authors also address the political nicety of portraying the Pueblos as largely peaceful as late as the 1960s and 1970s.

Recently, recognition that conflict was a meaningful component of Southwest prehistory has led to a concerted effort on the part of archaeologists to address this subject, focusing on time, place, and the broader cultural contexts and circumstances that led to and fostered hostilities and generating explanations for such encounters (LeBlanc 1999). Social conflict in the prehistoric Southwest was not engaged for purposes of hegemonic expansion and political dominance, however (Riley 1989, 138–39). From all indications, although whole villages were sometimes destroyed, hostilities took the form of raids. Raiding of one Pueblo village upon another or by outside groups could have been provoked by economic stress, revenge for social affronts, and, as a side benefit, the acquisition of scalps. In turn, defensive measures were established for protection. The archaeological record contains evidence of all of these possibilities and defensive responses.

In the past decade or so, there has been a noticeable growth in the number of volumes dedicated to warfare research, including, to name but a few, Haas and Creamer 1993; LeBlanc 1999; Rice and LeBlanc 2001; Schaafsma 2000; and Turner and Turner 1999. The numerous articles addressing the subject include Brooks 2002; Haas 1990; Haas and Creamer 1997; Kuckelman, Lightfoot, and Martin 2002; and Wilcox and Haas 1994.

Archaeological remains that indicate stress, hostilities, and conflict, however, are often circumstantial—settlement patterns involving population aggregation and settlement clustering, line-of-site communication between sites, defensive site situations and architectural design, and so forth. There is also the less frequent but more explicit evidence, such as burned rooms or villages, unburied bodies, and osteological evidence of violent deaths, including scalping (Allen, Merbs, and Birkby 1985). All of these pieces of information, both primary and secondary, were recently examined in detail for the entire Southwest by Steven LeBlanc (1999). In this chapter, I examine the evidence for prehistoric Pueblo warfare, giving special focus to the information encoded in rock art and kiva paintings.

The Colorado Plateau before AD 1300

In the Basketmaker period (early Anasazi, ca. 400 BC to AD 400) in the San Juan region (see fig. 5.1), skeletal remains suggest massacres as well as the taking of head trophies by these early practitioners of maize horticulture (Hurst and Turner 1993; LeBlanc 1999, 123, 140, table 4.1; Morris 1939, 19; Smiley and Robbins 1997, 47; Wilcox and Haas 1994, 229). Lethal conflict as exemplified by the skeletal remains in Cave 7 represent a devastating slaughter. Indeed, Winston Hurst and Christy Turner (1993, 169) conclude that "lethal conflict was a part of Basketmaker life." In addition, human trophies, occasionally found in burial contexts (Kidder and Guernsey 1919, 190–91, plates 87a and 87b; Morris 1925), were also pictured on cliffs and rockshelter walls. Depictions of fetish heads and scalps provide additional evidence that these items were not only taken by Basketmakers and their early Fremont neighbors but were also valued (Cole 1985, 1989; Howard and Janetski 1992; Reagan 1933; Schaafsma 2007).

LeBlanc (1999, 149) surmises that a decrease in hostilities after late Basketmaker II (ca. AD 400) was followed by an increase in Pueblo I (AD 750–900), and he cites numerous burned sites as evidence (LeBlanc 1999, 140–51, table 4.1). After AD 1200 there are multiple lines of archaeological evidence for a sharp increase in violence (Haas 1990, 187; Haas and Creamer 1996; Kohler and Van West 1996, 184; Kuckelman, Lightfoot, and Martin 2002), especially in the later 1200s (LeBlanc 1999, 197). Warfare is postulated to have been endemic across the northern Southwest in the thirteenth century (Haas and Creamer 1996, 205). The evidence for increased hostilities among the ancestral Pueblo Anasazi and possibly between them and the Fremont population includes paintings and petroglyphs of shields and shield-bearing warriors in Colorado Plateau sites in southeastern Utah by around AD 1250, if not before (Schaafsma 2000, 9–27). I have proposed that these paintings at defensive sites abandoned by circa AD 1280 represent a magical defensive strategy involving the perceived supernatural powers of the shield and its decoration, powers that appear to have carried over into the imagery itself (Schaafsma 2000, 22–27).

Indirect evidence of social problems on the Colorado Plateau during the thirteenth century involves site aggregation and building construction in elevated locations. Cliff dwellings with limited access were

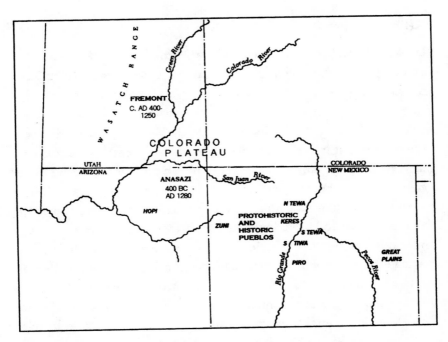

FIGURE 5.1 The northern Southwest, showing various cultural divisions.
Historic linguistic provinces of the Rio Grande Pueblos are believed to reflect
protohistoric linguistic patterns.

often protected by masonry walls with loop holes targeted toward trails,
springs, and storage units, indicating the need for protection while
defending strategic locations. More directly, unburied skeletal remains
and evidence of cannibalism at Sand Canyon Pueblo and Castle Rock
in southwestern Colorado in the late 1200s are direct testimonies to
violence (Kuckelman, Lightfoot, and Martin 2002).

Environmental degradation may have promoted competition
among various groups of Anasazi, who banded together and attacked
each other. Marauding bands of hunter-gatherers may have been
another disruptive factor at this time of drought and environmental
stress, although their presence so far is not visible in the archaeological
record (Ambler and Sutton 1989). In summary, population decimation
and/or migrations away from the Colorado Plateau and the San Juan
drainage marked the end of the thirteenth century, after which time the
area was depopulated altogether by Pueblo people.

PUEBLO IV, AD 1325–1600

Pueblo archaeology in Arizona and New Mexico after 1300 describes a demographic shift, a reconfigured settlement pattern, material culture, and cosmology. Following ideas proffered by Richard Burger (1988), these changes may reflect a revitalization movement in the wake of cultural crisis. During this period of accelerated change, a new ideology became manifest in the art beginning in the fourteenth century. Curiously, evidence for conflict does not diminish but becomes even more evident. In addition, the content of the visual documents also indicates that the motivations for conflict in the thirteenth century were different from those that followed, beginning with the late fourteenth century and continuing into the historic period. Except for an apparent belief in the magical power of shields, there is little continuity in the ideological content between the older and post-thirteenth-century work.

Following the abandonment of the Colorado Plateau by Pueblo people, the kiva mural iconography and Rio Grande rock art in Pueblo IV (ca. AD 1325–1600) (Schaafsma 2000) is rife with war themes. Shields, shield bearers, and other warriors armed with bows and quivers of arrows, war clubs, and more rarely, spears, speak for themselves as images embodying the presence of social strife. In addition, there are numerous portrayals of war-related supernaturals. Evidence of war societies is also present in this imagery; along with the kachina cult, war societies would have served to integrate the large towns characteristic of the period (Schaafsma 2000) while formalizing war-related activities and interaction with supernatural forces. An apparent environment of chronic warfare may have fostered social cohesion and promoted social complexity.

Religion and warfare are commonly inextricably linked. R. Brian Ferguson (1990, 46) has pointed out that war is a collective activity that involves group solidarity and survival and—a point that is important to this discussion—poses questions of meaning, as the participants confront hazards and risks. Thus, in Ferguson's words, "War is a virtual magico-religious magnet." In the Pueblo case, the synthesis of warfare, cosmovision, and religion among the late prehistoric Pueblos shows how ritual and real combat interrelated to maintain cosmic balance and to fulfill agricultural needs. An extraordinary emphasis on inducing rain permeates every Pueblo ritual (see Stephen 1936, for example). If warfare was irrevocably established in the thirteenth century as a way of life, it was certainly validated and rationalized in the following centuries by the adoption of a Mesoamerican-related ideology that interwove conflict with a belief system involving rain making. War and fertility were not only linked but also institutionalized, as the taking of scalps involved societal practices that transformed scalps into rain-makers. The underlying cosmology, which persisted into the ethnographic period, is spelled out in the visual text of rock art and kiva murals—importantly, the graphic voice of the Pueblo peoples themselves (Hibben 1975; Schaafsma 2000; Smith 1952).

CONFLICT, ART, AND COSMOLOGY, AD 1325–1600

The high visibility of shields and warriors along with other war-related themes in late prehistoric Pueblo rock art and kiva murals is direct evidence for the importance of warfare, as well as an indication of its cosmological implications. These depictions are not narrative statements like those pictured in Plains rock art and ledger drawings in the nineteenth century but involve symbols, serving as metaphors and representing other beliefs regarding conflict and the supernatural realm. War deities and other supernaturals, including warrior kachinas, the sun, stars—often feathered and taloned—and the sanctified predator-animal supernaturals as war and hunt patrons are represented in Pueblo IV art. This complex of figures embraces an ideology of conflict that fundamentally deals with both the need for the sun to warm the earth (for corn to grow) and the need for rain (for corn to grow). The deeper implications of these images involve the need for reciprocity, a Pueblo concept fundamental to the means for maintaining a balanced cosmology.

This prehistoric visual text fortunately lends itself to examination via the ethnographic record. Nevertheless, we must keep in mind that the images available from prehistory are but windows into a rich reservoir of concepts and oral traditions now lost or preserved by descendants in forms variously modified over time. Warfare and its concomitant ideology was on the wane by the late nineteenth century when the first ethnographers arrived in the Southwest, and the late prehistoric imagery cannot always be understood as having a one-on-one congruity with the ethnographic data now available. Nevertheless, overall, the good fit between Pueblo IV images and the ethnographic symbols and metaphors that they embrace demonstrates a general continuity of ideology since the 1300s.

Ethnographically, shield designs (see fig. 5.2) were chosen for their power and perceived magical protective qualities (Parsons 1939, 197; Wallis and Titiev 1945, 555). Although the social implications that these designs might have encoded remain unexplored, many of the elements decorating shields occur independently in the rock art and embrace symbolic and metaphorical meanings that relate to the deeper patterns in the Pueblo worldview.

In Pueblo IV rock art and kiva murals, sun symbolism appears commonly with shields. In fact, the sun's face is thought of as a shield or as being covered by a shield. That shields are replete with sun symbolism is not surprising in light of the fact that the sun is the ultimate warrior and the father of the warrior twins, to whom he supplies magical weapons. The sun is appealed to for power in war and hunting and is often referred to as a head-taker (Parsons 1939, 180). Human death is necessary to give the sun energy. Hopi oral traditions establish the need for human action to assist the sun in maintaining his proper movement across the sky (Lomatuway'ma, Lomatuway'ma, and Namingha 1993, 19–21).

Human intervention involves both conflict and the rituals that surround it, including ritual dramas by warrior societies during critical times of the year, such as the winter solstice and the equinoxes. Although warfare is not explicitly mentioned in Pueblo accounts of providing these requisite deaths, powdered human hearts of ancient enemies are described as present on Hopi winter solstice altars (Dorsey and Voth 1901, notes 22–23), and the parallels with Mexican sacrifices to keep the sun on track seem not too distant. At Zuni, if not elsewhere among the Pueblos, offerings of numerous prayer sticks to the sun at the winter solstice are viewed as sacrificial substitutes for human lives (Bunzel 1932, 625), embodying the reciprocity deemed necessary for sustaining life on the earth's surface.

FIGURE 5.2   A petroglyph of a shield bearer, circa AD 1350–1525, Galisteo Basin, New Mexico. The zigzag lines represent the sun's rays, while at least four of the interior designs are stars. The head of the figure is only roughly indicated, perhaps having been made at a later date and not part of the original image.

It follows that war society activities figure prominently in winter solstice rites. Rituals ensure the sun's seasonal reversals from the solstice positions, so that the world will be neither too hot nor too cold. Jesse Walter Fewkes (1897, 268) stated that the Hopi Soyaluna is strictly a warrior's observance. During winter solstice kiva rituals on First Mesa, mock battles between shield-bearing warriors appear to relate to the threats to the sun at its southernmost point of its journey along the horizon. These encounters are thought to "offset malign influences or to draw back the sun from a disappearance suggested by its southern declination" (Fewkes 1897, 271), while offerings to the Horned Serpent are made immediately prior. In this context, the serpent appears as a force threatening to the sun. Southern Tiwa and Piro petroglyphs of shield-bearing warriors confronting horned serpents appear to synthesize these solstice kiva dramas (Schaafsma 2000, figs. 4.10, 4.11).

Pueblo races were sponsored by Tewa war associations for the sun and as preparatory ritual for combat (Hill 1982, 345). Among the Tiwa, races were (are) held to regulate the sun's journey. In the Tiwa case, enemy scalps, ritually honored during races at Isleta, are not rain-makers (as described below) but are said to empower runners who represent the sun's movement during the equinoxes (Parsons 1932, 324–30; 1939, 962). In this way, the power of the honored enemy dead taken in battle is engaged to ensure the sun's proper motion (Schaafsma 2000, 116–17). The linking of racing to the sun at the equinoxes would seem to explain the running sun figures in Piro rock paintings (Schaafsma 2000, figs. 4.8, 4.9).

The Morning Star's role in warfare ideology is equally as complex as that of the sun, but with a focus on scalping, rain, and fertility. Venus, closely connected to the daily movements of the sun, is perceived as the sun's guardian and warrior. As warrior and protector, the star image as a shield motif is most appropriate and was commonly used prehistorically (see fig. 5.2). The star's frequency in the late prehistoric art (and the many ways in which it is utilized) suggests that it was a more popular icon and more complex in meaning in the Pueblo past than at present, although even today, all stars have an association with war (Parsons 1939, 181). Stars are depicted with four expanding points around a central circle that may have a face. The image is often conflated with eagle talons and tail feathers (Schaafsma 2000, fig. 3.26a), attributes of Knifewing, eagle-like supernatural of the zenith, who is identified with scalping (Schaafsma 2000, fig. 4.25). Stars may be perceived also as the warrior dead, uniting the concept of stars and scalps as such. Elsie Clews Parsons (1939, 181–82) found that among the Hopi-Tewa, stars and scalps were viewed as the same thing. These descendants of the Southern Tewa told her that scalps are called "Morning Star," or conversely, "stars are scalps" (Parsons 1939, 181–82).

The enemy scalp, as noted previously, has great significance as a rain fetish. Bloodletting associated with the act of scalping and long hair are references to fertility and rain. The scalp in Zuni poetry is alluded to as a "rain-" or "water-filled covering" or "cover of thin clouds" (Bunzel 1932, 676, 687, 764). Thus, one of the major benefits of conflict was to return with a few rain fetishes. Conflict appears to have been seasonally orchestrated, at least at Hopi; once the harvest was gathered, it was time to go on the warpath (Titiev 1944, 162), and this in turn would provide fresh scalps to ensure rainfall during the next growing season. The ceremonious return to the village by victorious warriors with the scalps they had taken was celebrated as women threw the scalps onto ground drawings of clouds as they proceeded into the pueblo (Stephen 1936, 97). The extensive Zuni prayers of the war cults documented by Ruth Bunzel (1932, 668–89) eloquently describe the ritual use of the enemy's scalp (usually Navajo) to bring rain, and thus corn, for the ultimate end of promoting Zuni well-being.

The model for scalping is provided by supernaturals. There are references in Zuni poetry to the Beast God war patrons ripping the scalp from the enemy (Bunzel 1932, 686–97). In contemporary Hopi mythology, the taking of scalps is sanctified by the Heart-of-the-Sky God, the initiator of scalping: "who kills and renders fertile" (Parsons 1939, 178). His unmasked face is a star (see fig. 5.3).

The Morning Star, or Venus, associated with warfare in both the Southwest and Mexico, is commonly represented in late Pueblo rock art, as mentioned above. This star is often conflated with eagle attributes. Other star-related deities are the War Twins, wearing pointed caps. The twin aspect of these sons of the sun is cosmologically expressed by Venus as Evening Star and Morning Star (Young 1992). Their caps may take

FIGURE 5.3 A Southern Tewa petroglyph of a star-faced war supernatural. This powerful warrior deity, associated with summer thunderheads and lightning, holds projectile-style lightning bolts as well as a (maize?) plant, and a bird is shown on his torso. The bird is believed to be Knifewing, supernatural of the zenith and in charge of lightning and scalping.

the shape and proportions of the point of a star (Schaafsma 2000, 53, fig. 3.16; Smith 1952, Fig. 65a). Their abilities as rain-makers as well as fighters are recounted in the oral literature (see especially White 1932, 150–54).

Other supernaturals pictured in the late prehistoric rock art that synthesize elements of warfare and fertility are kachinas. The appearance of the rain-making kachina cult simultaneously with the increase and elaboration of war iconography after circa AD 1325 is noteworthy and is probably not accidental (Plog and Solometo 1997). Stephen Plog and Julie Solometo (1997, 172–76), who rightfully point out that a separation of war and fertility is an artifact of twentieth-century analyses, focus on how kachinas relate to the interconnectedness and co-occurrence of warfare and fertility. These authors contend that early kachinas were warriors as such. While I think that the idea that early kachinas were warriors needs further scrutiny, there is no doubt that kachinas have a role in the Pueblo war cults.

Kachinas, as masked rain-bringing ancestral spirits, take many specific forms; and among these, numerous kachinas are warriors or have a warrior component (Schaafsma 2000, 129–36). Many of these kachinas appear in the prehistoric art, including the widely occurring Shalakos, Morning Star kachinas (whose frequent pairing suggests the War Twins), the Bloody Hand kachina, and Hilili. These kachinas unite warrior and fertility themes and are linked to contemporary Pueblo tales of conflict and revenge, which commonly end with head-taking or a scalping. In contemporary ritual, certain kachinas such as Hemsona at Hopi enact symbolic scalping by cutting the hair of spectators or other ceremonial participants (Wright 1973, 222).

Finally, there is the complex scene on Layer 1 of Kiva 2 at Pottery Mound, an early Pueblo IV ruin southwest of Albuquerque, New Mexico. This mural portrays a parade of varied warriors facing a line of cloud people ensconced in an atmospheric milieu of clouds and lightning. This meeting effectively unites the entire theme of war and fertility (Schaafsma 2000, Pl.12, 157), a complementarity that was prevalent as well in Mesoamerican cosmologies from which Pueblo IV ideology may have ultimately derived (Schaafsma 1999).

Spanish Documents and Oral Literature

Historical documents from between 1581 and 1601, prior to European impact on the indigenous scene, describe Pueblo weapons and shields, although they are sometimes ambivalent in regard to Pueblo warfare activities (Hammond and Rey 1953, 647; 1966, 82, 84–85, 87, 175, 221). Although some accounts describe the Pueblos as relatively peaceful, others note that the Pueblos were at war with each other as well as with Plains groups (Hammond and Rey 1966, 82, 87; Riley 1989, 142; Winship 1896). Unstable relationships between Pueblos and Plains nomads, mutually engaged in the exchange of maize for bison products, may have been conducive to volatile situations. (Although Judith Habicht-Mauche [1988, 161–71] emphasizes "interdependency and cooperation" over "coercion and conflict" between the Pueblos and Plains nomads during the Protohistoric period, she also details conditions that easily could have provoked hostilities between these groups [1988, 161–71].) The Eastern Piro and Eastern Tiwa (Tigua) are described as warlike and well armed, qualities possibly accentuated because of their proximity to the Plains. The emphasis on warfare in Southern Tewa rock art may be similarly explained (Schaafsma 1992).

Late-nineteenth- and twentieth-century Pueblo oral literature contains references to hostilities between Pueblos generated by feuds and perceived insults followed by revenge, as well as Pueblo confrontations with other ethnic groups (Lomatuway'ma, Lomatuway'ma, and Namingha 1993; Stevenson 1904, 34–45; White 1935, 176–77). One Santo Domingo story describes attackers from the east, whom the Santo Domingos overcame by supernatural means (White 1935, 179–82). These kinds of hostilities most likely predated the arrival of the Spanish.

Following a period of historic conflict between the Pueblos and their neighbors—the Spanish, Utes, Paiutes, and Apaches and Navajos—warfare and its related institutions and the social role they played in political and ceremonial contexts waned and were revised at the end of the nineteenth and early twentieth century. Nevertheless, even historically the war priest, representative of the sun, wielded authority equal to or second only to that of the *cacique* (the head priest-leader, with both religious and political duties), even sharing his responsibilities (Ellis 1951, 200; 1979, 361; White 1935, 37n9). Given these changes, it is not surprising to see the rain-bringing/fertility implications present in Pueblo warfare ideology during Pueblo IV being brought to the forefront during the historic period. Lending additional support to this premise is Leslie White's (1932, 45–46) observation that the primary function of the war chiefs in early-twentieth-century Acoma was to promote rain. Some of the former military functions among the Hopi-Tewa, by contrast, have been transformed into policing duties and dealing with outside matters (Dozier 1957; 1966, 27–28, 70–74).

WARFARE IDEOLOGY AND VISUAL IMAGERY

Unlike more-traditional archaeological data associated with conflict, war themes in rock art and kiva murals do not deal with defensive strategies or the direct social or economic causes of hostilities, nor are they primarily narrative or documentary in intent, as far as we can tell. However, the imagery is rich with symbolism that indicates how warfare and related activities were perceived and structured in terms of the supernatural, reflecting a Pueblo model of cosmological dynamics. Although differences in motivations for warfare before and after AD 1300 need further investigation, clearly only after 1300 were the cosmological and religious links to conflict made explicit in the art—and then, prolifically so. This suggests the rapid adoption of a new ideology in which a warfare cult was linked to a new and highly elaborated cosmology to promote rain (Schaafsma 1999; Schaafsma and Taube 2006), following the crisis precipitated by drought and the abandonment of the Colorado Plateau.

In conclusion, the graphic text provides the Puebloan perspective and statement, which complements the socioeconomic forces more traditionally considered by archaeologists to explain prehistoric conflict. Through the rock art and kiva murals of Pueblo IV, it is apparent that between AD 1325 and 1600, a religious ideology of warfare was in place that—to borrow the words of Clifford Geertz (1999, 13)—mystified power, sustained values, maintained morale, reduced anxiety, and justified unjust deserts, even while it empowered the horticultural base.

This ideology contributed toward psychological security and rationale in the face of conflict, as warfare was integrated with the cosmic forces in such a way that balance and harmony necessary for agricultural success were enforced. Between contributing toward the regulation of the sun's movement and the acquisition of scalps for rain, Pueblo warfare and its attendant rituals since the fourteenth century have worked to these ends.

6 CAHOKIA AND THE EVIDENCE FOR LATE PRE-COLUMBIAN WAR IN THE NORTH AMERICAN MIDCONTINENT

Thomas E. Emerson

The intensity, duration, and extent of native wars in the New World are tied by some researchers to the intrusion of European powers in the fifteenth century. Other scholars contend that the historic pattern of war is simply a continuation of existing prehistoric practices. Clearly the resolution of this debate lies in the evidence to be found in the archaeological record. The northern midcontinent of the United States, containing the Great Lakes and Missouri River valley regions, is an area that experienced endemic war during the historic period. The archaeological record for this area suggests that significant evidence of human skeletal trauma and fortification construction does not appear until after about AD 800–1000. Analysis of Late Woodland skeletal populations provides evidence that the recently introduced bow and arrow had been incorporated into local war practices. By about AD 1100, the construction of village palisades, often with bastions, had become widespread in the region. During the fourteenth century, we have two dramatic cases that indicate the intensity of pre-Columbian conflict: the Crow Creek massacre in South Dakota and the Norris Farms cemetery in Illinois. The archaeological record indicates that precontact war in the northern midcontinent was a part of everyday life. Scholars have attributed increased conflict to the appearance of sedentary lifestyles, resource scarcity, increasing population sizes, shifts in climatic regimes, and the introduction of chiefly sociopolitical forms that encouraged prestige war. All these variables may be possible contributing factors, but in this study I privilege the institutionalization of intergroup conflict within complex hierarchical societies as being pivotal (*sensu* Reyna 1994a).

These days, graphic visions of war, ethnic violence, terrorism, genocidal massacres, and their legacies of continuing hatred and new violence fill the media. The public is subjected to a grinding repetition of peril, injury, and death. Many believe that we are living in a period of accelerated violence, that the peaceful equilibrium of a long-gone, more idyllic past has been disrupted by modern tensions not previously experienced in the world. Often such violence is seen as a correlate to the rise of nation-states, as contrasted with the earlier "primitive" societies that lived in peace and harmony. Such perspectives envision past societal norms as ones of peace and cooperation, a prestate humanity living in a golden age seen through Rousseauian lenses. We find comfort in the belief that the violent behaviors expressed by modern societies are aberrations, deviances from the norm that can be corrected and improved. Such a perspective stems from a continuance of the great intellectual project of the Enlightenment—to "improve the human condition through scientific progress" (Reyna 1994a, xviii–xxi). In reaction to such philosophical and moralizing stances promoting the "pacification of the past," Lawrence Keeley (1996) produced his dramatic documentation of the violent nature of prestate societies.

As a group, social scientists have been especially reluctant to accept human violence. The number of scholars who consider human aggression, conflict, and violence as innate aspects of human nature and/or social makeup rather than pathologies is limited. Those with a sociobiological bent have been willing to contemplate the biological basis of violence. They frequently see human aggression as instinctual. As a consequence, such manifestations of violence as war do not need explanation, per se, because they are innate and, to some degree, inescapable. Such perspectives of human nature have deep intellectual roots reaching back to Hobbes and beyond. But although Thomas Hobbes saw society as the tamer of humanity's aggression, others have seen large-scale intergroup violence as its product. From such a viewpoint, war has been the essential ingredient in the march to civilization. Herbert Spencer ([1886] 1975) and in this century Robert Carneiro (e.g., 1994, 1998), among others, have ascribed the origin of civilizations and the rise of nations to the fundamental characteristics of organized war. Violence and war then can be seen as integral to the human experience, either because of innate human characteristics or because of the apparently virtually inseparable relationship between human societies and intergroup aggression.

But what is this phenomenon known as War? At least in historical and ethnographic circles, the scholarly deliberations on war often seem to have become a virtual war of and about words, a terminological and semantic field of battle occasionally devolving to sophistry. What makes the debate particularly contentious is the tremendous diversity of ways and means that humanity has employed to cause harm to their fellow humans and the multitudinous moral values attached to such actions. Unfortunately, many of these moral and value judgments seem to have been implicitly carried into the scholarly debates, thus further muddying the waters. There is very little agreement on what constitutes war. Murders, executions, brawls, family fights, feuds, massacres, skirmishes, ambushes, raids, battles (both sham and real), and genocide all have been filtered through the definition of war, excluded or included depending on the focus of the researcher. War researchers are also strongly influenced by body counts (perhaps a vestige of Vietnam), frequency, intensity, and to some degree intentionality. Conflicts that kill several individuals per encounter are demeaned as harmless (although that perspective might change if the researcher were counted among the dead), while only battles killing hundreds or thousands are considered as valid markers of real war. Infrequent, low-intensity conflicts for the purpose of revenge or anger are typically classified as "nonwar." Frequent, intense intergroup conflicts to destroy or control others are real wars.

War has been an important ingredient in socioevolutionary theorizing in which war is seen as a correlate of political development. In such approaches, scholars debate whether certain levels of sociopolitical complexity are or are not capable of engaging in war. Of course, the usefulness of such debates depends on employing a common definition of war (a commonality that is often missing). Typically, those who correlate sociopolitical complexity with war argue that smaller, less complex social entities, such as bands and tribes, do not participate in "real" wars, while chiefdoms, states, and empires are usually characterized as virtual war machines.

The ongoing documentation of war has, to a large degree, focused on its outward and obvious manifestations of intergroup violence—battles, casualties, weapons and accompanying paraphernalia, and the disastrous results that it has on the lives of people. From an external perspective, war really does seem logically, and even subjectively, inexplicable. However, as increasingly noted by observers, perhaps our perspective is what is flawed; the accumulation of more and more evidence of past human violence may not be sufficient to resolve the issues. The evidence in hand appears to clearly establish that human intraspecies violence, between both individuals and groups, is a demonstrable part of humankind's past. Without a doubt, humans have the latent potential to unleash violence against other humans, just as humans have the potential for amicable cooperation. The acknowledgment and identification of such potential is important but not explanative. Researchers now need to shift their attention to look within the historical trajectories of specific social groups to unravel the context of intergroup violence. The historical situations that encourage the practice of war should increasingly be the focus of our attention (e.g., Carman 1997a, 1997b; Otterbein 1997; Reyna 1994b).

THE LATE PRE-COLUMBIAN NORTHERN MIDCONTINENT

The geographical focus of this review can be summarized as encompassing a broad, fan-shaped area centered in the Mississippi River valley at

St. Louis, Missouri, and reaching west to the Missouri River valley of South Dakota and east to Lake Michigan (see fig. 6.1). The chronological focus is on pre-Columbian groups that inhabited this zone for the half millennium between roughly AD 900 and 1400, that is, just prior to European contact.

The people who inhabited this region were diverse, probably speaking languages attributable to several major language groups. At the beginning of the period, many of these groups were on the verge of becoming dependent on full-time maize farming as their primary subsistence source. As this dependence increased, it strengthened the likelihood that these groups would become more and more sedentary. Such a pattern of larger population agglomerations led to the development of new and different patterns of internal and external social and political interactions (Emerson, McElrath, and Fortier 2000; McElrath, Emerson, and Fortier 2000). During this time, distinct tribal and chiefly entities could be recognized on the archaeological landscape in major river valleys (Emerson and Lewis 1991). Other populations in the area, especially those outside of the major valleys or in the more northerly areas, continued a more mobile lifestyle, characterized by little or no dependence on maize growing. Bands, or perhaps loosely fashioned tribelets, of these part-time farmers(?), gatherers, and hunters appeared to exist throughout this five-hundred-year period, operating on the fringes of and interwoven with the clustered river-valley villages of the farming peoples.

What imprinted this time and this region, however, with a unique historical trajectory was the rise, at about AD 1000 in the St. Louis locality, of the largest polity ever to appear in pre-Columbian native North America—Cahokia (Emerson 1997; Milner 1998; Pauketat 1994, 2004; Pauketat and Emerson 1997). By AD 900, the American Bottom, the broad floodplain directly across the Mississippi River from St. Louis, was thickly populated by village farmers. Many of the inhabitants lived in clustered settlements that contained as many as 100 to 150 structures. Although we assume that such villagers lived in tribally organized societies, in some instances petty chiefdoms are likely to have been present or in the process of emerging. It is from this potentially politically volatile context that Timothy Pauketat (1994) surmises a series of collaborative chiefdoms arose that created the setting from which Cahokia emerged.

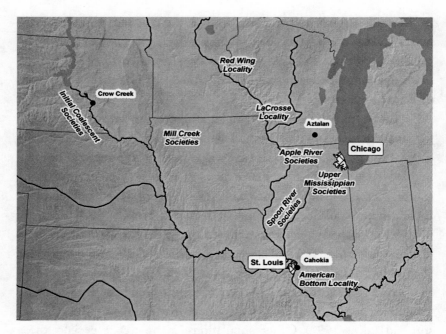

FIGURE 6.1 Selected sites in the northern midcontinental United States (AD 900–1400). (Courtesy of the Illinois Transportation Archaeological Research Program)

This great polity coalesced at about AD 1050 and expanded to control an immediate hinterland area of about 9,300 square kilometers, encompassing the surrounding floodplain and uplands zones of five to six modern Illinois and Missouri counties. The political administrative core of this center included a zone roughly 1 kilometer wide and 13 kilometers long containing over two hundred platform and mortuary mounds, extensive plazas, borrow pits, post-circle monuments, and elite housing. One of these monuments, a multistaged platform a hundred feet high called Monks Mound, is the largest such construction in North America.

Contemporaneous with the period of Cahokia's prominence, another fourteen mound centers were located within 25 kilometers of the administrative core (Emerson 2002). One-half of these outlying centers had multiple mounds. We may reasonably assume that these small centers and their residents were directly under the control of Cahokia or strongly influenced by the central elites. Interspersed around and between these centers were thousands of scattered households of family farmers, as well as the nodal households of minor elites, rural temples, small mortuary sites, and rural villages and nonmound centers (Emerson 1997; Mehrer 1995; Pauketat 2003). One gets the impression that there was little "unsocialized" or "unpoliticized" space within the Cahokian sphere of control.

It is within the archaeological remnants of this regional social and political mosaic that I seek the material reflections of late prehistoric human violence. We do not have far to look.

EVIDENCE OF REGIONAL VIOLENCE

Sometimes the historical and anthropological semantic overtones of the study of war almost seem to render such discussions moot. On the face of it, the archaeology of war appears to be a simpler, more straightforward task. To some degree, this may be simply because our data are more coarse grained than those of other social scientists. The vagaries of preservation and of sampling limit our access to evidential sources that we can use to measure the existence and intensity of past human violence. Traditionally, regional archaeologists, seeking to identify midcontinental pre-Columbian war, have sought evidence of fortifications, weapons, human remains that have demonstrable deliberate trauma, and an iconography of war.

In the current political atmosphere that often fosters disbelief in a violent past, in both professional and popular audiences, such archaeological evidence is not seen as convincing—there is a demand to produce a "smoking gun." The politics of the present have impacted archaeology in the past, and that is still true today. Despite the present hesitancy of some to accept the material remains that might imply a potentially violent pre-Columbian past for the North American midcontinent, a review of that supporting evidence here is useful (also see Dye 2006; Lambert 2002; Milner 1999).

FORTIFICATIONS

The appearance of wooden palisades around habitation areas can be recognized as virtually a horizon marker in the region during late prehistory. There is circumstantial evidence that some Woodland sites in the circa AD 900s to 1000s might have palisades (especially in southern Wisconsin), but the real explosion of these barriers began at about AD 1100 and continued relatively unabated into the historic period. This construction of palisades in the 1100s also correlates with the destruction of palisaded villages throughout the midcontinent. Examples of burned palisaded villages are known from the Illinois River valley, the Missouri Trench, and the northern Mississippi River valley. Essentially this pattern of twelfth-century defensive construction and offensive destruction is present across the area under discussion (Brown and Sasso 2001; Emerson and Brown 1992; Milner 1999).

In the west in the Missouri River Trench of South Dakota and on tributaries in western Iowa, compact villages with deep middens appear in the Initial Variant of the Middle Missouri Tradition in the AD 1000s. These South Dakota Initial Variant sites, along with Great Oasis and Iowa Mill Creek sites, are often surrounded by deep ditches and wooden palisades. Initial Variant sites in southern South Dakota were replaced in the late AD 1200s or very early 1300s by heavily fortified and bastioned Initial Coalescent villages, often on the location of the previous Initial Variant villages (Johnson 1998; Winham and Calabrese 1998). A testimonial of prehistoric conflict in the area is provided by the Crow Creek site (discussed below), as well as other excavated remains. The practice of living in heavily fortified villages continued into the historic period in this area.

Moving to the east, we also encounter large organized villages surrounded by bastioned palisades in the central Illinois River valley (Conrad 1989, 1991). Mississippian peoples moved upriver into the region from Cahokia in the early AD 1100s and lived in dispersed unfortified sites. But by the late AD 1100s, conflict in the area had apparently intensified so much that fortified villages became the norm. The Norris Farms 36 cemetery (discussed below) provides a graphic example of the duration and persistence of war in the region. By the AD 1400s, the chiefly societies involved had collapsed and disappeared from the archaeological record (Emerson 1999).

In the upper Mississippi River valley, southern Wisconsin, and the Chicago area of Illinois, fortified villages proliferated, ranging from small hamlets such as the twelfth-century Fred Edwards site in south-western Wisconsin and the post-fourteenth-century palisaded Oneota villages such as Valley View in the La Crosse area, to the ditched and palisaded fourteenth-century Upper Mississippian sites such as the Hoxie Farm site south of Chicago (Brown and Sasso 2001; Henning 1998; Jackson and Hargrave 2003). One of the more famous and enig-matic of these northern villages was the strongly fortified Mississippian site of Aztalan in southeastern Wisconsin.

The most impressive of the post–AD 1100 palisade lines were those constructed at Cahokia (Dalan et al. 2003; Trubitt 2003). This truly monumental construction began in the very late Stirling or early Moore-head phase (perhaps between AD 1175 and 1200). The bastioned wall enclosed somewhere between eighty and ninety hectares of the inner site, surrounding the nearly twenty-hectare Grand Plaza as well as Monks Mound. It was rebuilt at least four times within about two or three gen-erations and maybe more often. The earliest wall has circular bastions, while later versions have rectangular bastions. Each episode of palisade building consumed at least twenty thousand logs to complete the three-kilometer-long barrier. In addition, early aerial photos suggest that the palisade lines exposed by limited excavations were a small portion of what were, perhaps, numerous palisades and fences built at the site. The pattern is clear across the region—after AD 1100, palisades (often with bastions and accompanied by ditches) became an integral part of community life.

WEAPONS OF WAR

We do not have to look far to find the weapons used in hostilities in the midcontinent, for they were the items of everyday use. The first axes appear in the New World archaeological record during the Archaic period. Useful for both chopping wood and splitting skulls, axes were probably the preferred instruments for close-in, hand-to-hand conflict. In their late prehistoric version, the celt, such axes are found universally among the region's inhabitants but are especially common among the chiefly Mississippian societies. The importance of the celt as a shock weapon for the Cahokian warriors might be epitomized in the presence of a foundational cache of over seventy celts in an upland political/ritual center southeast of Cahokia (Pauketat and Alt 2004). The presence of war clubs of wood, antler, or bone is also probable, based on the evidence from some Crow Creek wounds and from the ethnohistoric records. The distinctive linear depressions in the skulls of the dead at sites including Crow Creek (Willey and Emerson 1993), Norris Farms 36 (Milner, Anderson, and Smith 1991), Material Service Quarry (Emerson and Hedman 1999), and others confirm that death resulted from blows to the head from an axe (e.g., Emerson 1999).

The introduction of the bow-and-arrow technology in AD 600–900, and its presumed replacement of the thrusting or throwing spear, must have transformed the ways in which people both hunted and fought (McElrath, Emerson, and Fortier 2000; Nassaney and Pyle 1999). The acquisition by native societies of bow-and-arrow technology may have contributed to the intensification of prehistoric war in much the same way as the acquisition of firearms appears to have escalated the levels of indigenous conflicts during the protohistoric and historic periods. The increase in firepower resulting from the increase in the range of the new weapons and the rapidity of fire certainly made the bow and arrow capable of inflicting a higher rate of casualties from a greater distance than the spear or axe/club. Embedded arrow points first appear in skeletons from near the end of the Late Woodland period and continue to be found in bodies up to and including the historic period (e.g., Milner 1999, 2005). We can assume that death by arrows was more common than the mortuary evidence suggests, since the arrows would likely have been removed from the body either by relatives or by the killers for reuse. Confirmed injury by arrows occurs only when the stone point hit and remained embedded in a bone. Considering this limitation of the archaeological record, the evidence of arrow-related deaths is not uncommon, with the most prominent example in our region reported from the fourteenth-century human remains buried in the Norris Farms 36 cemetery.

SKELETAL TRAUMA AND HOSTILE DEATH

The osteological evidence of intergroup violence in the northern midcontinent has been documented by many researchers—from across the region between AD 900 and 1400 are reports of violently crushed skulls, arrow points embedded in human bones, decapitation, and scalped heads. The numbers of such reported deaths are not usually large but range from one or two examples to perhaps a half dozen per site. However, the pattern is consistent and clear. The fear and likelihood of violent death at the hands of enemy groups must have kept the people in a constant state of anxiety.

Lawrence Keeley (1996), based on a cross-cultural examination of ethnographic and ethnohistoric data, has portrayed the devastating effects on a society of this ever-present, ongoing stress. It has been graphically demonstrated within Illinois by the work of George Milner and his colleagues at the early-fourteenth-century Norris Farms 36 cemetery (Milner, Anderson, and Smith 1991). About 16 percent of several hundred burials showed signs of having died a violent death, with evidence of decapitation, scalping, blunt force trauma, and arrow points embedded in bone. The bodies of the dead were apparently uncollected for some time, and their bones were gnawed by carnivores and bleached by exposure. The skeletal evidence also indicated that other members of the group had been scalped or injured previously but had escaped and their wounds healed.

As important as Milner's observations of the chronic violence that impacted the Norris Farms 36 villagers were, his demonstration of the dramatic effects that such threats had on community health is even more insightful. These people suffered from iron-deficiency anemia and various infectious diseases and had a low level of health. As Milner (Milner and Smith 1990) noted, this was a highly stressed population when their overall health is compared to that of other prehistoric peoples. As Keeley and Milner both demonstrate, there is more to war than simply the number of individuals killed and wounded. Perhaps the major impact of such long-term, chronic violence is its destabilization of a society's subsistence strategies, political and social patterns, and general lifeways. This pattern of low-scale, continuous, and persistent violence can destroy or entirely transform a society long before it kills large numbers of the society's members.

Correlated with such chronic war as experienced by the pre-Columbian inhabitants of the Norris Farms 36 village are those rare episodic attacks aimed at the total devastation of an enemy population. Pat Willey and I documented the aftermath of such an opportunistic attack at the now-famous Crow Creek massacre site in South Dakota (Willey and Emerson 1993). There, perhaps at dawn on a winter day in the early AD 1300s, raiders virtually decimated the population of a large fortified village. The mutilated bodies of nearly five hundred villagers were recovered in our excavations, with more bodies known to exist in the makeshift grave and in the site's burned houses. This truly was a massacre rather than a battle; most villagers appear to have been clubbed to death while fleeing. There is not an embedded arrow point in any of the bodies. Men, women, and children were indiscriminately killed. Their noses, hands, and feet were sometimes cut off, teeth smashed, and heads and limbs cut from the body. The victims, from babies to elders, were universally scalped and mutilated. The scale of the deaths suggests that most of the inhabitants were killed. Yet some survivors did return weeks or months later to bury the carnivore-gnawed, disarticulated remains of their kin and neighbors. The Crow Creek population, like that at Norris Farms 36, was suffering from depressed community health and poor diet. An enemy group sensing their weakness may very well have taken the opportunity to eliminate the population.

There is little doubt nor does it seem possible to reinterpret the existing evidence to signify anything except that the late prehistory of the northern midcontinent was marked by periods of chronic intergroup hostility and episodic hostilities that totally devastated communities. How widespread or frequent those hostilities were is difficult, if not impossible, to determine.

ICONOGRAPHY

Late prehistoric art that might reflect on the presence of war exists among the Mississippian peoples of the Southeast and Plains and has been discussed extensively in the literature. Such iconography, however, is fairly limited in the region under consideration. It includes such diverse forms as hawk-man carvings and copper plates, depictions representing maces or clubs, weeping eye motifs, decapitated human and animal heads, stone maces, knives, dance swords, and so forth. To some extent, war motifs appear more conspicuous by their rarity than by their presence.

However, an ongoing research project has provided new insights into Cahokia's iconography of war. For a long time, we have known that Mississippian people crafted a series of large, red stone figurines of exceptional quality and beauty. Only recently have we been able to demonstrate through archaeometric investigations that Cahokian artisans carved all of these figures in the twelfth century from a local flint clay source (Emerson et al. 2003). Two of these figures (called Conquering Warrior pipes), showing men in armor, provide valuable insights into aspects of Cahokian militarism. Both specimens show a large individual leaning over a crouched subordinate figure. In one case, the superior figure appears to be smashing the head of the smaller figure with a club (fig. 6.2). Each of the large warrior figures wears a protective open-top headband, a wide collar about the neck, and body armor that covers the back and chest. Both of these figures are elaborately carved with many details. This new awareness that the two large warrior figures represent Cahokian military regalia allows us to interpret some of the less elaborate figures recovered in the past. For example, a number of statuettes depicting nude men wearing only a thick, heavy, open-top headband have been recovered in the region (e.g., Emerson 1982). Given the presence of the distinctive "helmets," I now suspect that these figures depict warriors.

We have another example of a more obvious military connection in a flint clay figure illustrating a kneeling nude man holding a long, rectangular shield before his body (fig. 6.3). His head is wrapped in the distinctive thick headband. This suggests that such headgear was symbolic of the warrior role in Cahokian society. It was presumably designed to protect the head from club blows. With the recognition of these warrior figures, the symbolic repertoire of war gains a greater place of prominence in early Cahokian iconography.

This set of figures implies the existence of a class of military specialists who may have been an essential ingredient in the creation of the early Cahokian polity (e.g., Pauketat 1999). The heavy body and head armor and shields indicate that these warriors were involved in fierce hand-to-hand combat, most likely armed with heavy clubs. This was not the military equipment of light skirmishers engaged in hit-and-run tactics or the long-range exchange of arrows. They were prepared for, and must have engaged in, massed attacks aimed at creating maximum shock value among the enemy. Such warrior societies are known both

FIGURE 6.2 Cahokia-style drilled figurine showing an armored warrior smashing the face of a victim with a club. (Conquering Warrior pipe from the collections of the National Museum of the American Indian, Smithsonian Institution, 21/4088; photo by David Heald.)

in tribal and in chiefly level political entities and can form a powerful source of internal and external control. These organized military units are extremely effective against surrounding small-scale chiefdoms and scattered tribes and would be required in elite conflicts between comparably sized chiefdoms. Of course, one of the advantages that the early elite rulers of Cahokia possessed was that there were no peer polities to threaten it—it was without competition during its ascent. Only internal factional conflicts could have really jeopardized early Cahokia.

THE INSTITUTIONALIZATION OF WAR

An examination of the archaeological record from the northern midcontinental United States during the period between roughly AD 900

FIGURE 6.3 Cahokia-style figure pipe, showing a crouching warrior with shield. (Guy Smith Figure pipe; courtesy of the Illinois Transportation Archaeological Research Program)

and AD 1400 has provided strong evidence for the existence of organized intergroup violence in a pre-Columbian setting. Although evidence of earlier intergroup violence has been observed, the two-century period from AD 900 to 1100 was clearly marked by a dramatic peak in the evidence for violence. Scholars have attributed increased conflict to the appearance of sedentary lifestyles, resource scarcity, higher population densities, shifts in climatic regimes, and the introduction of chiefly sociopolitical forms that encouraged prestige war—all may be possible contributing factors. The most inherently convincing of these factors, however, seems to be the correlation between a higher level of intergroup violence and the establishment of more complex sociopolitical systems. High levels of violence become sustainable when societies are in a position to institutionalize such violence.

Prior to AD 900, the northern midcontinent was the home to primarily hunting-and-gathering, mobile band, and tribal-level societies—those that are typically classified as egalitarian in evolutionary stage typologies. The "performance of war" in such societies appears to follow the same general pattern as other daily activities. In these small-scale societies, hunting forays, residential shifts, work parties, spiritual encounters, and similar activities are carried out in a sporadic fashion by individuals, families, or small kin-related groups. Actions are often initiated by individuals and become group activities only to the degree of that individual's ability to inspire others to participate. Consequently, such activities have a low level of sustainability. The key to understanding leadership in such groups is to recognize that egalitarian status and prestige generally are achieved rather than ascribed and shifting rather than permanent. Such relationships may be profoundly unegalitarian but are restricted to domestic and kin situations. This social and political context does not allow for the initiation or pursuit of large-scale, intense, long-term conflict.

It is not the presence or absence of inequality, status delineation, prestige, or hierarchical organization that differentiates egalitarian from hierarchical societies, for these appear to be coterminous with human society. Rather, it is the appearance of institutionalized forms of these relationships that marks the threshold (Emerson 1995). Clearly, egalitarian societies have "powerful leveling mechanisms" (often both social and environmental) and an "ideology of equality" (Service 1975, 71) that serve to reinforce social homogenization and suppress the accumulation and consolidation of power by individuals or select groups. Such leveling mechanisms have been overcome in the development of more-complex and permanently organized hierarchical societies. A key variable is the relative ability of those possessing status or prestige in hierarchically organized societies to utilize *power over*. In egalitarian societies, leaders persuade and manipulate; in hierarchical societies, they command.

The restricted use of violence as a form of internal and external political and social control is possible only within a society that possesses a system of hierarchical political power. Although such power structures usually emerge in societies that have achieved a chiefly political level, they have been observed in tribal groupings, where they are described as "chieftaincies" (i.e., Redmond ed. 1998). The relationship between subsequent chiefdoms and these earlier situational chieftaincies is best visualized by seeing "chiefs" as the products of institutionalized "chieftaincies." Elsa Redmond (1998, 3–4) characterizes a "chieftaincy [as] a situational hierarchy occurring from time to time among nonhierarchical uncentralized tribal societies, which . . . exhibit a nested arrangement of consensual decision making." Such chieftains are usually able to exercise centralized power in the short term over an autonomous village, although occasionally such authority can be extended over several such villages on the basis of the chieftain's prestige, expertise, and authority. Usually the powers of such chieftains are ephemeral, but in rare instances they may continue for the life of the individual and even pass on to his or her descendants.

The studies of chieftaincy by Redmond and her colleagues (Redmond ed. 1998) are very insightful concerning the movement in classic so-called egalitarian societies toward a form of centralized authority in a chieftain. Equally as enlightening is the path to power that is available to future leaders. These scholars demonstrate that success in war, in trade, in ritual manipulation, in hunting, or in political leadership can all provide avenues to elevating and perpetuating central authority. Again, under the right conditions, such authority can become hereditary and perpetual, and when that happens, a chiefdom is born.

The critical break in the sociopolitical continuum is the appearance of institutionalized, hierarchically arranged, leadership positions; the correlation of these positions with power, prestige, and status; and the ability to pass these positions on to descendants. The simplest of such societies is the chiefdom. Its appearance marks the critical threshold: it breaks the equilibrium of egalitarianism. Chiefdoms, in fact, can be characterized by their opposition to earlier sociopolitical forms—they are not egalitarian, leadership is not transitory, there is no homogeneity in the control and exploitation of resources; rather, one might say simply that they are "governed" inequitable societies. From this point forward in the development of hierarchical organization, one finds only the increasing elaboration of and emphasis on the inequality of society, ultimately culminating in the appearance of the state.

The emergence of chiefdoms and chieftaincies in the midcontinent was a critical first step in the widespread institutionalization of war in the region. Carneiro has long been a proponent of the snowball effect of the rise of a chiefdom—adjoining societies must rapidly enhance their sociopolitical sophistication if they are to survive. It is a case of emulation or dispersion. This pattern of change can also be thought of as a domino effect or as the ripple on a pond. As Cahokia arose, it directly affected its nearest neighbors, whose changes in turn caused modification in the lifeways of their neighbors, and so forth. There is a case study documenting late prehistoric sociopolitical change in northern Illinois that illustrates this situation (Emerson 1999).

In the eleventh to twelfth centuries, migrants from Cahokia moved into the central Illinois River valley and began to establish a series of small-scale chiefly settlements. These fortified nucleated temple towns dominated the valley for the next two centuries (Conrad 1991). To the north, they were bordered by small groups of fairly mobile horticulturalists that were likely organized in extended family groups and loosely knit bands. They appear to have had some dependence on maize but in general wandered widely, hunting and gathering across the valley and adjacent uplands of the upper Illinois River valley (Emerson and Titelbaum 2000). Within a few generations, the small Late Woodland groups to the north had, through both emulation and resistance, transformed their lifestyle. Known as the Langford Tradition, these twelfth-century descendants of mobile hunters and gatherers had coalesced into large, widely spaced, sedentary villages; developed a major subsistence dependence on maize; and created large, multigenerational, accretional mounded cemeteries. I have proposed that these changes are a direct reflection and result of the impact of the intrusion of chiefly-level societies into the area, bringing with them new levels of institutionalized violence (Emerson 1999). The arrival of these chiefdoms correlates with the first appearance of fortifications and osteological evidence of violent death in the central Illinois River valley. In this instance, at least, it seems clear that the impact of Cahokia's ascendancy can ultimately be measured directly in the archaeological evidence of violence and social change in distant societies at least four hundred kilometers to the north.

A Horizon of Violence

The testimony of the archaeological evidence presented in this chapter strongly confirms that a peaceful midwestern pre-Columbian past is a product of the imagination. Proponents of such a harmonious vision, by romanticizing and idealizing past human relations, actually dehumanize such societies. They remove these peoples from their historical context and create a false impression of "otherness." Archaeology serves as an antidote to such imaginary pasts.

The archaeological evidence indicates that the post–AD 1100 period in the northern midcontinental United States saw an upsurge in activities that suggest the increased threat of intergroup hostilities. In this region, the sudden appearance of evidence of intergroup violence correlates with the development of intensive maize farming and population nucleation into large sedentary villages. While scholars debate the spatial extent and the sociopolitical impact of Cahokia on surrounding groups, the fact that it had considerable impact seems inescapable. We should heed Carneiro's observation (1970, 1981) that the emergence of chiefdoms had a "snowballing effect" on the sociopolitical development of their neighbors, driving them toward emulation or elimination. The rise of Cahokia in the AD 1000s was coupled with the subsequent appearance of chiefdom-level groups in central and northwestern Illinois, southern Wisconsin, the upper Mississippi River valley, and perhaps even into the Missouri River valley. But the post–AD 1100 "horizon of violence" does not signify the initial appearance of regional intergroup violence. There is sufficient osteological evidence from the remains of Woodland peoples to indicate that individuals were dying in violent encounters even though there is no evidence of large-scale, ongoing conflicts (e.g., palisaded and burned villages or numerous scalped and mutilated human remains) of the kind that marks the onset of the Mississippian period. Rather, the horizon of violence marks the institutionalization of war across the northern midcontinent, likely as part of chiefly sociopolitical agendas.

In fact, it may have played a critical role in local elite emergence (Pauketat 1999; Pauketat and Emerson 1999). The social and economic distance between the nobles and commoners in an emerging hierarchical system is encouraged by a dispersed elite pattern of relationships resulting from external marriages, political expansion and internal conflict, and exile that establishes the formation of an ideological division between the classes, buoyed up by mythological sanctions (à la Wright 1984). The mythological and ideological basis for dominance is naturalized to the extent that the elites are necessary mediators with the supernatural, protectors of the polity, and essential to the furtherance of society. Clearly, factors such as ideology, war, and economics played central roles in the genesis of institutionalized inequality. In this context, as others have argued previously, war—like economics, ideology, religion, and politics—is systematically controlled and often intensified by hierarchically organized societies as part of the larger process of their internal and external growth and development.

ACKNOWLEDGMENTS

My epiphany in recognizing the importance of violence in the pre-Columbian record of the midcontinent occurred when I directed the excavation of the Crow Creek massacre site. I appreciate Rick Chacon's invitation to reflect on this experience in the broader context of this volume. Timothy Pauketat and Rick Chacon commented on earlier versions of this work and made suggestions for its improvement. Michael Farkas and Mike Lewis assisted in creating the figures.

7 IROQUOIS-HURON WARFARE

Dean R. Snow

The Iroquois had a reputation for violence among Europeans from the beginning of their mutual contacts. Their name comes from a term meaning "killer people" in the pidgin Basque jargon used around the Gulf of St. Lawrence in the late sixteenth century (Snow 1994, 2). Archaeology and oral traditions both provide clear evidence that this reputation was not one that began with European contact but was deeply rooted in the Iroquois' relations with other American Indian nations of the Northeast (Milner 1999). There, as elsewhere in North America, no evidence exists to suggest that American Indians lived in peaceful harmony before European colonization (Keeley 1996). Keith Otterbein has shown that a rise in warfare typically accompanies the emergence of agriculture as a subsistence strategy, so we should not be surprised that warfare was common among the settled farmers of the Eastern Woodlands (Otterbein 2004).

The League of the Iroquois began the sixteenth century in a period of endemic warfare that saw them at war with virtually all their neighbors, including each other. Five nations—the Mohawks, Oneidas, Onondagas, Cayugas, and Senecas—came together in a nonaggression alliance that ended their mutual warfare and redirected it exclusively toward other neighbors, including other Iroquoian nations (fig. 7.1). The alliance was a weak confederation often referred to in modern literature as the League of the Iroquois but called "Hodenosaunee" by modern Iroquois (Snow 1994, 60). Recent research indicates that its inception dates to the late sixteenth century (Kuhn and Sempowski 2001).

Other sets of Iroquoian nations came together in similarly weak political confederations around the same time, expedient innovations made necessary by circumstances. The Hurons, Neutrals, and Eries were all multinational confederations. Independent Iroquoian nations such as the Petuns, Susquehannocks, and Wenros were fatally disadvantaged by these developments, but ultimately so were all the confederations save the Iroquois. Which confederation came first and thereby deserves credit for the innovation is not clear, but the League of the Iroquois was the only one to survive the seventeenth century, and as always, the survivors write the history.

IROQUOIS WARFARE

Iroquois warfare was personal by its nature. Most violence took the form of raids on enemy villages, mainly for the enhancement of the prestige of young males. Raids took place mainly during the warm months, while crops were growing. The Iroquois nations were strongly matrilineal and matrilocal. Women dominated domestic affairs in the villages, and men were in charge in the vast forests beyond the surrounding fields. After doing the heavy work of field clearing each spring, the men were free to leave on diplomatic, trading, and raiding expeditions, which often kept them away until the fall harvest. Young men sought credit for exploits on these long-distance trips, which they needed to advance socially and

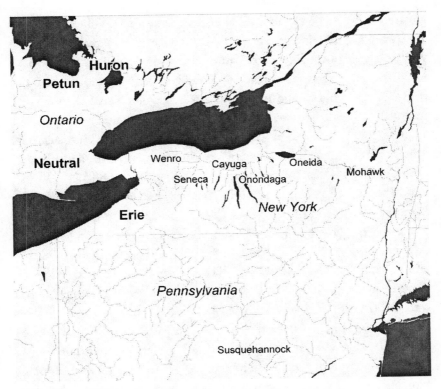

FIGURE 7.1 Northeastern North America, showing the distribution of Northern Iroquoian confederacies (bold) and selected nations.

politically at home. The successful returned with trophies and captives, the latter sometimes intended as replacements for lost relatives. The most desirable young women were unlikely to take on husbands who lacked these credentials.

An important cultural premise apparently believed by all Iroquoians at the time explains the high frequency of violence as compared to trade and diplomacy. The premise was that with the exception of drowning, any death was attributable to the conscious act of some evildoer. If the victim died violently, it was easy to argue that someone else was at fault. However, even if the victim died of heart failure while sleeping, the death was usually attributed to someone. The attribution in this case would be an accusation of sorcery, and the accused was usually (but not always) an enemy in a distant community. Whether a child died young or an elderly parent died of cancer at an advanced age, it was nearly always somebody's fault, and revenge was an appropriate response. The sharing of this belief among Northern Iroquoians guaranteed that cycles of revenge-motivated violence would percolate unabated in endemic form. The formation of confederations merely disqualified allies as potential evildoers and focused raids on more distant suspects. This pattern of belief and behavior is well documented in the legend of the origin of the League of the Iroquois (Snow 1994, 58–59).

The importance of this point is that it forces even the most ardent materialist to incorporate ideology into any adequate explanation of Northern Iroquoian warfare. Environment, subsistence, and technology alone are insufficient to explain the phenomenon. This point can be demonstrated by the case of two otherwise very similar modern South American societies that have very different patterns of violence and warfare. The Waorani of eastern Ecuador are among the most violent people on earth. Curiously, they are similar in almost every respect to the Barí, people who live in a similar South American environment but exhibit essentially no internal violence. Apart from their very different expressions of violent behavior internally, the major difference between the two peoples is that the Waorani share the Iroquoian view of causality when it comes to deaths (that is, the Waorani attribute nearly every death to some enemy or other and typically avenge it violently), while the Barí do not. The difference is ideological, and finding an adequate reason for the contrast through workings of materialist causes alone is difficult (Beckerman 2000).

SEVENTEENTH-CENTURY IROQUOIA

The first crowd infections introduced from Europe and Africa spread across Iroquoia in the fourth decade of the seventeenth century. The first smallpox epidemic killed about 60 percent in the villages it reached in 1634, and subsequent epidemics brought repeated devastation (Snow 1994, 94–108). The onset of epidemics prompted the elaboration of the curing ritual, the most visible expressions of which were the famous Iroquois False Faces. These cultural icons were carved from living wood with iron tools and equipped with brass and horsehair decorations, all of which point to seventeenth-century elaboration if not origin.

The epidemics also triggered a paroxysm of grief and revenge. The Iroquois lashed out at their traditional enemies, inflicting hideous deaths on some and using others to repopulate their decimated villages. Female captives were particularly valued in this matrilineal society, and most adapted quickly. Captivity accounts reveal that the Iroquois typically tortured and killed prisoners brought back to home villages. However, they also selectively spared individual captives and adopted these individuals to replace lost relatives, often after an episode of torture. They expected people thus spared to adapt quickly, and many did. Pierre Radisson's 1651 captivity in a Mohawk village is particularly informative. Radisson was spared to replace a lost son, and his adoptive parents and sisters expected him to become a Mohawk in every important way after a brief period of adjustment. They were baffled and heartbroken when he escaped by way of the Dutch outpost at what is now Albany, New York (Snow, Gehring, and Starna 1996, 62–92).

Most captives did accept their new identities. The epidemics and spiraling warfare that swept northern Iroquoia after 1634 created endless opportunities for this solution to demographic loss. There is no evidence that the Northern Iroquoian populations responded by increasing fertility rates (Engelbrecht 1987). At the same time, Jesuit missionaries often commented on the large numbers of people of foreign origins they encountered in Iroquois villages. The members of the League of the Iroquois survived the century while other Northern Iroquoian nations and confederacies did not, because the Iroquois were better at attacking, dispersing, and sweeping up remnants of their traditional enemies. There were substantial material reasons for this difference. The Mohawks and the other four Iroquois nations had access to Dutch (later English) and French firearms. They kept the Hurons, Neutrals, and Eries on the defensive, attacking them in their home territories almost at will. Meanwhile, attacks on the Iroquois nations by other native nations were rare or unknown. For example, although well-armed colonial French raiders attacked and burned Mohawk villages more than once, traditional native enemies never did. At the same time, the Mohawks were able to sustain their population by taking in refugees and captives. This included an entire village of Catholicized Hurons who moved to the Mohawk Valley in 1657 (Snow 1995, 403–10). Twenty-one years later, they left the valley with Catholicized Mohawks and resettled together at the nominally Mohawk village of Kahnawake outside Montreal.

It is not surprising that a Huron refugee community could become Mohawk over the course of two decades, complete with a shift in dominant language. However, today many may wonder at the passive acceptance of new identities demonstrated by individual Iroquoian captives, both men and women. Yet the cases of Patti Hurst, Elizabeth Smart, and countless similar but lower-profile modern kidnappings amply demonstrate that such behavior is not unique to that time and place. Captives often bond quickly with their captors. The phenomenon is sufficiently well known to have been named the "Stockholm Syndrome" (Havard 1987). People react to their immediate circumstances, with survival being their main concern, and there is often less to cultural conditioning than we may commonly prefer to believe.

By the middle of the seventeenth century, the Iroquois had become the scourge of the region, opportunistically befriended by nervous French and Dutch colonists (later the British as well) and feared by other Indian nations. They had vanquished the Hurons and Petuns by 1651. The Neutrals had been defeated and dispersed by 1653, and the Eries had suffered the same fate by 1656 (Snow 1994, 115–16). It might have been otherwise, but the Iroquois, particularly the Mohawks, were closest to the Europeans and thus both better equipped and perhaps better motivated by more severe epidemic losses. Defeated survivors of their attacks either fled westward or were incorporated as replacements into Iroquois communities. Despite the high mortality, particularly from disease, the Senecas actually maintained their population at around four thousand this way through this period (Snow 1994, 110).

DEFINING THE CURRENCY

All cultures operate with a prevailing currency. In modern industrialized nations, the currency is money and everyone knows how to use it. However, both skill and luck are unevenly distributed, and there is an inherent tendency for individuals possessing more than the average amount of wealth to attract even more of it, so there is a tendency for wealth to concentrate. The prospect of wealth concentration motivates individuals, for with it come fame, power, influence, well-being, and long-term security.

Left alone, economic systems will generate small numbers of very wealthy individuals and large numbers of poor ones. This tendency is both inherent and strong. Economists understood the phenomenon well in the nineteenth century, and two great political movements of the twentieth century tried very different means to control it. While fascists attempted to co-opt the process by seizing wealth and its principal generators, communists attempted to abolish them. Both failed. Meanwhile, liberal democratic systems discovered that the best solution was to attempt to neither commandeer nor abolish the phenomenon but rather to manipulate it for the greater good. Some politicians argue that wealth remains too concentrated, while others argue that the system is overtaxed by freeloaders, and the dynamic interaction between those extreme views keeps the system more or less in balance.

One can generate a curve showing the relationship of wealth per individual with some income size scale on one axis and the number of individuals in each income category on the other. A typical way of showing this is with the count of individuals on the Y axis and income level on the X axis. Let me stipulate for the sake of simplicity that there are about a billion people whose wealth levels are known and that the richest of them has about a billion dollars (fig. 7.2). The first thing that one should notice about such a curve is that it is not a normal distribution, not even a highly skewed normal distribution: there are many people with very low incomes and very few with high incomes. Indeed, the curve is very convex, like a half-life curve. There is no central tendency for individual cases to not trend toward some mean income level.

Within this distribution of wealth, there is only one richest person and a nearly countless number of poor ones. Twenty years ago, no one could have predicted that Bill Gates would today occupy the top position on a rank-size distribution, but anyone should have been able to predict that *someone* would. That is because the system tends to move toward equilibrium as a consequence of entropy, and in a system of this kind, equilibrium is reached when most wealth is concentrated, not when it is evenly distributed (see Barabási 2002).

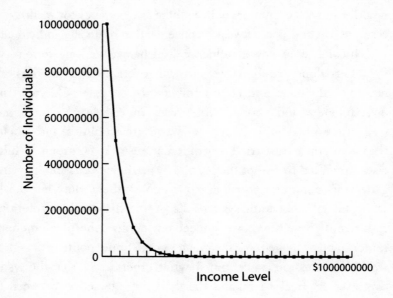

FIGURE 7.2 Wealth distribution displayed in a standard format.

The power curve generated by wealth distribution is remarkably similar to many other distributions of interest to anthropologists. Zipf's Law, for example, tells us that for any sufficiently large block of English text, there will be a few words that are used frequently and many that are used only once. "The" gets top honors, followed by "of," "to," "a," "and," "in," and so forth to rarer words. Networks that are not constrained by other factors often exhibit very similar power distributions.

As another example, Google went from nonexistence on the Internet a decade ago to being a network node with more links than any other. Now there is one node (Google) with a huge number of links and many nodes with only one or a few.

Airports offer still another example. Chicago and Atlanta are nodes with many links, while there are many small airport nodes with only a few. The same cannot be said of nodes on our highway network. Highways are built in a more-or-less two-dimensional plane, and no node can attract a very large number of links. It is not and never was true that all roads lead to Rome. Thus, there are sometimes constraints that prevent the formation of power distributions. Even airports have an upper limit to the number of links they can support as single nodes. O'Hare airport has probably reached its maximum. Google has yet to approach the maximum number of links it can handle.

The examples I have given are familiar ones that I have chosen deliberately to make the general concept clear. Wealth tends to concentrate and produce power curves. Networks of airports tend to seek equilibrium in the same way. Preindustrial societies often have or had other currencies, and so do certain subsystems in industrial societies, as in the case of Google. Sometimes those noncurrency distributions can translate into currencies, sometimes not. Both O'Hare airport and Google have successfully translated their links into dollars.

It should be no surprise for us to discover that there are power distributions in other currencies, whether they be the heights of temple mounds, the volumes of burial mounds, the lavishness of potlatches, or the number of citations in professional journals.

IROQUOIS CURRENCY

In the case of the seventeenth-century Iroquois, money (or some proxy for it) was clearly not the prevailing currency. George T. Hunt referred to the seventeenth-century wars of the Iroquois as the Beaver Wars and gave an economic spin to the phenomenon (Hunt 1940). However, José António Brandão has shown that even at the height of the fur trade, Iroquois war parties had little interest in seizing furs or in either interrupting or controlling the fur trade (Brandão 1997).

Clearly, then, if the Iroquois had some kind of currency as a raison d'être, it was not money or furs or some other proxy for money. If we examine Iroquois ethnohistory with a dispassionate eye, we discover that the prevailing currency was prestige, which could be acquired through generosity, bravery, and diplomatic acumen. Young men needed it if they were to be invited as husbands into the homes of the most desirable young women in this strongly matrilineal society. They needed it if they hoped to be selected as family heads or league chiefs. That it was unevenly distributed or that those who already had it in good measure were likely to acquire even more should come as no surprise. If we were able to go back and plot individuals and prestige on a simple graph we would discover that it conforms to the distribution of wealth seen in figure 7.2. At any given moment, one man in, say, Mohawk society enjoyed more prestige than anyone else, and there were many who had only a little of it.

Hunt missed discovering this because he was looking for the wrong currency. During the eighteenth century, money and the symbolic luxury items it could buy emerged as an alternative currency for the Iroquois. Prestige remained as a traditional currency, but some Iroquois, perhaps most notably Joseph Brant, stepped outside the traditional system and adopted the European currency of monetary wealth. Traditional chiefs continued to be selected for their generosity, bravery, and diplomatic skills; men such as Brant formed a new category, which came to be designated "Pine Tree Chiefs." D. B. Guldenzopf found documentation of the shift to the new currency in the records of Revolutionary War losses. Traditional chiefs had minor losses because they had maintained their positions through generosity and had little wealth in the form of cash or personal property left to lose. Only the Pine Tree Chiefs had major losses, because only they had accumulated monetary wealth, and the British government compensated their Pine Tree Chief allies accordingly after the war (Guldenzopf 1986).

THE NATURE OF TRADITIONAL IROQUOIAN WARFARE

Extreme interpersonal violence is a trait that is not easily assigned to unique times, places, or cultures. Violence is more latent than aberrant, even in the Apollonian cultures once celebrated by Ruth Benedict (Benedict 1989). Archaeology has demonstrated this for the Pueblo cultures of the Southwest, just as recent history has demonstrated it among the Khmer Rouge. Behaviors that we still denounce as "savage" or "barbaric" (to use the terms long since codified by Morgan) remain with us, swept under the rug we call civilization.

European colonists tended to regard peace as the natural state of things and war the exception. Traditional Iroquoians had the more realistic view that violence and warfare were the natural state of things and that peace had to be constantly tended and renewed if it was to prevail in the long term. Thus, we have a record of not just a few Iroquois peace treaties putting presumably permanent ends to various colonial wars, but many of them, most of which were little more than routine renewals (Jennings, Fenton, and Druke 1985). This pattern predated contact with Europeans. The ritual playing out of frequent treaty renewals provided Iroquois chiefs (sachems) with a regular mechanism for the generation of new prestige. When treaty maintenance failed, they had an alternative way to gain prestige, namely, warfare. European colonists went along with both because it was in their interest to do so. Both warfare and endless treaty conferences enhanced the Europeans' ability to acquire furs, land, and other proxies for the wealth that constituted the currency of greatest interest to them.

Revenge motivation and the currency of prestige combined with an increased demand for war captives to produce a paroxysm of warfare in the seventeenth century. It had little to do with the fur trade or monetary wealth and much to do with the traditional Iroquoian currency. The routine torture and execution of captives abated in the eighteenth century as monetary wealth emerged as a substitute currency and Iroquoians adopted a more European perspective on warfare. Prestige gained through warfare became a less important currency than money and property in that century (Guldenzopf 1986). Furthermore, both Catholic and Protestant missionaries had made significant inroads by that time, such that the torture of captives was no longer fashionable. But by then, the Hurons and other losers of the seventeenth century had vanished, the survivors long since absorbed by the Iroquois or displaced westward.

It has long been understood, particularly by U.S. Marine drill sergeants, that soldiers plunge into battle motivated not by patriotism or lofty altruism but rather by more immediate circumstances. Like warriors in other times and places, traditional Iroquoians competed for the admiration of their comrades and the affection of their close friends, their immediate families, and the women they hoped to marry. Like modern commandos, fighter pilots, and suicide bombers, they were mostly just ordinary men caught up in circumstances of time, place, and cultural imperative.

8 · DESECRATING THE SACRED ANCESTOR TEMPLES

CHIEFLY CONFLICT AND VIOLENCE IN THE AMERICAN SOUTHEAST

David H. Dye and Adam King

Spanish priests working among the Hasinai Caddo of eastern Texas in the early eighteenth century reported the destruction of a "fire temple" that had taken place around 1714. According to eyewitnesses, raiders from the neighboring Yojuanes polity destroyed the Hasinai sacred temple and its appurtenances and other buildings. The inquiring Spanish priests learned from the Hasinai that prior to the conflagration, the temple had housed two "boys," known to the Hasinai as "diviners" (coninisi). The two "boys" were perhaps the mythological or supernatural beings known throughout eastern North America as the Twins (Lankford 1987, 160–75; pers. comm. 2004). These twin diviners acted as intermediaries between the chief priest (Grand Xinesí) and the Hasinai supreme celestial supernatural, "Headman Above" (Caddi Ayo). In response to the Spanish priests' persistent (and undoubtedly tiresome, troublesome, and bothersome) requests as to the identity and nature of the two boys and why they could not be seen, the Hasinai used a recent historical event to explain the boys' invisibility and spiritual nature (Bolton 1987, 147–50).

According to the Hasinai, the Yojuanes raiders burned the sacred shrine or temple. The boys rose with the smoke, leaving only their spirits behind. Thereafter they resided in a newly constructed temple that housed a perpetual sacred fire maintained by special attendants. The Hasinai headman, priests, and elders provided offerings of food and tobacco to the boys. They consulted with the boys' spirits on important matters through a ceremony known as "Talking with God" (Bolton 1987, 148, 151).

Raiding behavior resulting in the desecration of an ancestral temple, as seen in the above ethnohistoric example, has been overlooked in the southeastern archaeological literature. While emphasis has been placed on other aspects of raiding behavior, southeastern archaeologists have paid little scholarly attention to ideological motivations in warfare, especially the destruction of elite temples[1] and associated ancestor sacra, ritual regalia, and ceremonial accoutrements.

In this chapter, we argue that raiding forces bent on the desecration of ancestral temples had a long history in the Mississippian Southeast and Midwest. Current archaeological and ethnohistorical evidence suggests that military attempts aimed at temple destruction occurred as early as the mid thirteenth century, when elites began targeting and desecrating their political rivals' sacred temples and temple contents. Destruction of temples was witnessed in the mid sixteenth century by members of the Hernando de Soto expedition and again in the early eighteenth century in the eastern Texas example cited above.

Ancestor temples, typically placed atop platform mounds and in close proximity to public plazas and elite residences, housed chiefly ancestral and cosmological connections. These links to the Other World were vital for a chief's claims to social identity, genealogical connections, religious legitimacy, and political authority. The preservation and protection of a chief's hereditary line was essential for the chiefdom's well-being. Defilement of the genealogical line through destruction of the temple, desecration of elite corpses, theft of sacred regalia, and defilement of ritual accoutrements would have been a high priority and strategic goal of rival chiefs and their militia raiders.

WARFARE IN THE MISSISSIPPIAN SOUTHEAST

Beginning with sixteenth-century French and Spanish explorations, European narratives document pervasive conflict among Mississippian polities (Anderson 1994a, 1994b; DePratter 1983; Dye 1990, 1993, 1995; Milanich 1995; Milner 1999; Rabasa 1997; Steinen 1992; Worth 1998). All written accounts have their biases, and European chroniclers who wrote about the Southeast may have exaggerated both the scale and the intensity of warfare as a result of their own experiences with European warfare and the nature of their audiences in Europe (Lankford 1993). However, a substantial body of archaeological and ethnohistoric evidence supports the contention that intersocietal armed conflict and aggression was a fact of life in the late prehistoric and early historic Southeast (Anderson 1994a, 1994b; DePratter 1983; Dye 2002a; Milner 1999).

Eastern Woodlands archaeology reveals a sharp increase in violence in the early centuries of the Mississippian period (Milner 2005, 166).[2] Warfare placed increased stress on late prehistoric populations, with elevated levels of strife and violent death. Settlement nucleation and unoccupied buffer zones clearly are evident (Anderson 1994a, 1994b, 1996; DePratter 1983), as are improved fortifications (Milner 2000). Palisades constructed around settlements can be viewed as evidence for the severity of warfare. Palisaded villages began to accompany the rise of Mississippian period societies shortly after AD 1000 (Milner 2000; Milner and Schroeder 1999, 104). In some areas populations nucleated, while in others households and hamlets remained dispersed but sought refuge in fortified centers during times of increased conflict (Anderson 1999, 224).

Osteological data indicate an increased incidence of weapons trauma on skeletal remains (Bridges, Jacobi, and Powell 2000; Milner 1995) despite the evidence that deaths from arrow wounds are underrepresented in the archaeological record (Milner 2005). Mutilation of slain enemies and trophy-taking are consistent features of Mississippian combat. Warlike themes in Mississippian artwork (Brown 1975, 1985) predominate the Southeastern Ceremonial Complex (Dye 2004; Knight, Brown, and Lankford 2001). Demonstrations of success in combat through trophy-taking elevated warrior status (Hudson 1976, 325–27; Rountree 1989, 101).

Armed conflict generally took the form of raids and ambushes, although on some occasions, organized large-scale attacks occurred (Bridges, Jacobi, and Powell 2000; Milner 1999). Raids were in part revenge oriented and individualistic (Gibson 1974; Hudson 1976). Narratives from sixteenth-century Spanish explorers clearly portray warfare as an integral component of competition among chiefly leaders for prestige and political aggrandizement (Anderson 1994a; Dye 1995; King 1999; Steinen 1992).

Archaeological evidence and historical accounts from the Southeast and Midwest allow several inferences to be made about Mississippian warfare. Intersocietal conflict, or at least some kind of armed combat, was a consistent and integral component of Mississippian life. Both the osteological data and historical accounts indicate that most warfare was conducted as small-scale raids and sniping, but occasional large-scale attacks did take place.

Finally, intersocietal conflict was part of an elite-coordinated strategy for wresting prestige goods and followers from neighbors. A key ingredient of this chiefly warfare strategy was the destruction of the sacred temples and desecration of their contents to annihilate or appropriate a rival's power, including severing ties with ancestors and deities and destroying ritual accoutrements, regalia, and paraphernalia.

THE SACRED ANCESTOR TEMPLE

The ancestor temple and the affiliated ancestor cult constitute one of the hallmarks of the Mississippian culture (Brown 1985; Knight 1986).

Indeed, as David Anderson has observed, "The cult surrounding the veneration of chiefly/elite ancestors appears to have been the central focus of the Mississippian ideological sphere" (Anderson 1994b, 79). Throughout the Mississippian world, major towns included at least one mound or restricted sacred space reserved as an ideological center or temple where elite bodies were honored. In addition to the noble dead (Knight 1986, 679), temples housed sacred fire and condensed symbols of ancestral power (Brown 1985, 106), including objects of wealth finance, symbolic weapons, and iconic statuary. Temple statuary associated with the Mississippian ancestor cult (Brown 1985, 2001; Knight 1986; Knight, Brown, and Lankford 2001) was the primary icon of the shrine. The humanlike statue was the object of respect and veneration and as such was restricted to elite viewing, care, and manipulation. The statue connected elites with the dead, as it was the materialized embodiment and incarnation of the ancestors. In fact, statues were treated as if they were living ancestors (Brown 2001; Waring 1968).

Mississippian great towns were surrounded by a palisade wall or some type of fortification (Holley 1999, 28), which "safeguarded the monuments used by highly ranked people to buttress claims to positions of exalted status, such as charnel structures that contained the remains of revered ancestors" (Milner 1999, 124). In addition to enclosing towns, wooden walls or other barriers also enclosed temples. These walls generally were less substantial (Anderson 1994b; King 2003). Presumably these fences served to demarcate, restrict, and protect the sacred and sanctified space around the temple and its contents, rather than protecting the temple from raiders (DePratter 1983; Payne 1994). Mississippian ancestor temples were restricted from public viewing in their role as elite mortuaries, shrines, and storage facilities, housing elite dead, human iconic statuary, ritual regalia, ceremonial paraphernalia, sacred fire, and hypertrophic/sociotechnic weaponry. In essence, Mississippian temples contained a chief's primary access to sources of political authority, social position, and materialized ideology that legitimized chiefly claims to rulership.

If Mississippian shrines embodied a chief's claims to ideological authority, then protecting them justified the massive labor requirements necessary to fortify an entire town and to fence, screen, or otherwise restrict and protect the chiefly temple. The powerful sacra housed in the shrine represented a potent force that could be used for either benevolent or malevolent ends. The temple would have to be protected from threatening outside forces, while the polity populace would need protection from its harmful or polluting effects; temple sacra could be viewed and handled only by those ritually protected to withstand its power. The materials stored there were both potent and powerful, being restricted, manipulated, and handled by priests and chiefs who were consecrated or possessed ritual purity sufficient to protect them.

The desecration of an enemy chief's ancestral temple, therefore, would destroy a key source of his authority. Connections would be severed to the ancestors and the use denied of instruments, accoutrements, paraphernalia, bundles, and regalia necessary for conducting the rituals that maintained, renewed, and protected the polity's well-being and the chief's sacred authority (Anderson 1994a, 67; 1994b, 80–81; Bolton 1987, 147–50; DePratter 1983, 63; Dye 1990, 219; 1993, 49–51; 1994, 47; Hudson 1997, 294; Milner 1999, 124; 2004, 165; Morse 1993, 64–65; Sabo 1993, 201–2).

The temple housed the source of sacred power that was dangerous, if not lethal. As Anderson notes, "Desecration of a rival society's temple, specifically its ancestral burials, was considered the ultimate insult and a primary goal in warfare" (1994b, 80). Consequently, the act of desecration would have been a primary goal in an attack upon a polity by Mississippian militia forces. As Chester DePratter (1983, 63) states, "By sacking the temple, not only were wealth items obtained, but past wrongs were redeemed. In addition, damage, perhaps irreparable damage, was inflicted on the spiritual center of the defeated chiefdom. With the sacred fire extinguished, the sacred items stolen, the bones of the ancient chiefs destroyed, how could any society hope to recover?"

ETHNOHISTORIC EVIDENCE FOR THE DESECRATION OF ANCESTOR TEMPLES

Ancestor cults and their associated temples and ritual paraphernalia began to be described in the Southeast as early as the sixteenth century, when European expeditions first encountered flourishing native chiefdoms (Anderson 1994b; DePratter 1983). Chroniclers of the de Soto expedition, for example, documented raiding parties who "thoroughly desecrated these charnel structures whenever they gained access to their enemies' settlements" (Milner 1999, 124). Throughout the sixteenth, seventeenth, and early eighteenth centuries, the ancestor cult institution was broadly distributed in the Southeast from the Mississippi River to the Atlantic Coast (Brown 2001; Swanton 1911, 1946). The French priest Jean-François Buisson de Sainte-Cosme, for example, in the early 1700s noted that the Natchez shrine housed a "stone statue enclosed in a wooden box" (St. Cosme in Swanton 1911, 172) and was located at the center of their principal town atop a platform mound. The statue was considered a source of political power (Brown 2001, 76). Accounts of the ancestor shrines of Virginian and North Carolinian tidewater chiefdoms, including that of Powhatan and his family (Arber 1910; Beverley 1947, 197; Lorant 1946; Swanton 1946), were similarly centered on human-like iconic temple figures. Virginian shrines were secluded in the "woods" rather than on platform mounds in towns, perhaps to protect them from raiders or protect the populace from power held within the temple.

Perhaps the earliest ethnohistoric description of the ransacking of a mortuary temple took place on the night of April 23, 1540, When Ocute-province warriors from the town of Cofaqui and under the command of the principal war leader Patofa looted the temple of their traditional enemies and neighbors who resided in Hymahi, a border town of the Cofitachequi chiefdom. Ocute was a complex, interior South Appalachian chiefdom located on the Oconee River, west of the Savannah River valley and to the south and east of Cofitachequi.

Hymahi was located on the Congoree River near its confluence with the Wateree River in central South Carolina. Cofitachequi was more complex and extensive than the chiefdoms to the south and exerted a powerful regional political force. The Cofaqui warriors appear to have been agents of the Ocute chiefdom—a broad, unoccupied buffer zone that separated the Ocute, Patofa (Cofaqui), and neighboring chiefdoms from the more complex and extensive Cofitachequi paramount chiefdom to the north, with whom they were at war (Anderson 1994b, 72–73; Hudson 1997, 168–69). The warriors accompanied Juan de Añasco, who was leading a reconnoitering party of ten horsemen in search of food for the starving and bewildered de Soto expedition (Hudson 1997, 170–71, 406).

The sixteenth-century chronicler Garcilaso de la Vega (1993, 280–81) described this event:

> During the night that they slept in the pueblo, General Patofa and his Indians sacked it and robbed the temple as secretly as they could, without the Spaniards knowing anything about their actions. The temple served only as a burial place, where . . . they kept the finest and richest of their possessions. They killed all the Indians they could find, in and out of the pueblo, without sparing sex or age, and they took off the scalps of those whom they so killed, from the ears up, with wonderful dexterity and skill. They carried off these scalps so that their curaca and lord Cofaqui could see with his own eyes the revenge they had taken on their enemies for injuries received, because, as it was learned later, this pueblo belonged to the province of Cofachiqui.

While recuperating at Hymahi for a week, the Cofaqui warriors, again under the command of Patofa, carried out a scorched-earth policy in the territory of their enemies in compliance with their chief's charge "to take revenge against his enemies and aggressors" (Garcilaso 1993, 283). Garcilaso (1993, 282) further noted,

> During this time Captain Patofa and his eight thousand Indians did all the harm and injury they could to their enemies, as secretly as possible. They scoured the country for four leagues in every direction, wherever they could do damage. They killed the Indians whom they could find, men and women, and took off their scalps to carry away as evidence of their exploits. They sacked the pueblos and temples whenever they could, but did not burn them, as they wished to do, so that the governor would not see or know about it. In short, they left nothing undone that they could think of to harm their enemies and avenge themselves.

A little over a year later, on June 27, 1541, members of the de Soto expedition observed the warriors of the Casqui chiefdom sacking the political and ideological center of their traditional enemy, the neighboring Pacaha chiefdom, located on the Mississippi River in present-day northeastern Arkansas (Anderson 1994b, 80–81; DePratter 1983, 63; Dye 1990, 219; 1993, 49–51; 1994, 47; Hudson 1997, 294; Morse 1993, 64–65; Sabo 1993, 201–2). As the warriors of Casqui sacked the town of Pacaha (in particular, the chief's house), they entered the sacred ancestor temple, located on the large public plaza, where the elite dead were kept. The Pacaha temple was the chiefdom's most venerated and sacred structure. In their destruction, the Casqui committed every act of desecration and offensive affronts that they could devise. In addition to pillaging and looting everything the temple contained—including riches, ornaments, spoils of war, and trophies that had been taken from the Casqui chiefdom—they knocked down to the ground the wooden chests that served as sepulchers for the Pacaha elite dead, throwing out the bones and bodies, smashing them to pieces, and kicking them with contempt and disdain. The Casquis, finding the skulls and decapitated heads of their own people impaled on lances by the temple door, removed these heads and substituted those of the Pacaha they had killed that day. The infuriated Casqui warriors wanted to set fire to the temple, the chief's houses, and the entire village, but de Soto convinced them not to burn the buildings because he planned to occupy the town for the expedition's much-needed rest and recuperation (Garcilaso 1993, 397–98).

By late April of 1542, de Soto had come to believe that the expedition was in danger. As he began preparations to descend the Mississippi River from the town of Guachoya near the mouth of the Arkansas River, he sensed that the expedition was vulnerable to attack from neighboring Mississippian polities. He ordered Nuño de Tovar to take fifteen horsemen overland and Juan de Guzmán to transport a number of footsoldiers by canoe up the Arkansas River to attack the town of Anilco. To terrorize the local polities, de Soto commanded his men not to spare any male lives. The horsemen attacked at dawn, quickly routing the town. After the horsemen had attacked, a number of Guachoya warriors rushed inside the town, looting the houses and the temple (Dye 1994, 48–49; Garcilaso 1993, 443–44; Hudson 1997, 346–48).

Garcilaso (1993, 43) noted,

The Guachoyas entered it as a pueblo of such hated enemies, and being an affronted people who desired vengeance, they sacked and robbed the temple and burial place of the lords of that state, where, besides the bodies of his dead, the cacique kept his best and richest and most valued possessions, and the spoils and trophies of the greatest victories that he had won over the Guachoyas. They consisted of numerous heads of the most important Indians that they had killed, placed on the points of lances at the doors of the temple, and many standards, and a large number of weapons that the Guachoyas had lost in the battles they had with the Anilcos.

The Guachoya warriors packed their plunder into canoes, arriving back at their town before the Spaniards to inform their chief that they had avenged themselves on Anilco. In addition to looting the temple, they had set fire to the houses (and presumably the temple) and indiscriminately killed a number of the inhabitants. They tried to conceal these acts from the Spaniards because de Soto had issued a decree that the town was not to be set on fire. The Spaniards tried to stop the Guachoyas from burning the town of Anilco, but the Guachoya warriors had already set several houses on fire by leaving burning sticks under the eaves of the houses, which erupted into flames shortly after they left.

The destruction of the Cofitachequi, Pacaha, and Anilco chiefdom ancestor temples was instigated and planned by the Cofaqui, Casqui, and Guachoya warriors, not the Spaniards. As a high-priority military target, it was the first or one of the first locations destroyed by the invading raiders upon entering the town. Garcilaso's accounts do not indicate that de Soto requested or ordered the warriors to preferentially target the temples. In fact, at Cofitachequi and Anilco, they took pains to hide their acts from de Soto; at all three polities, they wished to burn the temples but refrained from doing so because de Soto asked them to avoid burning the towns. Thus, it would appear that the temple as a specific military target was an act of traditional, indigenous chiefly warfare rather than a response to Spanish intervention.

Although Garcilaso's three accounts of the desecration of Mississippian temples may be exaggerated, they are consistent with the Southeastern belief system. George Sabo (1993, 202) notes that in societies with hereditary lineages, the ties that a group maintains with its ancestors serve to transmit down through the lineage the sacred powers or "mana" that ancestor spirits acquired through heroic deeds performed in some former era (i.e., in "myth time"). . . . If access to the ancestors were to be impeded or disrupted, through desecration of remains of the ancestors or of other ritual spaces or paraphernalia, then the effects upon the living community could be devastating and might include such consequences as loss of social identity, loss of community solidarity, and loss of social control. Thus, the acts of retribution attributed to the Casqui in the de Soto accounts may be indicative of the degree of animosity that existed between these two neighboring polities.

ARCHAEOLOGICAL EXAMPLES

Archaeological examples of desecrated chiefly ancestor temples in the Mid-South include buildings erected on Mound B at Toqua (Polhemus 1987), a mound at Jonathan Creek (Schroeder 2003a, 2003b), Mound C at Etowah (King 2001, 2003; Larson 1971), Mound 2 at Towosahgy (Price and Fox 1990), and Mound B at Chucalissa (Childress and Wharey 1996; Dye 2007; Nash 1972, n.d.) (see fig. 8.1). These building destructions span a 250-year period between approximately AD 1200 and 1450, the time during which Mississippian temples were widespread throughout the Mid-South (Brown 2001).

One of the principal iconic markers of the ancestor cult and associated mortuary shrine was materialized in the thirteenth century in the form of seated male and female human effigy sculptures crafted from pottery, wood, and stone. Recovered from archaeological contexts dating from approximately AD 1200 to 1400, the most numerous are dated to the fourteenth century (Brown 2001), a time of heightened elite political and religious activity. These mortuary statues were given special treatment by placement in the sacred mortuary structure that also housed elite burials and ritual regalia. At the time of their disposal, they were interred in graves or otherwise accorded mortuary treatment typically reserved for human elite burials. The ancestor statues were buried with elaborate grave goods and sometimes with retainers. They were

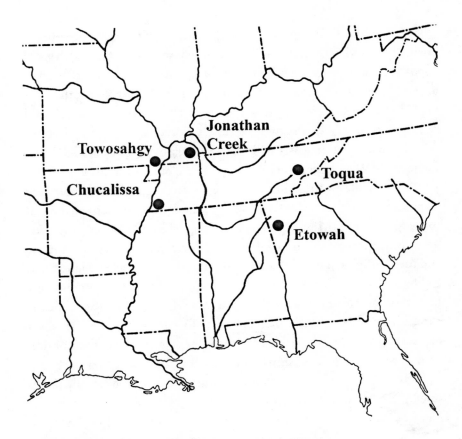

FIGURE 8.1 Archaeological sites mentioned in the text.

placed in highly restricted contexts in or near the floors of sacred mortuary structures built atop platform mounds.

The archaeological evidence for desecrated ancestral temples is well documented, but these incidents are not usually mentioned in discussions of overall patterns of warfare. Destruction episodes generally are characterized by burned buildings; abandoned political centers; hidden or secreted ritual objects, including hypertrophic or sociotechnic combat weaponry; desecrated human remains, especially those of elites; and sacra that have been destroyed, including the destruction and burial of human statuary, the diagnostic cult artifact. The incidence of burned towns, including the destruction of temples, after AD 1200 suggests intensive political stress (Holley 1999, 37) in much of the Mississippian world.

An anticipated temple attack might result in the ancestor icon being hurriedly buried. As a "human elite," its burial would be replete with grave goods and perhaps retainers. Symbolic weaponry should be destroyed or unceremoniously secreted in residential areas of the town in otherwise mundane cache pits. Scattered and scorched elite human remains should be recovered in contexts suggesting desecration of a shrine.

Such a situation exists with the 1894 discovery of the Duck River cache at the Link Farm site in Humphreys County, Tennessee (Brehm 1981; Dye 2002b). In addition to a set of male and female limestone statues, forty-six flint artifacts were located in a residential area of the large Middle Mississippian bluff-top town. The bifaces included "swords," raptor talon effigies, maces, hypertrophic knives, solar discs, and turtle effigies. James Brown (2001) suggests that caches such as that of Duck River conform to what one would expect of the contents of a mortuary temple and that their burial in a residential area would constitute the final act in the abandonment of a site and the loss of power by local elites. The failure of later recovery suggests that the political demise was more or less permanent and catastrophic.

These acts of violence often constitute the final or nearly final closure of the ancestor shrine, followed by a period of substantial abandonment. As a terminating event, site abandonment would be linked to the extinction of the social group as an autonomous polity. The statuary would conceivably remain in use only as long as the chiefly elite held power; their burial would mark a dramatic, catastrophic, and devastating loss of power likened to a polity's spiritual death. The burial of temple contents thus constitutes the final act in the abandonment of a site and the loss of power by local elites (Brown 2001).

In the Mississippian Mid-South, the earliest evidence for the destruction of a mortuary shrine occurred in the early thirteenth century at the Toqua site in the upper Tennessee Valley. The initial occupation of Toqua took place during the Hiwassee Island period, shortly after AD 1200. The palisaded town seems to have been attacked shortly after it was settled. Richard Polhemus (1987, 1216) notes, "The town was destroyed by a fire, as indicated by the burned condition of the palisade, Structure 6, Structure 60, the structures on the Phase A-1 summit of Mound A, as well as village structures within the Palisade Perimeter

A. Only a short period of time is represented by this rather spacious town plan as none of the public buildings . . . show signs of repair or replacement."

The mortuary temple, Structure 60 (Polhemus 1987, 330–32), was a large rectangular building. Polhemus states, "The large size of the structure, coupled with its lack of a hearth of any sort and the presence of [a] disarticulated circular mass of human bone representing a minimum of seventeen individuals on its floor, suggest a special function for this structure, such as a charnel house" (Polhemus 1987, 332).

Slightly later in the mid thirteenth century, archaeological evidence from the Jonathan Creek site suggests that a conflagration destroyed a mortuary temple located on top of a small mound at the plaza's edge. The Jonathan Creek site is located in the lower Tennessee Valley of western Kentucky. The mound area originally had been a residential area on the edge of town that had been dramatically reorganized and transformed into a sacred precinct devoted to mortuary rituals. Three building episodes are evident in the mound stratigraphy. The second and third building stages were destroyed by fire. The third catastrophically burned building was never rebuilt. The pyro-archaeological data indicate that the burnings were deliberate, rather than accidental acts. The final burning was a terminating event for the town (Schroeder 2003a, 2003b). Associated with the final mortuary temple burning was the building of a massive palisade. This final palisade line (Feature 3), unlike previous palisades, was a visually impressive towering wall replete with closely spaced bastions that had substantial towers. The palisade had not been dismantled or repaired; instead, the posts appear to have been "left to rot in place, as might happen following complete and relatively rapid abandonment of the community" (Schroeder 2003a). The site was not reoccupied after the abandonment.

There is further evidence at the Etowah site in northwestern Georgia of a destructive ancestor temple event during the mid fourteenth century, a time of increased warfare in the Mid-South. The event is possibly linked to warfare and the abandonment of the site (Brain and Phillips 1996, 174–75; King 2003, 78–81; Moorehead 1932, 75). One of the last burials to be interred at Etowah's burial mound, Mound C, was Burial 15, excavated at the base of the mound's ramp. In that burial were found marble male and female painted iconic figures, along with the disarticulated (or dismembered) remains of as many as four individuals, whose bones had been scattered across the floor (fig. 8.2), in addition to shell beads, copper-covered ear discs, antler projectile points, fragments of sheet copper ornaments, and stone and clay pipe bowls. The marble figures were found broken, one atop the other, as if they had been hurriedly placed in the tomb (King 1996; Larson 1971, 65) (fig. 8.3).

Statues such as these are believed to represent the mythical founders of ruling lineages (Brown 2001; Knight 1986; Waring 1968). They were treated much the same as other elite dead in Mound C, suggesting that they were buried in the same fashion as elites. In fact, their interment has been interpreted as the hurried burial of the founding ancestors of Etowah's ruling chiefly lineage (Kelly and Larson 1957; King 2003, 80). The nature or state of Burial 15's contents implies that it was created under some duress, perhaps the threat of armed conflict.

The suggestion that the temple was sacked by raiders or a militia force is made more compelling by two other potentially related events. One is the deposit of a middenlike smear of human bone and ceremonial objects on the face of the Mound C ramp. These materials, recorded as Burial 1, were deposited shortly after the interment of Burial 15 (Larson 1971). As was the case with Burial 15, Burial 1 contained portions of four people along with a stone palette, shell beads, copper-covered ear discs, a pipe bowl fragment, antler projectile points, pieces of ceramic vessels, and whelk and oyster shell. Jeffrey Brain and Philip Phillips (1996, 174–75) suggest that the deposit may have been the result of the ransacking of the ancestor temple. The scattered ceremonial goods and human remains of Burial 1 may have been the last contents of the Etowah mortuary temple, with both human remains and sacred objects having been tossed from the temple as it was pillaged by invaders.

The other event that may indicate an armed attack or raid is the burning of the palisade. According to Adam King (2003, 79), the palisade was destroyed at roughly the same time as the interment of Burials 1 and 15. The palisade was never rebuilt, and the site was abandoned almost immediately after its destruction, implying that the palisade's burning was intentional and directly related to the site's abandonment. With the destruction of the palisade and possible sacking of the site,

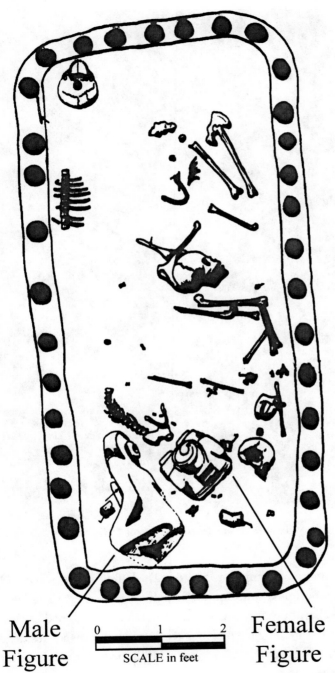

Male
Figure

Female
Figure

0   1   2
SCALE in feet

FIGURE 8.2
Etowah Burial
15. (From Larson
1971, fig. 5)

FIGURE 8.3 Etowah statues in situ. (Kelly and Larson 1957, 40)

including the ancestor temple, the site was abandoned around AD 1375 and not reoccupied until approximately one hundred years later. The Etowah Valley, however, was never completely abandoned during this time (Southerlin 1993), which suggests that the Etowah resident population shifted its political allegiance or affiliation to a neighboring regional political center.

An early-fifteenth-century temple conflagration has been recorded at the Towosahgy site, a large fortified town located in the Cairo Lowland of southeastern Missouri (Price and Fox 1990). The town was fortified by an elaborate system that included a system of palisade walls, a ditch, and embankments. Four palisade events have been recorded at the site (Cottier and Southard 1977; Price and Fox 1990). Palisade A was constructed around AD 1300 and later burned (Lafferty and Price 1996, 13). The final fortification event was the construction of a massive earth embankment 2,700 feet long, 11 feet wide, and approximately 5 feet high, raised in conjunction with a ditch 2.5 feet in depth and 20–22 feet wide. The embankment called for the excavation of some 148,500 cubic feet of earth. The archaeological excavations "showed that a complex sequence of building took place over a long period of time, culminating in the formidable ditch and embankment that surrounded the site" (Price and Fox 1990, 66). Presumably, a palisade wall accompanied the final embankment and ditch.

Excavations at Mound 2 revealed a two-foot-thick deposit of burned structure(s): "Scattered through this zone were pieces of mica, sherds of a negative painted vessel, pipe fragments, and other exotic artifacts. This zone is a deposit of huge quantities of building rubble and refuse that was cast down from the top of the mound. It is debris from the large public structure or structures that once stood on top of the mound that burned by the force of nature or the act of humans and was pushed, hauled, or dumped down the mound slope" (Price and Fox 1990, 17). Included in the dump were sherds from a large negative painted bottle, "fluorite and quartz crystals, mica, a crinoid stem bead, a red-painted elbow pipe, earplugs, an earspool, sherd paint palettes, and fragments of miniature jars with caked paint pigment in them" (Price and Fox 1990, 40). Other materials found concentrated in the temple dump were "plate sherds, red ochre, limonite, ferruginous sandstone, lumps of white kaolin, and fragments of effigy vessels and bottle sherds" (Price and Fox 1990, 40). The nonlocal sherds represent trade vessels. Exotic cherts—including Fort Payne, Mill Creek chert, and novaculite—were also found in the dump. After the building burned and was pushed off the summit edge, a clay cap was added to the mound summit as a final act to ritually bury the mound prior to final site abandonment in the early to mid fifteenth century (Price and Fox 1990, 65).

The Chucalissa site, located in southwestern Tennessee, provides an example of the possible destruction of a mortuary temple in the mid fifteenth century. Some 241 fragmentary human remains are securely associated with a thick ash layer that sloped down the face of Mound B (fig. 8.4). An additional 179 human skeletal elements also appear to be associated with this layer. Human remains from the ash layer consist almost entirely of adult cranial fragments representing a minimum of 34 individuals (based on the number of occiputs). The remains are highly weathered, partially exfoliated, and completely disarticulated. They exhibit rodent gnawing, suggesting exposure to the elements for some time prior to burial or eventual natural deposition (Childress and Wharey 1996).

The ash-layer skeletal remains represent elite individuals. For example, the males are 5.3 centimeters taller than the average male at Chucalissa, and the females are 5.6 centimeters taller than the average female (Nash 1972, 19). The suggestion that these were elite burials is also based on their physical separation from the general village interments; the accompaniment of worked, curated, and unmodified human bones, including human crania and forearms; their distinctive "sitting" position; and the possible association of copper. In addition, Charles Nash noted that the mound burials had a distinctly different burial and preburial treatment from the remains found in neighboring residential areas (Nash 1972, 19).

The humic ash layer was the final addition to the mound, representing the terminal use of the mound during the early part of the Walls phase. Mound B "yielded numerous burials, indicating the earthwork was symbolically and physically linked to mortuary activity associated with the final disposal of a segment of the village population" (Childress and Wharey 1996, 75). The ash layer may represent a mortuary shrine that was burned and not capped by a clay layer. Thus, the building may have been reduced to ash. Unfortunately, plowing and erosion appear to have removed any traces of structures that may have existed on the mound summit, but Charles Nash, who excavated Mound B, believed that the mound had supported a temple (Nash n.d.).

These Mid-South sites offer confirmation that mortuary temples were targeted by Mississippian militias at a time when elevated rates

FIGURE 8.4 Chucalissa, Mound B (Unit 4). (Childress and Wharey 1996, fig. 9.7; courtesy of the Chucalissa Museum, University of Memphis, 4SYI165)

of warfare are signaled by increases in skeletal trauma (Bridges, Jacobi, and Powell 2000; Milner 1995), trophy-taking behavior (Dye 2005), buffer zones (Anderson 1994b), nucleated towns (Holley 1999), warfare-related iconography (Brown 1985; Dye 2004), and fortifications (Milner 2000). Burned structures associated with temple statuary, elite remains, and prestige/exotic goods, on mounds located along plazas, suggest that archaeologically identifiable ancestor shrines were purposively destroyed by raiders.

CHIEFLY WARFARE AND THE DESTRUCTION OF SACRED AUTHORITY

Among the goals of chiefly warfare are the seizure of wealth finance, the appropriation of exchange routes, and the theft of ritual paraphernalia and exotica. To capture or destroy a polity's sacred temples that housed a chief's wealth, exchangeable products, and ritual accoutrements would yield access to the legitimacy supported and endowed by the polity's institutions. The objective of war was thus to increase a ruler's effectiveness by seizing the bases of power that one's enemies possessed, including the contents of sacred ancestor temples (Earle 1997, 206).

These five fortified sites of the Mid-South, dating between AD 1200 and 1450, reveal varying levels of confirmation for sacred mortuary temple destruction. Etowah, Jonathan Creek, Toqua, and Towosahgy were heavily fortified with palisades. Chucalissa is located on a hundred-foot-high bluff overlooking the Mississippi River alluvial valley. Each site indicates evidence of a conflagration, although this is manifested in several ways. The entire town of Toqua appears to have been burned, while Chucalissa, Jonathan Creek, and Towosahgy have mound-summit ash or burn layers. Etowah and Chucalissa have a smear of fragmented human bones across the mound flanks. Towosahgy exhibits massive debris from a burned building, including exotic artifacts that were dumped down the mound slope. Finally, each destructive episode was either a final, terminating event or initiated a temporary abandonment. Chucalissa, Etowah, and Toqua reveal evidence of a series of periodic abandonments followed by resettlement throughout the site histories. Toqua, for example, was rebuilt soon after the town's destruction, while Etowah was abandoned for over a century before being reoccupied. The temple burning at Towosahgy was associated with the final abandonment of the site.

Archaeological and ethnohistoric information clarify that warfare was a salient part of Mississippian life and a crucial component of elite strategies that include competition with neighboring elites for prestige, power, and social labor. We suggest that one of the key elements of chiefly political strategies was the desecration and looting of ancestral temples. The sources of chiefly authority in Mississippian society centered on the ancestor temple and the attendant rituals that connected ruling elites with their ancestral spirits (Knight, Brown, and Lankford 2001). The ancestor shrine, primarily accessible to chiefs and secondarily to their priests, was a sacred place where sources of power were materialized and the divine presence manifested to the greatest degree (Brown 1985, 2001). An enemy's destruction or appropriation of these links to chiefly sources of power would have been an attractive if not obligatory military target. The appropriation of a defeated chief's ancestors, ritual accoutrements, and symbolic weaponry would have played a vital role in a new chief's or polity's ascendancy to power. The destruction and desecration of the ancestor shrine—which housed the elite dead, sculpted ancestral figures, symbolic weaponry, sacred fire, and ritual regalia—would have ensured the destruction of a polity's political and religious existence and the source of a chief's power, his sacred authority.

NOTES

1. In this chapter, we use the term *temple* rather than *shrine* to describe Mississippian religious buildings. *Temple* typically refers to a building or place dedicated to the worship of or the presence of a deity or anything considered to contain a divine presence. A temple can be any place or building serving as the focus of a special activity or of something especially valued. *Shrine*, by contrast, usually refers to a container or receptacle for sacred relics, but it can also refer to the tomb of a venerated person or a site hallowed by a venerated object or its associations (see Morris 1978).

2. The Mississippian period in the Mid-South dates to approximately AD 1000–1600.

9 WARFARE, POPULATION, AND FOOD PRODUCTION IN PREHISTORIC EASTERN NORTH AMERICA

George R. Milner

Only archaeology provides a perspective on warfare that spans many thousands of years. Yet despite the importance of warfare to our understanding of the human condition, until recently there have been few systematic attempts by archaeologists in the United States to study the nature, intensity, frequency, and effects of fighting among prehistoric small-scale societies, those often labeled bands, tribes, and chiefdoms (Keeley 1996, 2001). In eastern North America, archaeologists for several decades prior to the 1990s steadfastly clung to a romantic view of a peaceful prehistory, an idea with deep roots in Western thought about humankind's natural state. A focus on cultural adaptations to local environments, including cooperation to minimize risk in inherently unpredictable settings, contributed to this perception of life in prehistoric times. Interestingly, the widespread denial of significant warfare in the distant past came at a time when cultural anthropologists were directing considerable attention toward conflicts among historically or ethnographically known small-scale societies (Chagnon 1988; Ferguson 1984, 1992; Ferguson and Farragher 1988; Otterbein 1994, 1999; Reyna and Downs 1994; Turney-High 1949; Vayda 1974). Even there, however, some scholars viewed warfare as stemming largely from the disruptive effects of European contact rather than being a common characteristic of societies deeper in the past.

The situation in archaeology has now changed: evidence for warfare in many geographical and temporal settings is widely acknowledged in North America and elsewhere (Guilaine and Zammit 2005; Haas 2001; Keeley 1996, 2001; Lambert 1997b; LeBlanc 1999; Maschner 1997; Milner 1999; Rice and LeBlanc 2001). Such a statement, however, does not get us very far. With the data now available on the prehistory of eastern North America (the Eastern Woodlands), it should be possible to identify variation across time and space in the prevalence of intergroup conflicts, the way warfare was conducted, and how it was related to different social and natural settings. We must be content with the general conditions associated with broadly delineated periods of war or peace. The long-term effects of warfare on population distribution, settlement characteristics, technology, and political centralization can be monitored effectively with archaeological remains. In contrast, archaeology is ill suited for detecting the proximate causes that motivated warriors in particular circumstances, such as seeking revenge and capturing women or livestock.

THE PRESENT STATE OF KNOWLEDGE

It is best to begin by defining what is meant by warfare (compare Keeley 1996 with Turney-High 1949). Here, warfare is considered potentially lethal fighting among separate communities that is viewed as a legitimate, even desirable, means of advancing a group's position relative to that of its neighbors (following Webster 1999). It does not need to be a highly organized endeavor involving structured formations of trained men who possess specialized weaponry and meet in large numbers on a battlefield. Warfare involves a collective rather than an individual element. Antagonisms are directed toward groups of people, so that many or all members of a particular community or society are classified as enemies (Kelly 2000). In that respect, warfare is distinct from homicides, in which specific individuals are targeted because of personal grudges or some real or imagined acts, such as witchcraft. Warfare is typically carried out between different villages, although tensions leading to outright fighting could begin within a single community before the quarrelsome factions split to occupy separate settlements. Thus, warfare covers fighting conducted in various ways for different purposes, from opportunistic ambushes to planned attacks, and it does not involve a specified number of participants or casualties.

Warfare in the prehistoric Eastern Woodlands can be recognized in several ways. Most of the people struck with arrows, spears, and clubs were undoubtedly casualties of war. A few of them, however, might have died in accidents or were perhaps killed because they were perceived as posing a danger to their communities. Good evidence for warfare includes multiple skeletons with conflict-related injuries in a single grave. It is unlikely that several people were simultaneously killed accidentally or intentionally by fellow community members before being ceremoniously buried in their village cemetery. Mutilated victims and palisaded sites are also clear signs of intergroup fighting.

Other indications of warfare include weapons, artwork, and settlements in easily defended locations. Specialized weapons include clubs or axes; noteworthy in this regard are ceremonial Mississippian period (ca. AD 1000–1600) monolithic axes and chipped stone maces possessed by highly ranked people. Yet for the most part weapons are difficult to distinguish from spears, atlatl darts, arrows, and axes used for everyday purposes. Stone projectile points embedded in skeletons, regardless of whether they tipped arrows or spears, display a wide range of workmanship. So it appears that victims were often struck with whatever was readily at hand, even if weapons were occasionally fashioned specifically for war. Artwork includes Mississippian period depictions of elaborately costumed figures brandishing weapons. Defensive positions are most easily recognizable as sites on high hilltops commanding good views, such as many late prehistoric villages in hilly parts of the Northeast.

Since there are several generally accepted signs of warfare, we might naturally ask what we already know about it in eastern North America (Bridges, Jacobi, and Powell 2000; Mensforth 2001; Milner 1999; Milner, Anderson, and Smith 1991; Smith 1997, 2003). The following list is not exhaustive, but it includes a number of the more important findings. First, the existing literature, especially for skeletons, underestimates evidence for warfare. Second, conflicts took place over the entire period for which there is sufficient skeletal evidence (most skeletons date to the past six thousand years). Third, mobile to sedentary hunter-gatherers and subsistence agriculturalists who were members of tribes and chiefdoms found themselves embroiled in conflicts. Thus, conflicts were not limited to particular kinds of societies, however they might be classified. Fourth, anybody, regardless of age or sex, could fall victim to an attack; nobody was spared. Fifth, despite the fact that anybody might be killed, conflict-related mortality fell most heavily on adults. Sixth, weak and debilitated people who were least able to fight or flee were most likely to be killed. Seventh, ambushes (planned or not) of just a few people apiece were the most common form of attack. Eighth, warfare-related mortality could on occasion reach as high as that in recent conflict-prone tribal societies, including those reeling from contact with aggressively expanding nation-states. Ninth, the intensity and frequency of conflicts varied greatly over time and space, although regional patterns are poorly understood.

The last of these nine findings—variation in the severity and number of conflicts—demands more attention. Most studies are still oriented toward the single skeleton, wall, or cluster of nearby sites. While such work does little to push us beyond what was already known more than a decade ago, individually described skeletons and palisades remain important because they are the stuff of broad-based analyses of temporal and geographical patterns (for North America, see Lambert 1997b, 2002; LeBlanc 1999; Maschner 1997; Milner 1999; and Rice and LeBlanc 2001). But even the recognition that the intensity of warfare varied over time and space only points us in the right direction. The next step that must be taken—and it is admittedly difficult with archaeological materials—is to identify the cultural and natural conditions associated with periods and places of harmony or hostility. Here, at last, a point is reached at which archaeological and osteological studies can make a useful and unique contribution to knowledge about this important, if distasteful, aspect of human behavior. We must identify the natural and cultural settings that covaried with warfare to contribute to an understanding of the conditions that fostered or dampened conflicts throughout the lengthy period spanned by prehistory.

TEMPORAL AND GEOGRAPHICAL CATEGORIES

Societies distributed across this culturally diverse region are lumped together into just a few categories as a first approximation of the nature of prehistoric warfare. Such categories permit the use of available data to highlight general patterns that, in turn, can be refined further as additional information becomes available. The temporal units conform to those commonly used in eastern North America. Grouping sites by culture period permits a broad-stroke view of changes over time, although it obscures potentially informative differences in the experiences of people in quite different social and natural settings.

For the late prehistoric period (AD 1000–1600), a distinction is also drawn between groups in the northern and southern Eastern Woodlands. Once again, this separation masks considerable diversity in population size, societal organization, intergroup contact, and natural landscapes. Yet it still captures differences in the intensity and practice of warfare that should serve as a springboard for more fine-grained future studies.

During late prehistoric times, the southern Midwest and Southeast were for the most part dominated by large and small chiefdoms, many referred to as Mississippian (fig. 9.1). Societies in the remainder of the Midwest, the Great Lakes area, the Northeast, and the mid-Atlantic region for the most part consisted of aggregates of roughly equivalent villages that tended to conform loosely to what anthropologists often label as tribes. While such classifications facilitate the identification of general patterns, the diverse nature of these societies in terms of their size and organizational structure means that they do not all fit comfortably into whatever sociopolitical categories might be devised. There was, in fact, considerable overlap between the northern and southern late prehistoric societies in subsistence practices, population size, vertical and horizontal differentiation among kin-based groups, and leadership roles, including the nature of community-wide decision making.

WARFARE IN DIFFERENT KINDS OF SOCIETIES

Before embarking on a discussion of general trends over time and, to a lesser extent, distinctions among geographical regions, we might find it useful to know whether warfare was practiced differently in various cultural settings within eastern North America. For the most part, the answer is no. Ambushes of just a few victims were the most common form of attack by hunter-gatherers and subsistence agriculturalists, the latter being members of both tribes and chiefdoms. That being said, the general picture of little difference in the practice of warfare is not entirely correct. Palisades, most of which date from the eleventh century onward, indicate that late-prehistoric people often perceived a threat that was sufficient to prompt the erection of defensive works. Furthermore, variation in wall construction shows that the danger posed by attacks varied from one place to the next.

The members of many of the late prehistoric southern chiefdoms apparently felt a greater need for substantial and well-planned defensive works than did their contemporaries to the north who were part of tribal-scale societies (Milner 1999). Walls around settlements in chiefdoms encompassed residential areas as well as public plazas and mounds associated with high-ranking people. The stout wooden walls were often straight and reinforced by substantial bastions, deep ditches, and high embankments. Bastions tended to be regularly spaced at an average of thirty meters, well within the distance covered by overlapping bowshot. Most of the known palisades were built at the biggest sites in any particular area. In many places, therefore, there was an emphasis on protecting the seats of hereditary chiefs at the expense of outlying settlements.

These defensive works could be quite elaborate. One of the most remarkable was built at Angel in southwestern Indiana (Black 1967).

FIGURE 9.1 The approximate distribution of late prehistoric chiefdoms that are mostly referred to as Mississippian. To the north were many tribal-scale societies.

There, attacking warriors had to cross a ditch and scale a fence before reaching a strong wall studded with bastions, each large enough to hold several bowmen. To do so would have meant considerable loss of life, assuming that the attackers faced alert defenders. The main wall was built on the crest of an embankment that accentuated its height, thereby making it a more formidable barrier.

The situation was different in the northern Eastern Woodlands

(Milner 1999). There, walls were often flimsy, being constructed from narrow poles, and surrounded no more than was absolutely necessary. They usually lacked reinforcing bastions, ditches, and embankments, and many appear to have been expedient constructions thrown up to meet the needs of the moment. Bastions, when present, were much smaller than those along the walls of many settlements in the southern chiefdoms; ditches and embankments, which were rare, were likewise typically shallower and lower, respectively. Each northern village apparently felt compelled to meet its own defensive needs, so on occasion virtually all well-documented contemporaneous settlements in a particular area possessed palisades. Only in the area occupied by the predecessors of the historic-period Huron and Iroquois were robust walls common. They consisted of multiple lines of posts or thick bands of posts and appear to have conformed to seventeenth-century descriptions of palisades (Heidenreich 1978; Trigger 1976). Yet even there, defensive works did not exhibit the regular layout of walls that surrounded many of the palisaded settlements in the southern Eastern Woodlands.

Differences in the strength of walls and the effort spent acquiring building materials can be illustrated by the diameters of soil stains (postmolds) where support posts once stood. In figure 9.2, postmold sizes are presented for 166 palisades at 116 sites in the northern Eastern Woodlands and 54 palisades at 36 sites in the south. Information in site reports is not reported uniformly, so postmold means and range midpoints were combined to obtain the largest sample possible. While these two measures are not the same, the intent is only to provide a rough approximation of patterning in existing information. Even with poor-quality data and a coarse cultural classification, it is clear that palisade posts in the south were typically larger than those in the north.

Such marked distinctions in palisade construction indicate that something different was happening in these two areas. In the southern Eastern Woodlands, the threat of attacks in strength must have been greater, necessitating better-planned, stronger, and well-maintained defenses to protect the principal settlements of chiefs. To judge from historical accounts, warriors who successfully gained entrance to a town did whatever they could to desecrate the charnel house containing the remains of the chief's illustrious ancestors (Anderson 1994b; DePratter

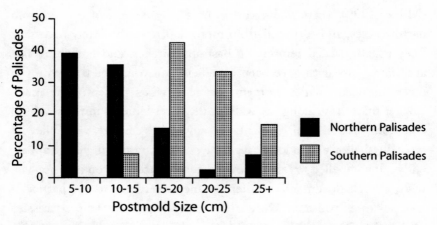

FIGURE 9.2 Approximate postmold sizes (means and range midpoints combined) for 166 and 54 palisades in the northern and southern Eastern Woodlands, respectively.

1991; Varner and Varner 1951). To do so struck a mortal blow at the core of a hereditary chief's power—it was a sure sign of feeble leadership. Through impressively strong walls, chiefs were also able to project an aura of strength to deter external enemies and intimidate internal rivals supported by their own constituencies.

Leading figures in chiefdoms exerted influence over their followers, no doubt more so in some places than in others, thereby providing them with opportunities to promote war or peace with their neighbors as circumstances dictated. They were also able, on occasion, to direct large bodies of men for short periods in concentrated attacks, to judge from the experience of the mid-sixteenth-century de Soto expedition (DePratter 1991; Varner and Varner 1951). An illustration from a somewhat later French expedition even shows a Florida chief accompanied by warriors on the march (Lorant 1965). Specific details, however, should not be given great weight, because the arrangement of men conforms to conventionalized treatments of soldiers in the European art of that period (Hale 1990). This particular illustration likely says as much about the European artist as it does about its Native American subject.

The northern villagers, in contrast, were concerned with protecting their settlements against small parties of warriors. Most walls were little more than screens that prevented a few men from slipping up to unwary or sleeping villagers, not formidable defenses that could keep numerous determined enemies at bay. While the threat of attack was sufficient for people to surround their communities with walls, the villagers seem to have been mostly concerned about a few warriors seeking targets of opportunity.

TRENDS OVER TIME

In terms of temporal trends, the story starts about six thousand years ago, in the last half of the Middle Archaic (the Middle Archaic spans ca. 6000–3000 BC). That is when skeletons with grievous wounds first become reasonably common in cemetery samples, although they are not the first evidence for conflict-related death (Mensforth 2001; Milner 1999; Smith 1997). Most of the late Middle Archaic through Late Archaic skeletons were excavated from long-occupied midden and shell heaps in the midcontinent (the Late Archaic spans ca. 3000–1000 BC or somewhat later). The inhabitants of these sites spent much of the year tethered to rivers or wetlands where there were abundant, spatially fixed, locally productive, and highly dependable foods, including shellfish (Anderson 1995; Dye 1996; Jefferies 1995; Milner 2004; Smith 1986). The cultivation of native plants, specifically weedy species that thrived in the continually disturbed and organically enriched soils at long-occupied camps, had by around five thousand years ago resulted in the appearance of several domesticated varieties (Fritz 1990; Smith 1989, 1995; Smith and Cowan 2003; Watson 1989).

In contrast to their mobile predecessors, these semisedentary hunter-gatherers were less likely to have been able to defuse tense situations by simply moving away from the sources of problems. Perhaps that is why skeletons with projectile points embedded in bone appear repeatedly at these sites. Yet the association between settled life and conflicts may be partly, or even largely, an artifact of uneven sampling. Middens in the midcontinent are often loaded with burials, particularly when compared to sites elsewhere; bone preservation is often good; and large-scale excavations have produced many skeletons. As a result, it cannot be said with assurance that hunter-gatherers from Kentucky southward to northern Alabama, which is where many of the middens and skeletons have been excavated, were any more likely to fight than other people (despite Kentucky's ill repute as that "dark and bloody ground," a result of the much later European-generated turmoil). Nevertheless, the semisedentary hunter-gatherers frequently found themselves at odds with one another, and they killed each other over those differences.

The last half of the Archaic period, when conflicts were common, spanned the end of a lengthy interval of population stagnation and the beginning of growth that continued unchecked until contact with Europeans. This shift has been identified through the use of 83,000 components (often sites have more than one occupation) dating to the past ten thousand years from eight states: Alabama, Arkansas, Illinois, Kentucky, Mississippi, New York, Tennessee, and Wisconsin (Milner 2004). The overall pattern from stasis to a 0.06 percent annual increase lasting from about four thousand to five hundred years ago is only a coarse-grained approximation of what occurred over very long periods across a vast area. Not all places conformed to the general trend, as shown by separate state and regional sequences. Within local regions—most systematically examined areas are no larger than several hundred square kilometers—there were undoubtedly population increases and declines, as indicated by largely qualitative assessments of the relative numbers of sites.

What can be said at this point is that the several thousand years bracketing a subtle, but ultimately momentous, shift in population-growth regimes were associated with intergroup conflicts in at least those areas that, by the standards of the time, were heavily occupied and had semipermanent sites. That the stasis-to-growth transition around four thousand years ago followed the earliest evidence for domesticated varieties of native cultigens is probably no coincidence (Smith and Cowan 2003). Regardless of any benefits the cultivation of weedy plants might have provided, this shift in subsistence strategies did not immediately relieve intergroup hostilities.

The situation reversed itself about two thousand years ago during Middle Woodland times (ca. 100 BC–AD 400). Skeletal evidence for interpersonal violence is uncommon for a period spanning as long as a half millennium (Milner 1999). This apparent easing of tensions cannot easily be attributed to poor sampling. Numerous Middle Woodland skeletons, many of which are well preserved, have been examined by osteologists. Although the Middle Woodland period was not entirely free of violence, there seems to have been a decline in conflicts that erupted into outright fighting.

This drop in intergroup conflict coincided with a rapid change in subsistence strategies in the midcontinent, which is where many of the skeletons are from. Native cultigens became a major component of midcontinental diets about two thousand years ago (Smith 1989; Smith and Cowan 2003). In fact, Bruce Smith (1989, 1569) has argued that the Middle Woodland period is notable for the appearance of "food-producing economies." That change is shown graphically in figure 9.3, in which the dots represent previously published water-screened (flotation) samples (Milner 2004). The sites vary in terms of location, duration, and function; all that was required for inclusion in the graph was the presence of a hundred or more identifiable seeds or nutshells. The top graph shows the percentage of cultigens, both native and introduced (maize and beans), expressed in terms of cultigens plus nutshells, mostly hickories. Nutshells, which tend to be well preserved, serve as a measure of wild plant foods. The bottom graph shows the introduced crops, principally maize, relative to all cultigens, including the native plants. Until late in the first millennium AD, virtually all of the cultivated plants were native weedy species that yielded great numbers of nutritious starchy and oily seeds. For the most part, the bottom graph highlights the shift to maize because the other introduced plant, the common bean, is so poorly represented that it has no discernible effect on the overall pattern. Archaeological materials cannot be directly translated into ancient diets, but marked changes in sample composition indicate shifts in the relative importance of general categories of food—in this instance, plants that were purposefully tended versus those that were collected.

Thus, the road to agriculture appears to have been long, spanning several thousand years, but it was not at all gradual when considered from an archaeological perspective rather than a single individual's lifetime. The process is better characterized as steplike, with the first evidence for a significant intensification of subsistence strategies based on cultivated plants appearing in some places around two thousand years ago. This sort of profound shift in food production must have been

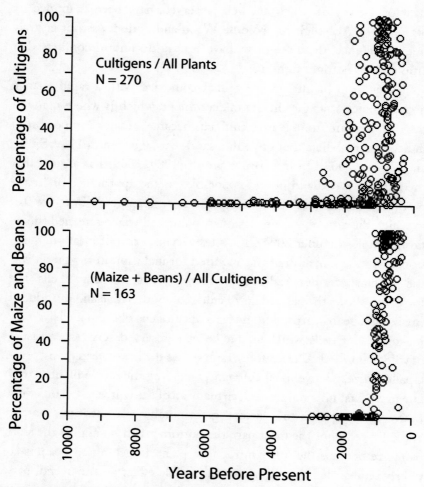

FIGURE 9.3 The temporal distribution of the contents of water-screened samples from separate occupations at Eastern Woodland sites, mostly in the midcontinent.

accompanied by alterations in other aspects of life as group mobility, labor needs, and social relations correspondingly changed. The Eastern Woodlands population was also increasing, but the coarse temporal resolution currently available is not precise enough to identify episodes of increase, stasis, and decline that likely took place at century-long or even generational time scales at local and regional levels.

Enhanced productive output coupled with only small gains in population meant that, on average, the Middle Woodland time horizon was a transitory period of Malthusian surplus. Surpluses could be produced with little extra effort once a commitment to native cultigens had been made. These cushions would have dampened competition for critical resources among small, self-sufficient communities that were always threatened by fluctuations in the yield of wild plants and animals. It is precisely these surpluses that would have been available in average to good years for mobilization by local descent groups to underwrite the impressive ceremonial activities, including mound building, that occurred in many places, especially in the midcontinent.

The Middle Woodland period is also known for increased exchanges of materials and artifacts, which occasionally ended up far from their points of origin. Several decades ago, researchers noted that people might have traveled to distant sources for some of these materials, a position that continues to receive support (Carr 2005; DeBoer 2004; Griffin 1967; Milner 2004). Two great hoards of Yellowstone, Wyoming, obsidian at the Hopewell site in Ohio are the most dramatic indications of what was likely to have been a direct acquisition of some rare and prized objects, although they are not the only such items. Apparently, for perhaps up to a half millennium, people occasionally crossed long distances carrying highly valued objects that, considering their eventual deposition, had profound ritual significance. Such trips would have been unlikely during most of prehistory, when people regularly fell victim to warlike neighbors. It is probably no coincidence that this unusual time of harmony, indicated by skeletons, occurred precisely when social group boundaries were relatively permeable, far more so than they were either earlier or later in time.

This generally pacific period was not destined to last. Relations between groups took a turn for the worse in the last half of the first millennium AD during Late Woodland times, as indicated by numerous skeletons with injuries (in the Midwest and Southeast, the Late Woodland period spans ca. AD 400–1000). A decline in exchanges of nonlocal materials and more localized pottery styles are consistent with diminished contact and sharper distinctions among groups. Bow-and-arrow technology also spread rapidly at that time (Blitz 1988). The widespread adoption of this technological innovation was no doubt related to new hunting practices, but people soon found arrows, a superb stealth-attack weapon, ideal for killing one another.

Groups often fought from this time onward into the historic period, when existing antagonisms played into the hands of newly arrived Europeans intent on pursuing their own political and economic agendas. Late prehistoric cemeteries often contain the skeletons of people shot with arrows, clubbed with stone axes, or mutilated by scalping, decapitation, and the removal of limbs. Not until the eleventh century, however, did palisades begin to be a common feature of settlements in both the northern and the southern Eastern Woodlands. Their appearance signaled a new level of concern over defense in many, but by no means all, places.

Around a thousand years ago, people across much of the Eastern Woodlands were gravitating toward one another, forming distinct clusters of settlements, a process that would continue into historic times (Anderson 1991; Hally 1993; Milner 2004; Snow 1994). Communities in close proximity to each other meant that local population densities increased far in excess of what would have happened from overall population growth, assuming that the long-term growth rate approximated what was actually taking place at that time. The pockets of people tended to be separated by large vacant areas. In the historic period, these places were often dangerous no-man's lands where hunting game or gathering wild plants invited attack, and the same was likely true of earlier times (Anderson 1994b; DePratter 1991; Hickerson 1965). Pressure on resources near settlements increased accordingly. The most serious consequences would have been felt when people desperately tried to find alternative foods during hard times. A reliance on maize increased the efficiency and flexibility of food procurement during harvest, when scheduling demands were greatest on the limited labor that individual households could muster (Milner 1998). That many people in the Eastern Woodlands turned to maize as a major part of their diets therefore comes as no surprise.

In the southern Eastern Woodlands, palisades became common in the eleventh century, around the time when the number and spatial distribution of large and small chiefdoms increased (Milner 1999).

Defensive walls remained a common fixture of settlements, particularly important ones, from that point onward. Artwork associated with high-ranking people shows men or mythical figures in warlike poses, some clutching maces and severed heads (Brown 1985; Dye 2004). Regardless of what was being depicted, a link was made between success in war and elevated social positions. There also appears to have been a connection between an upward ratcheting of warfare and the origin and spread of chiefdoms across a broad area. This finding provides empirical support for what Robert Carneiro (1998), among others, has argued is a common feature of chiefdom development (also see Haas 2001; for warfare and southeastern chiefdoms, see Anderson 1994a, 1994b, and DePratter 1991).

In the northern Eastern Woodlands, the processes of population aggregation and dietary change resembled in some respects what was happening at roughly the same time to the south, but the sociopolitical outcomes were different. What is most interesting about evidence for intergroup conflict in the north, as distinct from the south, is the unidirectional increase in the number and distribution of palisades (fig. 9.4). Palisades became more common as climatic conditions deteriorated during the bumpy slide into the Little Ice Age. This cooling trend, aggravating uncertainty over anticipated yields from one year to the next, represented a serious problem for villagers at the margins of maize agriculture. They included Iroquoian groups in southern Ontario and upstate New York, where the most elaborate and strongest of the northern palisades were erected. There, living on anything less than ample optimal land could prove difficult, if not fatal.

After AD 1400, palisades began to become a common feature of settlements in the mid-Atlantic Piedmont and Coastal Plain (Milner 1999). This expansion of hostilities among ever-changing constellations of villages was probably related to an increasingly desperate jostling of populations for the most advantageous social and natural settings. There is archaeological evidence for changes in the distribution of populations in the mid-Atlantic region, including a downstream movement along the Potomac River (Potter 1993; Rountree and Turner 1998; Stewart 1995). Not all such groups would have been responding to a climatic downturn sufficient to cause shortages in critical resources. Hard times

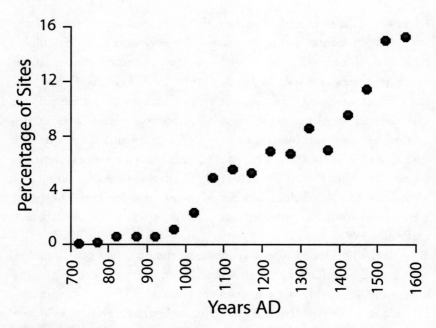

FIGURE 9.4 The temporal distribution of 231 palisaded sites in the northern Eastern Woodlands.

affecting the most vulnerable groups, however, would have resulted in a cascade of movement and conflict, and these disruptions eventually made themselves felt in distant places as population distributions changed over time. In short, greater numbers of palisades along with their broader distribution after circa AD 1400 are the clearest signs so far for a climatic contribution to worsening intergroup relations across much of the northern Eastern Woodlands.

Groups at the leading edges of population expansions could have experienced staggering conflict-related mortality, even to the point of threatening community survival. The best example comes from the central Illinois River valley, where at least one-third of the adults in one cemetery, Norris Farms 36 (dated to circa AD 1300), had been killed by their enemies (Milner, Anderson, and Smith 1991). This particular community included members of one of the earliest Oneota groups (if not the first) to move from the north into this part of the Illinois Valley, an area previously occupied by Mississippian groups. Distinctive artifacts, especially pottery, along with cranial morphology indicate that this group was, indeed, a new arrival in the river valley (Esarey and Santure 1990; Steadman 1998).

COSTS TO COMMUNITIES

Although evidence for fighting in prehistoric times is now generally acknowledged, warfare's effect on communities, other than contributing to some deaths, is hotly debated. Maria Smith (2003), for example, has dismissed fighting as inconsequential when only several percent of a cemetery's skeletons show unambiguous signs of conflict-related trauma. This view is not at all uncommon, despite the low archaeological visibility of warfare (skeletal trauma underestimates combat fatalities) and the fact that, relative to all deaths, conflict-related mortality in single communities at times approached or exceeded that of wars in the recent past (Gat 1999; Keeley 1996, 2001; Milner 2005).

Archaeologists must direct more attention toward estimating the cost of conflicts as measured by excess mortality, labor demands for defense, interference with food production, population movement, and the like. Confict-related deaths are only the start of the story. The sudden loss of key productive people from self-sufficient households must have increased the risk of death for remaining family and community members. Thus, warfare deaths—no matter how few might be identified in a cemetery sample—likely had ramifying effects throughout the once-living population.

Problems stemming from warfare deaths would have been compounded to the extent that hard-pressed groups were forced to modify subsistence practices or move to safer, but less productive, places. For example, only two hundred years ago, the Lewis and Clark expedition on their journey to the Pacific encountered Shoshone who had "to remain in the interior of these mountains at least two thirds of the year where the[y] suffered as we then saw great heardships for the want of food sometimes living for weeks without meat and only a little fish roots and berries" (Moulton 1988, 91; original spelling). A narrowing of subsistence pursuits also took place in the late prehistoric community that buried their dead at Norris Farms, as indicated by small samples of plant and animal remains from village contexts (King 1993).

INTERPRETIVE FRAMEWORKS

With all the recent archaeological interest in prehistoric warfare, we should be wary of substituting one perception of facts for another, that is, a state of Hobbesian "warre" replacing a Rousseauian peace. It would not be the first time such reversals have occurred. In the early twentieth century, Alfred Kroeber (1939, 148) viewed warfare as "insane, unending, continuously attritional . . . and it was so integrated into the whole fabric of Eastern culture, so dominantly emphasized within it, that escape from it was well-nigh impossible." He had no solid information to back up such a claim. Neither do more recent portrayals of prehistoric North America as a time of near-universal peace (Sale 1991). Such flip-flops, in which broad characterizations outdistance any semblance of solid evidence, serve no end other than the promotion of particular ideological positions.

There is a more reasonable middle-ground interpretation of the archaeological evidence: conflicts varied in intensity from one place and time to another. Although the underlying causes can only dimly be seen at a coarse-grained level, apparently no single cause can be associated with periods of greater or lesser intergroup conflict. Population size and distribution, environmental settings (including climatic change), technology (particularly as it pertains to subsistence practices), and society (such as the organization of labor) all played a part in determining whether warfare was common. Some of these factors had a greater effect on intergroup relations in certain times and places than they had in others. Nevertheless, in combination they are reducible to pressure on resources, which varied greatly from one time and place to the next.

To move our understanding forward, we must conduct research at different temporal and geographical scales. More descriptions of skeletons, walls, and other evidence of warfare are certainly needed. But that is the easy part. We must also refine information on temporal and spatial variability in the intensity and conduct of warfare in regions ranging from parts of river valleys to the entire continent. Then we must determine how this variation is related to measurable past social and natural conditions. That is the only way to explore why warfare in various places waxed and waned throughout prehistory, and for archaeology to contribute to a greater understanding of this aspect of the human experience.

10 THE OSTEOLOGICAL EVIDENCE FOR INDIGENOUS WARFARE IN NORTH AMERICA

Patricia M. Lambert

The bioarchaeological record provides one of the most definitive and nuanced accountings of prehistoric warfare in North America: the tale of the biological impacts of war on individuals and populations, the ultimate accounting of its costs. To reconstruct patterns of warfare, a bioarchaeologist begins at the end of the story, with the skeletal record of the injured and dead. The task is then to work back from patterns of injury and mortality to the behaviors responsible for these patterns, and thence to the larger social and environmental contexts in which the injuries were sustained. Through this approach, it is possible to establish various parameters of violent conflict that are otherwise difficult to ascertain from archaeological data, such as the age and sex of victims and participants, the type and sequence of weapons used, the relationship between weaponry and mortality, the spatial relationship of attackers to victims, the practice of taking human trophies, and stress levels in individuals and populations engaged in violence. This survey assembles such data from six regions of North America to permit examination of patterns and trends in violent conflict. Within each region, case studies illustrate the nature of violent conflict at different times and places, as well as the different methods that bioarchaeologists have employed to document and reconstruct this behavior.

The six regions included in this survey are California and the western Great Basin, the Southwest and periphery, the Great Plains, the Eastern Woodlands, the Northwest Coast and Plateau, and the Western Arctic and Subarctic. In four of these regions (California, Great Plains, Northwest Coast, and Western Arctic), foraging economies predominated, although many were highly specialized and on the Great Plains horticulture became more important after AD 900 (Blakeslee 1994; Brooks 1994a). In the other two regions, farming economies began to develop in the first millennium BC and became more prominent after AD 1 (Gumerman and Gell-Mann 1994; Smith 1992). Hence, a range of economies is represented by societies covered in this study.

The osteological evidence for violence and warfare includes several classes of injuries that tend to occur in violent contexts: embedded projectiles (spears, arrows, darts, bullets) or scars from these weapons; depressed skull fractures, nasal fractures, tooth fractures, broken ribs, and forearm and hand fractures from parrying blows to the face and upper body; decapitation, scalping, dismemberment, and other signs of trophy-taking; more extensive perimortem bone breakage, cut marks, punctures, and other damage suggestive of torture, corpse mutilation, and/or cannibalism; and more subtle evidence such as carnivore tooth marks or other signs of corpse exposure that suggests unnatural death. Victim profiles identifying those at risk can help to sort out the nature of violence (e.g., Lambert 1994; Milner, Anderson, and Smith 1991), while demographic profiles can reveal population-level impacts of war, such as the loss of young males killed in battle or young women captured by enemies (e.g., Hurst and Turner 1993; Willey 1990).

The mere presence of violent injuries does not necessarily demonstrate intergroup aggression, as conflicts between individuals can involve violence, and injuries resulting from such encounters may be difficult to distinguish from those sustained in intergroup conflict. However, group-level conflicts involve more people and therefore tend to result in archaeologically distinct signatures such as individuals with multiple embedded weapons (multiple assailants), multiple victims in cemeteries, and mass graves containing mortally wounded individuals. Signs of trophy-taking also suggest intergroup conflict (Lambert 2002).

It is important to note, however, that the absence of osteological evidence does not necessarily imply an absence of war. Aspects of mortuary behavior may have resulted in differential disposal of war victims (e.g., in situ burial at the site of the killing, cremation, or aboveground burials), skeletal material may be rare overall owing to poor preservation or mortuary practices such as cremation, or skeletal assemblages may not have been examined for this kind of evidence. Reexamination of extant osteological collections has significantly changed perceptions of prehistoric violence in several regions of North America (e.g., Bridges, Jacobi, and Powell 2000; Lambert 1994; Milner 1999; Smith 1997), so the absence of reported cases needs to be evaluated in light of efforts made to systematically investigate warfare in this way.

CALIFORNIA AND THE WESTERN GREAT BASIN

Systematic study of warfare in prehistoric California has concentrated on the southern coast (Kennett 2005; Kennett and Kennett 2000; King 1982; Lambert 1994, 1997b; Lambert and Walker 1991; Walker 1989; Walker and Lambert 1989), although there is abundant osteological evidence of violent injury and death elsewhere in the region (e.g., Andrushko et al. 2005; Courville 1952; Jurmain 1991, 2001; Loud 1924; Rackerby 1967; Schenck 1926; Tenney 1986; Tyson 1977; Wedel 1941; Wiberg 1988). Depressed cranial vault fractures and wounds from projectile weapons are the two types of injuries most commonly studied for the purpose of documenting patterns of violence and war (e.g., Jurmain 1991; Lambert 1994; Walker 1989). Forearm parry fractures (Grady, Latham, and Andrushko 2001; Jurmain 1991, 2001; Lambert

1994) and nasal injuries (Lambert 1994) have also been observed and discussed as possible evidence of violence, although such injuries may occur in nonviolent contexts and thus are more difficult to interpret. There is also evidence for trophy-taking of human forearm bones and possibly also crania and other body parts (e.g., Andrushko et al. 2005; Grady, Latham, and Andrushko 2001).

The osteological record of violent injury for semisedentary hunter-gatherers of the Santa Barbara Channel area currently offers the broadest temporal and geographic perspective on prehistoric violence in California (Lambert 1994, 1997b; Lambert and Walker 1991; Walker 1989; Walker and Lambert 1989). Data on over 1,700 individuals spanning a 7,500-year period from thirty archaeological sites provide a diachronic perspective on sublethal and lethal violence in maritime societies of this region (Lambert 1994, 1997b). Sublethal violence primarily involved blows to the head, apparently from some sort of wooden clubbing implement. These injuries, mostly healed, are evident in crania from throughout the 7,500-year period (128/753, or 17 percent affected) but are most prevalent (25 percent affected) in those dating to circa 1500 BC–AD 1380 (Lambert 1994, 1997b; Walker 1989). Typically small and round, evincing the contour of the weapon used to inflict them, these injuries are much more common in males than females and suggest some form of male-oriented, ritualized violence like the club fights of Yanomamö men (Chagnon 1992; Lambert 1994; Walker 1989). This hypothesis is supported by evidence for the concentration of these fractures on the forehead, particularly in males, which suggests that participants were facing each other when blows were dealt (Lambert 1994, 1997b; Walker 1989). Healed cranial fractures are common in periods long before lethal violence became prominent, demonstrating a long history of social tensions but also the apparent effectiveness of social mechanisms for constraining them (Lambert 1994, 1997b; Walker 1989).

Projectile weapons appear to have been favored for lethal engagements in the Santa Barbara Channel area. Recorded injuries from projectile weapons there include stone or bone spear, dart, and arrow points embedded in bone; scars in bone that retain the shape of a stone or bone projectile tip; and projectiles found lodged between bones or in body cavities (Lambert 1994). Like depressed cranial fractures, projectile injuries are more common in males than females (3:1 overall) and tend to affect 18–40-year-old males. This age and sex patterning in wound distribution implies that projectile wounds were a more important cause of death for young and mature adult men than for older men, women, or children of either sex (Lambert 1997b). Temporally, victims are relatively uncommon in samples antedating AD 580, ranging in frequency from about 0 to 5 percent of individuals in these samples (Lambert 1994). They are much more frequent in samples dating to between AD 580 and AD 1380 (Lambert 1994, 1997b; Lambert and Walker 1991; Walker and Lambert 1989), affecting 10 percent (39/402) of the collective sample from this time period in frequencies ranging from 0 to 22 percent for individual archaeological sites (Lambert 1994). Victims from this time period also tend to have more injuries (as many as 16, or perhaps even more) than in previous or subsequent time periods, suggesting the participation of multiple individuals in a "kill" (Lambert 1997a, 1997b, 2008). Among the Yanomamö of Venezuela, feuding often results in victims with multiple injuries due to the desire of kinsmen to participate in a kill to avenge the death of a loved one (Chagnon 1992; Lambert 1997a). Clustering within and among graves is also present in some Santa Barbara Channel area cemeteries (Lambert 1994, 141–47), though mass graves are rare, suggesting constant but small-scale forms of engagement that nonetheless resulted in a high death toll overall. The concentration of victims in centrally located sites rather than on cultural peripheries and the predominance of projectiles made from locally available lithic materials in wound contexts suggest that conflicts primarily involved culturally affiliated groups (Lambert 1994).

The causes of this late prehistoric escalation in violence are likely complex and synergistic. As Douglas Kennett demonstrates using archaeological settlement data (Kennett 2005; Kennett and Kennett 2000), this was a time of increasing population consolidation, territoriality, and concern with defense on the Northern Channel Islands. Proxy measures of population size also suggest a general increase through time in the human population of the region that positively correlates with increased lethal violence overall (Lambert 1994). Highly unstable, drought-prone conditions between AD 450 and 1300 (Kennett 2005; Kennett and Kennett 2000; Lambert 1994; Lambert and Walker 1991;

Raab and Larson 1997; Stine 1994; Walker and Lambert 1989) in particular may have fostered mistrust and deadly competition as the population became too large to respond through settlement shifts and other nonviolent mechanisms for alleviating resource shortages. This hypothesis finds support in human skeletal evidence of unprecedented health stress during these years (Lambert 1993, 1994, 1997b; Lambert and Walker 1991; Walker and Lambert 1989). A shift from large to small projectile points in wound contexts (Lambert 1994) and archaeological tool assemblages (Glassow 1996; Moratto 1984) also documents the introduction of the bow and arrow into California AD 500–900, and this technological innovation likely changed how war was conducted there, as occurred elsewhere in North America (Blitz 1988; Lambert 1994). The decline in warfare after AD 1380 corresponds with improving climatic conditions, the elaboration of trade systems, and the appearance of more complex social systems (Arnold 1992, 1993; Kennett 2005; Kennett and Kennett 2000; Lambert 1994, 1997b; Lambert and Walker 1991) that may have functioned to mitigate disputes and suppress feuding.

There is abundant osteological evidence for violence and warfare elsewhere in California (e.g., Andrushko et al. 2005; Grady, Latham, and Andrushko 2001; Jurmain 1991, 2001; Lambert 1994). To the east of the Santa Barbara Channel area in the southern San Joaquin Valley, 3.4 percent (19/551) of individuals from four cemeteries at Buena Vista Lake (AD 600–1500) had at least one projectile injury (Lambert 2007; Wedel 1941). All of the victims for whom sex could be determined were male, and 8 percent (15/188) of identified males in the sample were thus affected. Although most common in human remains dating to circa AD 900–1200 (10.7 percent of males), projectile injuries were also fairly common in a large sample dating to circa AD 1200–1500 (8.5 percent of males affected). Although dating imprecision makes comparisons between the two areas challenging, the late prehistoric decline in violence evident in the Santa Barbara Channel area appears not to have been paralleled in the southern San Joaquin Valley. To the north in the San Francisco Bay area, many archaeological sites have produced individuals with projectile wounds and other types of violent injuries, and there is some evidence for an earlier peak (1000 BC–AD 1) in violence there than in the south (Andrushko et al. 2005; Lambert 1994). For example, forearm mutilation and trophy-taking were recently identified in human skeletal remains from a two-thousand-year-old site (SCL-674) in the San Francisco Bay area (Andrushko et al. 2005; Grady, Latham, and Andrushko 2001). There, fourteen individuals were discovered with missing forearms, and twelve of these had cut marks on the distal humeri, verifying the intentional removal of these limb segments. Most of those with missing forearms were male (12/14), and 20 percent (12/59) of the males identified in the SCL-674 sample were thus affected; a few of these had other violent injuries as well. Later samples from the San Francisco Bay area show relatively high frequencies of projectile wounds and parry fractures (e.g., Jurmain 1991; Lambert 1994), but evidence of trophy-taking is at present more problematic. On the eastern California periphery, historic sources report very warlike behavior among indigenous desert peoples (e.g., Kroeber 1980; Kroeber and Fontana 1986; Stewart 1947), but there appears to be very little archaeological evidence for such interactions. The absence of osteological evidence for war there and in some other regions of California may well be a product of cultural practices such as cremation of the dead (Kroeber 1925), rather than the absence of war.

THE SOUTHWEST AND PERIPHERY

Osteological evidence of violence and warfare is also fairly abundant in the Southwest, though it is more prominent to the north in the Anasazi region (LeBlanc 1999; Rice and LeBlanc 2001; Turner and Turner 1999; Wilcox and Haas 1994). The osteological record of violence in the Southwest extends back at least two thousand years, to the early years of maize agriculture and increasing sedentism. Evidence of violence includes cut marks from scalping (and a few scalps), other signs of trophy-taking, projectile wounds, cranial fractures, body mutilation, and unburied bodies (e.g., Allen, Merbs, and Birkby 1985; Baker 1990; Billman, Lambert, and Leonard 2000; Dice 1993; Farmer 1997; Howard and Janetski 1992; Lambert 1999; LeBlanc 1999; Luebben and Nickens 1982; Malville 1989; Martin 1997; Turner and Turner 1999; White 1992; Wilcox and Haas 1994; Wilcox, Robertson, and Wood 2001). In the Southwest, unlike California, cranial trauma is the more prominent form of lethal violence, suggesting differences between the regions in how war was conducted.

In his major treatise on warfare in the prehistoric Southwest, Steven LeBlanc (1999, 142–43) identifies thirty-two sites with evidence of violence antedating AD 900 (see also Farmer 1997; Howard and Janetski 1992). Whereas most cases involve a relatively small number of individuals and some do not include clear evidence of violence, others are hard to dispute. Two of these stand out in terms of number of victims and types of injuries: Wetherill's Cave 7 in southeastern Utah (Farmer 1997; LeBlanc 1999; Hurst and Turner 1993; Turner and Turner 1999) and Battle Cave in northeastern Arizona (LeBlanc 1999; Morris 1939; Turner and Turner 1999). Wetherill's Cave 7, a Basketmaker II (ca. AD 400) site in Cottonwood Wash, contained the remains of at least ninety-two individuals interred in a single event. Some of the bodies had projectile or knife wounds, many heads and jaws showed signs of bludgeoning, and cut marks on some crania provided evidence that scalps and ears were taken as trophies. Biases in the age and sex distribution of the sample further suggest that some women and children may have been captured instead of killed (Hurst and Turner 1993; Turner and Turner 1999, 59–65), a practice common in recent tribal warfare (e.g., Chagnon 1992; Otterbein 2000b). The human skeletal remains from Battle Cave consisted of eleven individuals from a Basketmaker II (ca. 500 BC–AD 500) cist deposit (LeBlanc 1999; Turner and Turner 1999, 133–41). Included were the remains of men, women, and children, many exhibiting perimortem cranial trauma. Both of these cases provide evidence of serious, group-level violence and document at least episodic outbursts of intergroup violence in the northern Southwest early in the Puebloan sequence.

In later archaeological contexts, various types of injuries are apparent in human remains (e.g., Lambert 1999; Martin 1997; Wilcox, Robertson, and Wood 2001), but one type of trauma is most notable: disarticulated bodies with cut marks, extensive perimortem fracturing, percussion scars, and burning (Lambert, Billman, and Leonard 2000; Turner and Turner 1999; White 1992). As many as forty assemblages of broken and butchered human remains, each containing from one to thirty-five (or possibly more) individuals, have been identified from sites in the northern Southwest. Most date to between AD 900 and 1200 (Baker 1990; Billman, Lambert, and Leonard 2000; Turner and Turner 1999; White 1992). These assemblages have variously been interpreted as evidence of cannibalism (e.g., Billman, Lambert, and Leonard 2000; Dice 1993; Malville 1989; Nickens 1975; Turner and Turner 1999; White 1992), violent mutilation without cannibalism (e.g., Bullock 1998; Dongoske, Martin, and Ferguson 2000), witch-killing (Darling 1998), and mortuary behavior (e.g., Bullock 1998). Recent biochemical verification of human processing and consumption of human flesh at Cowboy Wash, a twelfth-century site in southwestern Colorado, indicates that cannibalism played a role in the formation of at least one of these assemblages (Billman, Lambert, and Leonard 2000; Lambert, Leonard et al. 2000; Leonard, Lambert, and Marlar 2001; J. Marlar et al. 2000; R. Marlar et al. 2000). At Cowboy Wash, human blood was discovered on two cutting tools found in association with processed human remains, residues from human muscle tissue were found in a cooking pot, and both human muscle tissue and brain tissue were recovered from a human coprolite.

LeBlanc (1999) and Christy Turner and Jacqueline Turner (1999) argue that cannibalism was a strategy used by an expansionist polity centered at Chaco Canyon to intimidate and control its populace. However, this explanation has yet to be reconciled with evidence such as the early (AD 880–910) appearance of cannibalism in southeastern Utah (Cottonwood Wash; see Turner and Turner 1999, 269; White 1992) before the northerly expansion of Chacoan influence (Varien et al. 1996), and the concentration of mutilated assemblages in the Mesa Verde region (Billman, Lambert, and Leonard 2000; Turner and Turner 1999) after the depopulation of Chaco Canyon early in the twelfth century (see Frazier 1999; Stuart 2000; Varien et al. 1996). On the southern piedmont of Sleeping Ute Mountain in southwestern Colorado, corpse mutilation, cannibalism, and community abandonment around AD 1150 strongly suggest that serious intergroup violence was important in the formation of the Cowboy Wash assemblage (Billman, Lambert, and Leonard 2000; Lambert, Billman, and Leonard 2000).

Unburied bodies with and without obvious trauma are prominent at some locations after AD 1250 (LeBlanc 1999; Rice and LeBlanc 2001), but evidence for cannibalism is at present less common (Billman, Lambert, and Leonard 2000; Turner and Turner 1999). At Castle Rock, a fortified village in southwestern Colorado (AD 1256–85), the unburied and in many cases mutilated remains of 41 individuals were deposited within and outside of structures during a massacre that terminated the site occupation (Lightfoot and Kuckelman 2001). At Sand Canyon Pueblo, a contemporaneous fortified pueblo in the vicinity, 20 bodies were recovered from nonburial contexts (Bradley 1992; LeBlanc 1999; Lightfoot and Kuckelman 1995). Recent reanalysis of the human remains suggests that cannibalism may also have occurred at these sites (Kuckelman, Lightfoot, and Martin 2002), extending evidence for the practice well into the thirteenth century. On the southern piedmont of Sleeping Ute Mountain, four (of eight) individuals recovered from a small village site (5MT9943) also appear to have died violently, as attested to by perimortem cranial trauma and nonformal body disposal (Lambert 1999), although evidence of cannibalism is lacking. These cases help to explain the extreme defensive measures (e.g., fortification, village relocation to inaccessible/defensible land forms) that people began to take throughout the northern San Juan basin after AD 1250 (Haas and Creamer 1993, 1996; LeBlanc 1999; Lightfoot and Kuckelman 1995).

Massacre may also account for the demise of Casas Grandes in northern Mexico, a large and important cultural center during the fourteenth century. There, the skeletal remains of 127 unburied bodies have been recovered (DiPeso 1974) from what LeBlanc (1999, 252) estimates may have been a massacre of over 1,000 residents. If he is correct, then Casas Grandes may represent the largest prehistoric massacre in the American Southwest (LeBlanc 1999) and possibly all of native North America.

In the eastern Great Basin on the northern Puebloan periphery, evidence for war exists but is sporadic. A partial skull from a Fremont site on the eastern shore of the Great Salt Lake has scalping cut marks on the frontal bone and documents trophy-taking of scalps around AD 650–990 in northern Utah (Lambert 2002). Three skulls and associated upper cervical vertebrae from the Hysell site, a Fremont village in central Utah, provide evidence of violence and trophy-taking at a slightly later date (AD 960–1180) (Owsley et al. 1998; Rood 2001). Perimortem fracturing from decapitation is present on one skull and mandible and on cervical vertebrae of both children and an adult female; the latter also has cut marks on the face and mandible (Owsley et al. 1998). Discovered below a collapsed pithouse roof, the heads appear to have been centrally placed or hung for display (Rood 2001). To the east at the Turner-Look site in east-central Utah, seven human bone fragments with perimortem damage hint at the presence of cannibalism in the cultural territory of the Fremont around AD 1075 (Turner and Turner 1999, 170–72). Shield images in Fremont rock art overlap in time with this osteological evidence (AD 900–1200; Loendorf and Conner 1993; Madsen 1989; Schaafsma 2000), and Fremont defensive sites appear on the southeastern Anasazi periphery during the twelfth century AD (LeBlanc 1999, 192). This evidence raises intriguing questions about the nature of intergroup relations on the northern Puebloan frontier.

THE GREAT PLAINS

Human remains provide some of the best archaeological evidence for intergroup violence in the Great Plains region, including evidence of scalping and other forms of mutilation, projectile injuries, and skewed sex ratios indicative of differential treatment of men and women (e.g., Miller 1994; Neiburger 1989; O'Shea and Bridges 1989; Owsley and Berryman 1975; Owsley, Berryman, and Bass 1977; Owsley and Jantz 1994; Owsley, Marks, and Manhein 1999; Willey 1990; Willey and Bass 1978; Williams 1991). Skeletal evidence of war antedating AD 950 is minimal (Blakeslee 1994; Brooks 1994b; Owsley 1994). A few cases of scalping have been reported from Archaic and Woodland period sites on the northern Plains (Owsley 1994; Tiffany et al. 1988; Williams 1994). Although these hint at an early origin for practices such as counting coup, fortification and other archaeological signs of warfare are largely absent from sites dating to this time (Blakeslee 1994; Brooks 1994b). These indicators become more apparent in the archaeological record after AD 1200, particularly at major cultural boundaries on the northern Plains (Bamforth 1994, 2001; Owsley and Jantz 1994). The movement of populations both southward (Extended Middle Missouri) and northward (Initial Coalescent), perhaps as a consequence of drought in the thirteenth century, appears to have brought several groups into contact and competition with each other and with the resident population (Initial Middle Missouri) during the late prehistoric period (Bamforth 1994, 2001; Blakeslee 1994; Holliman and Owsley 1994; Owsley 1994).

Although the scale of engagement appears to have varied considerably, evidence for the massacre of whole villages attests to the virulent nature of some late prehistoric warfare on the northern Plains. At the Fay Tolten site, a fortified Initial Middle Missouri (AD 950–1250) village on the Missouri River in central South Dakota, limited data recovery suggests such an attack. There, five unburied bodies were recovered from the floor or features of the only two houses excavated at the site (6 percent of identified houses). Two bodies had been partially burned while fleshed, one had a perimortem projectile injury, and one (a child) had been scalped a short time before the terminal event (Holliman and Owsley 1994). Although most of the village remains unexcavated, the sampled portion extrapolates to a massacre of some note.

At Crow Creek—a large, Initial Coalescent village in South Dakota with a terminal occupation around AD 1325—a mass-burial deposit containing the remains of a minimum of 486 men, women, and children was discovered in 1978 in a fortification ditch that partially surrounded the village (Willey 1990; Willey and Emerson 1993; Zimmerman and Bradley 1993). Most of the bodies had been mutilated, and many showed signs of exposure before interment. At least 89 percent of 415 identified frontal bones had cut marks indicative of scalping, and 41 percent of 101 identified skulls had round or ellipsoid depression fractures from round or axelike clubbing implements. Decapitation and possible tongue removal by humans was also evident by anatomical placement of cut marks on occipital bones, cervical vertebrae, and mandibles. Hands and feet may also have been purposefully removed, although damage from carnivore teeth indicates some scavenger activity. Isolated bones and body parts in other contexts (Willey 1990; Willey and Emerson 1993), as well as burning of all identified structures (Bamforth 1994), support the annihilative intent of the attack. However, a pronounced bias against 15–24-year-old females, as well as the act of burying almost 500 bodies, suggests that some people survived through capture or escape (Willey 1990; Willey and Emerson 1993). In scale, the Crow Creek massacre is unparalleled anywhere in prehistoric North America, except possibly that at the broadly contemporaneous center at Casas Grandes described above.

Contemporaneous sites on the southern plains in Oklahoma and the Texas panhandle have not produced evidence for similar levels of strife, although both archaeological and osteological evidence for violence during the late prehistoric period has been found, particularly on the western frontier of this region (Bovee and Owsley 1994; Brooks 1994b; Owsley, Marks, and Manhein 1999). Evidence of conflict includes possible lookout sites and burned structures, and skeletal injuries such as healed and unhealed perforations, embedded arrow points, scalping cut marks, and depressed cranial vault fractures. Some osteological evidence in contemporaneous populations of central Oklahoma also suggests violence, but with fewer victims. Overall, the archaeological evidence for late prehistoric violence on the southern plains suggests small-scale raiding, with some evidence for intertribal conflict in frontier regions of northern West Texas (Bovee and Owsley 1994; Brooks 1994b).

Evidence from human skeletal remains documents the continuance of hostile engagements in the protohistoric and historic periods on the northern Great Plains that involved both indigenous peoples and Euroamericans (Bamforth 1994; Gill 1994; Owsley 1994). Lack of evidence for large-scale loss of warrior-age males and the presence of small victim counts overall (compared to sites such as Crow Creek) are consistent with small-scale raiding as the primary form of engagement in the region (Owsley 1994). However, more serious violence continued to erupt on the frontier, as archaeological discoveries at the Larson site (1750–85) in South Dakota reveal. Remains of seventy-one people were found on house floors and scattered about this village, and musket balls, metal arrowheads, and extensive burning attest to the nature of their demise (Bamforth 1994; Owsley, Berryman, and Bass 1977). As at Crow Creek, there was evidence of crushing blows to the head and face, scalping, decapitation, missing hands and feet, and disembowelment (Owsley, Berryman, and Bass 1977). Intergroup violence also escalated on the southern plains at this time but was not as pronounced (Brooks 1994a).

THE EASTERN WOODLANDS

In the Eastern Woodlands, osteological evidence of intergroup violence long predates archaeological evidence such as the appearance of stockades and other signs of fortification. Evidence for some form of war has been reported at a number of Archaic period sites (e.g., Bridges, Jacobi, and Powell 2000; Milner 1999; Smith 1996, 1997; Walthall 1980). In western Tennessee, for example, projectile wounds, scalping, and/or limb dismemberment in 2.3 percent (all males) of 439 interments from Archaic contexts (6000–1000 BC) strongly suggest intergroup aggression (Smith 1997). In northern Alabama, embedded spear points in 2.7 percent of individuals (four males and three females) at the late Archaic (4000–1000 BC) Perry site similarly imply intergroup hostilities (Bridges, Jacobi, and Powell 2000). Violent trauma appears to have declined after this time (cf. Seeman 1988) but increased again after AD 500 and peaked during the millennium preceding sustained European contact (Milner 1999).

Most Eastern Woodland sites with evidence of violent trauma contain only a few victims, mostly males (80 percent of 140 adult victims identified by Milner [1999]), suggesting a pattern of warfare that emphasized feuding and small-scale raiding. There are some exceptions, however. At Pinson Cave in Alabama, the remains of forty-four to one hundred people deposited in the cave around AD 1040 suggest the possibility of a massacre, although the evidence—seven projectile points embedded in bone and fifty scattered throughout the remains—is more circumstantial (Bridges, Jacobi, and Powell 2000). At Koger's Island, a smaller Mississippian center in northern Alabama, four mass graves each containing between five and eight individuals also indicate more serious intergroup aggression. Six individuals from these graves have perimortem scalping cut marks, and one has an unhealed depression fracture, supporting the hypothesis that all of the associated individuals in these graves died violently. High rates of trauma (cranial and post-cranial fractures, scalping) there and at other small to midsized settlements in the Deep South suggest that risk of violent injury and death was greater at these locations than at large centers such as Moundville (Bridges, Jacobi, and Powell 2000).

To the north on the Mississippian periphery in west-central Illinois, the high toll of constant, small-scale raiding is evident at the Norris Farms site. At least 43 of 264 (16 percent) inhabitants of this fourteenth-century Oneota settlement died violently, as indicated by embedded projectile points, scalping cut marks (n = 14), decapitation (n = 11), and carnivore damage from corpse exposure prior to interment (n = 30) (Milner, Anderson, and Smith 1991). The relatively equal sex ratio of victims and the frequent association of same-sex individuals in multiple graves, coupled with evidence for preexisting debilitating conditions in many, suggest that these were opportunistic killings of vulnerable adults (Milner, Anderson, and Smith 1991). This constant onslaught appears to reflect efforts of resident Mississippians to oust Oneota intruders from the north (Milner 1999; Milner, Anderson, and Smith 1991). Although there is no evidence for a massacre on the scale of Crow Creek, Norris Farms represents another form of deadly intergroup violence in indigenous North America.

The archaeological record also provides some evidence of hostile interactions between Native Americans and early European troops and colonists. Although possible sword injuries at the sixteenth-century King site in Georgia (Blakely and Matthews 1990) have recently been discounted (Milner et al. 2000), evidence of such wounds is present in an early historic sample from the Tatham Mound in northern Florida (Hutchinson 1996; Larsen 1997). A gunshot wound in a Native American male from Mission San Luis de Talimali (AD 1656–1704) is additional osteological evidence of conflict involving European weapons (and probably Europeans) during early years of Spanish contact (Larsen, Huynh, and McEwan 1996). Farther north at Fort Laurens, Ohio, the eighteenth-century burials of twenty European males between the ages of ten and forty-five document an ambush by local Native Americans (whose villages were slated for destruction by the U.S. military) of unwary Continental troops out gathering firewood and stray horses. Eleven of thirteen suspected ambush victims had perimortem cranial injuries from heavy, bladed implements, and five of these also had fractures attributable to blunt force trauma. In addition, all twelve crania that could be scored for trauma had fine cut marks indicative of scalping. This osteological evidence accords well with historic eyewitness accounts of the ambush (Williamson et al. 2003).

THE NORTHWEST COAST AND PLATEAU

The osteological record of the Northwest Coast and Plateau has also produced abundant evidence for violence and war, at least in some regions. However, because of a shift in mortuary practices from burial to aboveground interment on the coast after AD 200, the coastal record is biased against late prehistoric burials and the information these might provide (Maschner 1997). The earliest evidence of violent injury in this region dates to the eighth millennium BC and comes from the Columbia Plateau near Kennewick, Washington. A projectile wound in the pelvis of "Kennewick Man" shows signs of healing and bears witness to at least one violent encounter during the life of this adult male (Preston 1997; Slayman 1997). Other Archaic (10,500–4400 BC) skeletons from the Columbia Plateau also show signs of violence, but small sample sizes make interpreting the nature and scale of this violence difficult (Ames and Maschner 1999). However, several sites postdating AD 300 have yielded victims of violence, including two mass graves containing five individuals each, some with embedded stone arrow points (Chatters 1989). These cases suggest more serious strife on the plateau after this time.

On the coast, skeletal series analyzed by Jerome Cybulski (1990, 1992, 1994, 1999; see also Ames and Maschner 1999) suggest a long but uneven history of violence. Violent injuries reported for Northwest Coast remains include projectiles embedded in bone, skull and facial fractures, tooth fractures, forearm and hand fractures from parrying blows to the face and upper body, decapitation (Cybulski 1990, 1992, 1994, 1999), and scalping cut marks (see Ames and Maschner 1999, 190). The earliest cases (3500–1500 BC) come from coastal sites in British Columbia, where violent trauma is evident in 21 percent of fifty-seven observable individuals (Cybulski 1994). Although most of these injuries are nonlethal, reported injuries include a projectile wound in a male dating to 2200 BC and several instances of decapitation dating to the end of this time period. Considerable disparities also exist between samples: violent trauma is almost nonexistent in remains from the Queen Charlotte Islands and common in those from the central mainland coast (Ames and Maschner 1999; Maschner 1997).

A similar rate of violent trauma (21.2 percent) is evident in remains dating to 1500 BC–AD 500 (Cybulski 1994), but this figure also masks important regional differences (Ames and Maschner 1999; Cybulski 1990). Over 32 percent of individuals from northern-coastal contexts, primarily Prince Rupert Harbour, show signs of violent trauma, whereas only 6 percent of those from contemporaneous sites to the south are thus affected (Ames and Maschner 1999; Maschner 1997). Fractures from club blows predominate, but instances of decapitation are also present (Cybulski 1999; Maschner 1997). Large villages began to form during these years, and war paraphernalia such as slate daggers and stone clubs appear in northern-coastal archaeological sites of the period (Ames and Maschner 1999; Fladmark, Ames, and Sutherland 1990; Maschner 1997), so alternative lines of evidence support the interpretation that intergroup violence was on the rise in some locations. Human remains are rare after AD 500 (Ames and Maschner 1999), but a small late prehistoric sample studied by Jerome Cybulski (1992, 1994) does exhibit a higher rate of violent trauma overall (28 percent), consistent with evidence for increased concern with defense late in the prehistoric period.

THE WESTERN ARCTIC AND SUBARCTIC

Skeletal evidence for violence in the Western Arctic is present but sporadic and disparately distributed in time and space (Maschner and Reedy-Maschner 1998). The oldest bioarchaeological evidence of serious violence dates to between 1500 BC and AD 1000 and comes from two sites on Kodiak Island in the Gulf of Alaska: Crag Point and Uyak (Hrdlička 1944; Simon and Steffian 1994; Urcid 1994). At these sites, disarticulated remains with cut marks, punctures, and other signs of extensive processing suggest mutilation and possibly cannibalism, although some deposits have been interpreted as mortuary behavior (see Simon and Steffian 1994). Decapitation, scalping cut marks, and perforations at joint surfaces of postcranial skeletal elements also hint at trophy-taking (Maschner and Reedy-Maschner 1998; Simon and Steffian 1994; Urcid 1994).

Late prehistoric examples of violent injury are rare in the literature, but two have been reported for the Aleutian area: a male skeleton with an apparent projectile injury at Peterson Lagoon on Unimak Island (AD 1575) and a male mummy from the north coast of Unalaska Island with a crushing injury to the skull (Maschner and Reedy-Maschner 1998). Far to the northeast on the MacKenzie Delta in the Northern Territories, the disarticulated, defleshed, and broken remains of a minimum of thirty-five people at the fourteenth-century Saunaktuk site bear witness to lethal violence on a very different scale (Melbye and Fairgrieve 1994; Walker 1990). Knife cuts, slash wounds, piercing, gouging, and split long bones evident in human skeletal remains from the site accord well with Inuit oral traditions in the Saunaktuk region. According to these accounts, at some time in the past, the Inuit settlement at Saunaktuk was attacked by Athabaskans while the men were away whaling. Old men, women, and children were tortured, murdered, and mutilated. Although Inuit accounts do not describe cannibalism, bodies do appear to have been treated in ways consistent with this interpretation (Melbye and Fairgrieve 1994). These cases illustrate extremes in the bioarchaeological evidence for prehistoric violence in the Arctic, but the dearth of systematic data make conclusions regarding frequencies and trends impossible at this time.

THE TIMING AND TEMPO OF VIOLENCE IN PREHISTORIC NORTH AMERICA: CLUES TO CAUSATION

The osteological record of war in North America reveals several broad patterns. First, despite the range of lifeways represented in this survey, human skeletal evidence documents the existence of war prehistorically in all six regions covered in this review. Although the nature of intergroup violence clearly varied by region in terms of weaponry, scale, timing, and duration, in no region was it absent or inconsequential. Second, most of the osteological evidence suggests that relatively small-scale engagements, such as those that tend to occur in the context of feuding and raiding, predominated. However, quantitative assessment of victim frequencies reveals that this "low-level" warfare could result in very high death tolls overall, particularly for some sex and age classes (e.g., Bridges, Jacobi, and Powell 2000; Jurmain 2001; Lambert 1994, 1997b; Milner, Anderson, and Smith 1991). Third, mass graves or large numbers of unburied bodies showing signs of trauma are known from four of six regions surveyed and document outbreaks of highly lethal, intergroup violence. Large-scale massacres are perhaps best known at sites on the northern Great Plains (Crow Creek, Fay Tolten, Larson), but apparent massacres have also been identified at sites in the northern Southwest (Wetherill's Cave 7, Battle Cave, Castle Rock, Sand Canyon Pueblo) and southern Southwest (Casas Grandes), as well as the Canadian Arctic (Saunaktuk) and possibly the Southeast (Pinson Cave). Other such outbreaks likely also occurred but were not preserved archaeologically, because no one survived to bury the dead.

Chronological evaluation of the North American osteological data reveals some important temporal trends. Violent injuries are present in many skeletal assemblages antedating AD 500; these include projectile wounds, fractures from clubbing implements, and evidence of trophy-taking. The considerable variability within and between regions in the frequency of these injuries, however, suggests that local social and environmental conditions may be central to understanding outbreaks of violence and war in these early years. This situation began to change around AD 500, as indicated by a substantial increase in the frequency of reported injuries attributable to violence. These injuries are most evident in human remains from throughout North America dating between AD 1000 and 1400, when most of the massacres described above occurred.

Several explanations have been posited to account for this post–AD 1000 escalation in warfare. These include critical population threshold (e.g., Haas 1999), global impacts of the Little Ice Age (e.g., LeBlanc 1999), and technological innovations such as the introduction of the bow and arrow (e.g., Blitz 1988) and sinew-backed bow that changed the way war was conducted (e.g., Maschner 2000; Mason 1998). All find some evidence in the archaeological record of North America, and some combination of these and other factors is likely what led to the increase in intergroup violence between AD 1000 and AD 1400. There can be little doubt that the North American population increased substantially during much of the Holocene, and population thresholds may very well have been reached at several points in prehistory, fostering social and economic change. The transition to agriculture in the Southwest and Eastern Woodlands may have come about in this way. Also, climatic indicators show that climate was not stable but varied throughout the Holocene; the medieval climatic anomaly is one of the better known of these perturbations.

Neither climate change nor population increase necessarily leads to competition and war, but when the balance of populations and the resources they depend on shifts in a manner potentially detrimental to at least some, violence is one strategy that individuals and the groups they comprise may adopt to shift or maintain the balance in their favor. This choice may be more attractive in terms of cost-benefit analysis when populations in a region become sedentary, because alternative strategies such as mobility for dealing with local shortages are no longer an option. Those adopting such a strategy could (but need not) be those in greatest peril; those in a favorable position may take advantage of others' misfortunes to promote their own fitness. Technological improvements in war weaponry can also advantage those who possess them and might serve to encourage such offensive action. Once one group adopts such a strategy, for whatever reason, other individuals and groups must respond in kind; in this way, patterns of enmity and cycles of feuding ensue that can last for generations. Causal factors such as these likely combined in an unprecedented manner late in the prehistory of North America and explain the post–AD 1000 surge in violence documented in this chapter.

11 ETHICAL CONSIDERATIONS AND CONCLUSIONS REGARDING INDIGENOUS WARFARE AND VIOLENCE IN NORTH AMERICA

Richard J. Chacon and Rubén G. Mendoza

Despite the evidence for conflict and violence in aboriginal America, revisionist historians argue that anthropologists have conspired to invent "bloody worlds" by exaggerating the scale of warfare and ritual violence identified with Amerindian societies (Montejo 1993). Some elements of this revisionist school of thought argue that scholarly misrepresentation is but one facet of a malicious colonialist legacy determined to denigrate and dehumanize indigenous cultures, societies, and histories (Hassler 1992; Means and Wolf 1995; Montejo 1993, 1999a, 1999b; Tlapoyawa 2003).

Scholars such as Peter Hassler contend that the conquistadors generated propaganda designed to offend the sensibilities of their Christian audience (1992). According to Victor Montejo, the corpus of European and American scholarship produced over the course of five centuries has been dominated by racist, derogatory, and demeaning colonialist characterizations of indigenous peoples (see Cojti Ren 2004). Such scholars hold that colonialist narratives have been manipulated to political and ideological ends to justify a five-hundred-year pattern of indigenous land expropriations, forced relocations, and assimilationist political agendas affecting indigenous peoples to this day.

For example, Vine Deloria holds that Native Americans did not engage in the procurement of human trophies, such as the taking of scalps, prior to European contact; rather, he claims, English colonials introduced the practice of taking scalps. Deloria argues that this was accomplished through the introduction of incentives born of bounties placed on enemy scalps by the English on the eve of the French and Indian Wars of 1754–60 (Deloria 1969). Robert Heizer (1974, 267) in turn reports that "many anthropologists believe that (scalping) was not an aboriginal custom, but was a practice introduced by the French and English, from whence it spread westward."

Some revisionists go so far as to argue that documenting Amerindian warfare and ritual violence only serves to promulgate further violence and aggression against indigenous peoples (Means and Wolf 1995; Montejo 1999a; cited in Cojti Ren 2004). Where established patterns of indigenous warfare are concerned, A. Vexnim Cojti Ren (2004) contends that such "interpretations lead us to believe that in preconquest times our People were already in a state of oppression from our governors leading to the notion that our present situation as targets of violence and national policies is just the continuation of the past; we have just changed oppressors." Deloria in turn argues that for Native Americans, "the struggle of this century has been to emerge from the heavy burden of anthropological definitions" (1995, 65).

We acknowledge that many early European colonists and their early American counterparts bear significant responsibility for the killing and enslavement of indigenous peoples in the Americas throughout the fifteenth though twentieth centuries. We similarly acknowledge that

European and American colonial powers have been less than forthcoming in accepting responsibility for those atrocities. One needs only to review the particularly ethnocentric early accounts of Hernando de Soto (1539–43) and his companions in *La Florida* to recognize their propaganda value as moral justification for the conquest and subjugation of native peoples. One need only consider some of the many abuses visited upon native peoples by various Catholic and Protestant missionaries along with western soldiers to understand the motivation behind the creation of many ethnocentric accounts of Native American life. Both religion and politics clearly conspired to disinherit and disenfranchise Amerindian culture and civilization by way of the Eurocentric frameworks of analysis prevalent in that time and place. The pernicious nature of colonial-era Spanish "misinformation" systems and propaganda have been documented (Petersen and Crock 2007).

We are also pressed to acknowledge that Native American groups too have a history of having engaged in the killing and enslavement of one another for some of the very reasons explored in this volume. As such, we are in accord with Montejo, who is on record as saying that "as a people, we do not deny the fact that warfare, violence and human sacrifice were practiced as this information is well documented by archaeology" (cited in Cojti Ren 2004). However, despite the large-scale massacres documented in chapter 10 and by other contributors to this volume, we do not observe the existence of an unrestrained genocidal tendency among Amerindians. Moreover, we do not equate indigenous warfare and ritual violence with that pattern of wholesale genocide conducted by some European groups through the course of the colonial era. To do so would constitute a significant misrepresentation of the facts as we currently understand them. We contend, therefore, that to argue otherwise would constitute a blatant disregard for those millions of native peoples who suffered unspeakable cruelties at the hands of Westerners over the course of the past half millennium.

We thus must concur with observations made by Russell Means and Marvin Wolf (1995) and Victor Montejo (1993, 1999a, 1999b), who contend that early Euro-American ethnohistories are often based on those blatantly ethnocentric and racist assumptions formulated by said groups to legitimize the expansion of Western powers in the Americas. However, scholars need only consider accounts produced by the likes of Alvar Núñez Cabeza de Vaca, Hernando de Soto, Francisco Vasquez de Coronado, Samuel de Champlain, James Adair, George Catlin or missionaries such as Jacques Marquette, Eusebio Francisco Kino, Joseph Lafiteau, or Francisco Garcés to more fully appreciate the utility of these same narratives for addressing the catastrophic consequences of culture contact and the triumphs of Amerindian civilization. We thus call for the judicious use and critical reassessment of those same documentary resources that are often maligned by the revisionist movement, because assuming that such works convey only half truths and propaganda would be a mistake.

We also believe that various scholars (see, e.g., Biolsi and Zimmerman 1997; Cojti Cuxil 1995; Cojti Ren 2004; Deloria 1969, 1995; Means and Wolf 1995; Montejo 1999a, 1999b; Wilson 1991) are essentially justified in claiming that many anthropologists have fundamentally fallen short in their valuation of the human rights of indigenous peoples. We are therefore troubled by the fact that many of our colleagues have not always conducted anthropological research with the best interests of native peoples at heart. The sad realization of this painful and shameful truth leads us to empathize with those who have been injured and or exploited by members of the anthropological community. Frankly, we are not at all surprised that many native peoples, and their nonnative advocates, look upon those of us within the anthropological community with some degree of suspicion or outright contempt. Not surprisingly, therefore, many Native Americans are reluctant to acknowledge scholarly evidence or findings that unmask the persistent specter of indigenous warfare and ritual violence purportedly committed by their ancestors. Unfortunately, some of those anthropological findings have been exploited by outsiders hostile to the idea of indigenous self-determination and political and social empowerment. Indeed, we are in accord with those (e.g., Biolsi and Zimmerman 1997; Cojti Ren 2004; General and Warrick 2004; Nicholas 2004; Walker 2000) who encourage anthropologists to forge collaborative engagements with indigenous communities to remedy or avert further transgressions (for examples of this perspective, see Chacon, Chacon, and Guandinango 2007; Chacon and Dye 2007; Dongoske, Aldenderfer, and Doehner 2000; Nicholas 1997; Swidler et al. 1997).

Accordingly, we believe it a mistake to deny the fact that native peoples are equally capable of lethal engagements with one another and with outsiders. The failure to objectively report on the substantive defensive and offensive capabilities of Amerindian groups, even where motivated by the noblest of intentions, may exacerbate conditions in which violence may provide the only alternative medium for effecting self-defense, particularly where such conflict may entail engagements with nonnatives (Heath 2004). As Keith Otterbein has acknowledged, "classifying peoples as non-violent could position them to be victimized as easily as calling a people fierce could make them a target of attack" (2000a, 843).

Beth Conklin advocates the development of an engaged anthropology that empowers marginalized peoples. She nevertheless condemns the tailoring of research findings "to produce the images that certain activists or advocacy groups want" (2003, 5). Further, she contends that the promotion of an idealized depiction of society, however well intended, will backfire when distorted claims are exposed or, as she aptly asserts (Conklin 2003, 5), "when the gap between rhetoric and realty is revealed" (also see Edgerton 1992; Krech 1999; Rothstein 2004; Scheffel 2000; Stearman 1994; Vargas-Cetina 2003). Given the many serious threats confronting indigenous peoples today, social scientists would do well to heed Conklin's assertion that idealized (mis)representations are shaky ground on which to stake indigenous rights claims.

We similarly acknowledge that Deloria is correct in characterizing the current state of affairs regarding the pervasive rendering and re-rendering of Native American representations. Deloria contends that "it becomes impossible to tell the truth from fiction or facts from mythology. Experts paint us [Native Americans] as they would like us to be . . . the American public feels most comfortable with the mythical Indian of Stereotypeland. . . . To be an Indian in modern American society is in a very real sense to be unreal and ahistorical" (1969, 9–10).

Rather than distort research findings to conform to the prevailing political and cultural agenda of the day, we should seek to provide indigenous peoples with an escape from the "noble savage slot trap" (Conklin

2003, 5). For that and related reasons, the promulgation of a politically expedient (i.e., nonviolent) aboriginal America hinders progress toward indigenous self-determination. Heeding Conklin's admonition, this volume seeks to dispassionately document the multidimensional sources and consequences of Amerindian warfare and ritual violence in a manner consonant with the facts and, at the same time, faithful to those indigenous traditions and beliefs that explain from an emic standpoint the phenomenon under study.

The failure to acknowledge the specialized role that warfare and ritual violence plays in the lives of indigenous peoples is itself a vestige of colonial repression, as it denies indigenous warriors their legacy of armed resistance. This thereby minimizes how participation in acts of violence were traditionally perceived or justified at the emic levels of analysis. Even a cursory review of the literature reveals that one of the most highly prized social distinctions available to Native American males was that specific to the warrior tradition. To be considered a fierce warrior ready and willing to battle in defense of the people was the ultimate honor.

Therefore, revisionist arguments stating that the very act of reporting data or findings on Amerindian warfare and ritual violence only serves to justify further violence and aggression against native people are untenable. Indeed, Amerindian groups have long maintained warrior societies through which the strength and valor of combatants and defenders were celebrated (Moore 1996; Schaafsma 2000; Taylor 1975). Amerindian peoples clearly believed that there was absolutely nothing savage or degrading about a warrior who courageously fights on behalf of his people.

Denying or suppressing dialogue regarding organized violence in native society is patently Eurocentric, as it lends itself to abuse by those researchers who then choose to evade the discussion altogether, thereby fostering the growth and perpetuation of misrepresentations of mythic proportion. A secondary consequence of such a pattern of denial is that traditional Amerindian perspectives and worldviews concerned with validating and celebrating participation in combat are suppressed and thereby lost. One additional consequence of denying indigenous traditions a voice in this discourse is that it lends itself to having perspectives on indigenous conflict and ritual violence defined and evaluated exclusively through the prism of a nonnative value system.

Should we seek to obscure the fact that for many Native Americans the most effective means by which to garner prestige was by way of membership in warrior sodalities (Moore 1996; Schaafsma 2000; Taylor 1975)? Similarly, how is it possible to negate the existence of Plains Indian traditions centered on the commemoration of the military exploits of their war heroes by depicting these events on bison hide tipi liners and robes (Afton, Halaas, and Masich 1997; Taylor 1975)? Such efforts conflict with the fact that among such groups as the Sioux, honor and the achievement of the most exalted status was reserved for the *blotahunka*, or "war leader" (Larson 1997). Prior to battle, Cheyenne warriors chanted, "I do not wish to die an old man. The day is mine to die" (Greene 1994, 21). How then does one reconcile these recorded indigenous warrior traditions with the radical revisionist perspective of late? And what of the words of Sauk leader Black Hawk, who proudly recalled, "I was once a great warrior" (Jackson 1955, 181)? Are we then to censure the Sioux warrior Tokala-luta for vowing, "I will give my flesh and blood that I may conquer my enemies" (Taylor 1975, 44)? The radical revisionist perspective is clearly at odds with the Thunder Society war chant of the Omaha, which asserts, "Before me stands, awaiting my touch, coal-black paint, heavy black clouds filling all the sky o'er our head. Upon our faces now we put the black, coal-black cloud. Honoring war, wearying for the fight, warrior's fight, waiting to go where the Thunder leads warriors on" (Mails 1973, 272). Similarly, the Cheyenne victory song (like that of many other indigenous warrior traditions) proclaims, "Brother, pull up my dog rope. I will clean it and use it again. Where are the enemies that taunted me? They are dead now. I will see one more summer; it's too soon for me to go. I will surprise my sweetheart; she thinks that I am dead. I have another scalp for my mother; she will be proud" (Moore 1996, 108). Given the inherent power and pride so proclaimed, should we not therefore acknowledge that the very survival and integrity of indigenous communities rested on the tenacity and courage of such armed combatants? We believe that to deny voice to this warrior tradition of self-sacrifice is to plunder the most ancient and valued systems of belief to be found within these proud cultural traditions.

As Cojti Ren (2004) has acknowledged, human societies everywhere have had to cope with conflict emanating from within their own ranks. Native Americans are no exception in this regard. The first European colonists in the New World encountered many sophisticated societies replete with rich cultural traditions and remarkable technological achievements. European colonials also confronted native societies in the throes of interminable and bloody conflicts. Moreover, Europeans often found allies in native North American Indian groups who had grown weary of the onslaught and subjugation to which they had been subjected by their more powerful neighbors. As a result, such groups were often quite willing to join forces with Europeans bent on overthrowing native overlords. The earliest sixteenth-century accounts by Spanish explorers in North America—including those of Alvar Núñez Cabeza de Vaca, Hernando de Soto, and Francisco Vasquez de Coronado—all record intertribal slavery and internecine warfare in native North American contexts (Castañeda 1966; Champlain, cited in Axtell and Sturtevant 1980; Day 1964; Duncan 1996; Garcilaso de la Vega 1993; Hallenbeck 1971). Garcilaso de la Vega (1993), one of the chroniclers of the ill-fated expedition of Hernando de Soto, reported that on several occasions the Spaniards destroyed indigenous villages with the assistance of Indian allies who sought revenge against traditional enemies. The Pecos warriors of New Mexico similarly formed an integral part of Spanish-led punitive expeditions against nomadic Plains groups who preyed upon the Pueblos (Kessel 1979; Rohn 1989).

There can be no doubt that early European colonials and their descendants committed untold atrocities against the peoples of native North America. However, given those examples cited in this volume, there can also be no question that deep-seated antagonisms and intertribal conflict characterized interactions between native groups long before initial European landfall in the Americas. Therefore, violence, bloodshed, and the brutality of warfare and subjugation were not entirely foreign concepts to Amerindian peoples prior to 1492. A host of similar observations have been made by other noted scholars (e.g., Ewers 1975; Martin and Frayer 1997; Topic 1989). We do not contend that precontact Amerindians were the bloodthirsty predators that their portrayal within many colonial-era documents suggests. Rather, we seek to establish that preconquest peoples of the Americas did not inhabit the "Paradise lost" often championed by revisionists, with precontact life in the New World summed up in edenic statements such as "the Great Mystery had given us everything we need, a heaven on earth" (Means and Wolf 1995, 15).

We therefore reassert the need to more fully explore and understand Amerindian warfare and ritual violence from cross-cultural and interdisciplinary frames of reference. We believe that such a call to action constitutes a more forthright, albeit challenging, alternative to that which currently seeks to deny or denounce anything that challenges the notion of the passive American Indian victim of Western aggression. As social scientists and humanists, we feel an obligation to our respective communities to accurately, objectively, and faithfully convey our findings in a respectful and scholarly manner.

While we jointly support and encourage community endeavors intended to bolster indigenous self-determination and native self-esteem, we do so only as long as such efforts do not come to fruition at the expense of scholarly integrity and accuracy. When scholars and researchers recover significant evidence for warfare and ritual violence in the anthropological record, they are obliged to report the facts critically and unequivocally. To do otherwise constitutes an inexcusable violation of ethical and scholarly protocols. This is the objective that we kept in mind when we set about bringing together significant new research produced by those scholars represented in this collection devoted to the study of Amerindian warfare and ritual violence.

This work has generated a multitude of new insights and observations regarding indigenous armed conflict in native North America. We believe that we have collectively extended the scope of research devoted to warfare and ritual violence by way of our inclusion of corollary forms of civil and religious conflict reconciled by means of ritual violence. What then can we conclude from those studies presented? Ultimately, we have identified and defined war and ritual violence, and its origins and affinities in North America, in terms of several idealized patterns or dynamics that include the following observations:

1. The inherent multicausality of organized violence. This volume advances a variety of materialistic and nonmaterialistic explanations

cited as the causal or primary motivations for warfare and other forms of human conflict and aggression. Moreover, we hold that it is entirely reasonable to assume that human beings may be motivated to do battle as a consequence of multiple or even conflicting factors, conditions, and variables (material and otherwise).

2. Variance in the reason or rationale for fighting and the intensity of organized violence through time. This volume illustrates that the incipient rationale for initiating armed conflict may vary significantly from those reasons that underlie its persistence through time (see chapter 3). The intensity of warfare in turn may covary or fluctuate through time irrespective of its initial impetus (see chapters 9 and 10).

3. Significant loss of life in tribal warfare. Clearly, a serious misconception is at work in presuming that tribal warfare was, or is, of little demographic consequence. Some revisionists nevertheless seek to minimize the demographic consequences of nonstate (or tribal) conflict interaction (e.g. Blick 1988; Means and Wolf 1995). Several of the contributions to this volume document the fact that tribal populations may be significantly reduced by way of "primitive" warfare (see, especially, chapters 6 and 10), and other scholars have reported similar findings (e.g., Chagnon 1988; Keeley 1996).

4. Corroboration of European and American chronicles in archaeological evidence. Despite revisionist claims that seek to dismiss ethnohistorical sources (reporting indigenous warfare) as mere propaganda (e.g. Cojti Ren 2004; Means and Wolf 1995; Montejo 1993, 1999a; Tlapoyawa 2003), contributors to this volume provide a refutation, as in chapter 8, which reports the extent to which the archaeological record testifies to the accuracy of key ethnohistorical accounts of Southeastern warfare.

5. Variation in the intensity of indigenous warfare upon contact with state-level societies. Some studies report that under certain conditions, groups inhabiting the tribal zone experience an escalation of hostilities as predicted by those models of conflict interaction advanced by R. Brian Ferguson and Neil Whitehead (1992). We, however, found that in the wake of the expanding tribal zone, the opposite may also accrue, and Western influence may diminish preexisting patterns of conflict and violence. Some contributions to this volume (chapters 1

and 2) report that in some instances, contact with the expanding world system of European colonialism had the effect of suppressing tribal warfare, and the most intensive levels of tribal warfare occurred prior to the establishment of the expanding tribal zone in question (chapter 10).

The complex nature of the nexus that forms between state and tribal peoples is exemplified in Joan Lovisek's work (chapter 3), which indicates that the intensification of tribal warfare on the Northwest Coast was the result of direct engagement with the Euro-American fur trade. This was followed by a diminishing pattern of violence that coincides with the introduction of British colonialism. Lovisek's findings should therefore serve as a cautionary tale to scholars exploring the role that state-level societies play with respect to the intensity of indigenous conflict in any given tribal zone.

Ultimately, we believe that this volume, devoted to the exploration of war and ritual violence in native North America, will necessarily supplement extant theoretical frames of reference and bolster new research regarding the causes and consequences of human, not just Amerindian, armed conflict and ritual violence.

REFERENCES

Ackerman, Robert E. 1998. Early Maritime Traditions in the Bering, Chukchi, and East Siberian Seas. *Arctic Anthropology* 35 (1): 247–62.

Afton, Jean, David Halaas, and Andrew Masich. 1997. *A Ledgerbook History of Coups and Combat*. Niwot: University of Colorado Press.

Allen, Wilma H., Charles F. Merbs, and W. H. Birkby. 1985. Evidence for Prehistoric Scalping at Nuvakwewtaqa (Chavez Pass) and Grasshopper Ruin, Arizona. In *Health and Disease in the Prehistoric Southwest*, ed. Charles F. Merbs and Robert J. Miller, 23–42. Arizona State University Anthropological Research Papers 34. Tempe.

Ambler, Richard J., and Mark Q. Sutton. 1989. The Anasazi Abandonment of the San Juan Drainage and the Numic Expansion. *North American Archaeologist* 10 (1): 39–53.

Ames, Kenneth M. 2001. Slaves, Chiefs and Labour on the Northern Northwest Coast. *World Archaeology* 33:1–17.

Ames, Kenneth M., and Herbert D. G. Maschner. 1999. *Peoples of the Northwest Coast: Their Archaeology and Prehistory*. London: Thames and Hudson.

Anderson, David G. 1991. Examining Prehistoric Settlement Distribution in Eastern North America. *Archaeology of Eastern North America* 19:1–22.

———. 1994a. Factional Competition and the Political Evolution of Mississippian Chiefdoms in the Southeastern United States. In *Factional Competition and Political Development in the New World*, ed. Elizabeth M. Brumfiel and John W. Fox, 61–76. Cambridge, U.K.: Cambridge University Press.

———. 1994b. *The Savannah River Chiefdoms: Political Change in the Late Prehistoric Southeast.* Tuscaloosa: University of Alabama Press.

———. 1995. Recent Advances in Paleoindian and Archaic Period Research in the Southeastern United States. *Archaeology of Eastern North America* 23:145–76.

———. 1996. Chiefly Cycling Behavior and Large-Scale Abandonments as Viewed from the Savannah River Basin. In *Political Structure and Change in the Prehistoric Southeastern United States*, ed. John F. Scarry, 150–91. Gainesville: University Press of Florida.

———. 1999. Examining Chiefdoms in the Southeast: An Application of Multiscalar Analysis. In *Great Towns and Regional Polities in the American Southwest and Southeast*, ed. Jill E. Neitzel, 215–41. Albuquerque: University of New Mexico Press.

Andrushko, Valerie A., Kate A. S. Latham, Diane L. Grady, Allen Pastron, and Phillip L. Walker. 2005. Bioarchaeological Evidence for Trophy Taking in Prehistoric Central California. *American Journal of Physical Anthropology* 127:375–84.

Arber, Edward, ed. 1910. *Travels and Works of Captain John Smith.* Edinburgh: John Grant.

Archer, Christon I. 1993. Seduction before Sovereignty: Spanish Efforts to Manipulate the Natives in Their Claims to the Northwest Coast. In *From Maps to Metaphors: The Pacific World of George Vancouver*, ed. Robin Fisher and Hugh Johnston, 127–59. Vancouver: UBC Press.

Archibald, Robert. 1978. *The Economic Aspects of the California Missions.* Washington, D.C.: Academy of American Franciscan History.

Arima, Eugene Y. 1984. Caribou Eskimo. In *Handbook of North American Indians.* Vol. 5: *Arctic*, ed. David Damas, 447–62. Washington, D.C.: Smithsonian Institution.

Arnold, Jeanne E. 1992. Complex Hunter-Gatherer-Fishers of Prehistoric California: Chiefs, Specialists, and Maritime Adaptations of the Channel Islands. *American Antiquity* 57:60–84.

———. 1993. Labor and the Rise of Complex Hunter-Gatherers. *Journal of Anthropological Archaeology* 12:75–119.

———. 2001. The Channel Islands Project: History, Objectives, and Methods. In *The Origins of a Pacific Coast Chiefdom: The Chumash of the Channel Islands*, ed. Jeanne E. Arnold, 21–52. Salt Lake City: University of Utah Press.

Axtell, James, and William Sturtevant. 1980. The Unkindest Cut: Who Invented Scalping? *William and Mary Quarterly*, 3d ser., 37:451–72.

Baker, Shane A. 1990. *Rattlesnake Ruin (42Sa18434): A Case of Violent Death and Perimortem Mutilation in the Anasazi Culture of San Juan County, Utah.* Master's thesis, Department of Anthropology, Brigham Young University.

Bamforth, Douglas B. 1994. Indigenous People, Indigenous Violence: Precontact Warfare on the North American Great Plains. *Man* 29:95–115.

———. 2001. Radiocarbon Calibration, Tree Rings, Climate, and the Course of War in the Middle Missouri. Paper presented at the 66th Annual Meeting of the Society for American Archaeology, New Orleans.

Bancroft, Herbert Howe. 1886. *History of California.* Vol. 3: *1825–1840.* San Francisco: History Company.

Barabási, Albert-Laszló. 2002. *Linked: The New Science of Networks.* Cambridge: Perseus Publishing.

Barrow, John, ed. 1852. *The Geography of Hudson's Bay: Being the Remarks of Captain W. Coats, in Many Voyages to That Locality, Between the Years 1727 and 1751.* London: Hakluyt Society.

Beckerman, S. 2000. *Warfare and Social Institutions: Some Ethnographic Examples.* 50th International Congress of Americanists, Warsaw.

Beechey, Frederick William. 1831. *Narrative of a Voyage to the Pacific and Bering's Strait to Co-operate with the Polar Expeditions; Performed in His Majesty's Ship "Blossom" . . . in the years 1825, 26, 27, 28.* 2 vols. London: Colburn and Bently.

Belcher, Edward. 1843. *Narrative of a Voyage Round the World Performed in Her Majesty's Ship* Sulphur *during the Years 1836–1842.* London: Henry Colburn.

Benedict, Ruth. 1934. *Patterns of Culture.* New York: Mentor Books.

———. 1989. *Patterns of Culture.* New York: Houghton Mifflin.

Benson, Arlene, ed. 1997. *The Noontide Sun: The Field Journals of the Reverend Stephen Bowers, Pioneer California Archaeologist.* Menlo Park, Calif.: Ballena Press.

Beresford, William, and George Dixon. 1968. *A Voyage Round the World: But More Particularly to the North-West Coast of America.* Amsterdam: N. Israel.

Beverley, Robert. 1947. *The History and Present State of Virginia.* Chapel Hill: University of North Carolina Press.

Billman, Brian R., Patricia M. Lambert, and Banks L. Leonard. 2000. Cannibalism, Warfare, and Drought in the Mesa Verde Region during the 12th Century A.D. *American Antiquity* 65:145–78.

Biolsi, Thomas, and Larry Zimmerman. 1997. *Indians and Anthropologists: Vine Deloria and the Critique of Anthropology.* Tucson: University of Arizona Press.

Bird, Louis. 1999a. Oral history told by Louis Bird. Title: 0083. Our Voices—Stories. Bird Number: 2061. Recorder: Louis Bird (date recorded: October 18, 1999). Transcriber: Amelia LaTouche (date transcribed: February 18, 2003). Our Voices website: www.ourvoices.ca.

———. 1999b. Oral history told by Louis Bird. Title: 0093. Our Voices—Oral History of Cree. Bird Number: None. Recorder: Louis Bird (date recorded: June 30, 1999). Transcriber: Tamara Robinson (date transcribed: February 15, 2003). Our Voices website: www.ourvoices.ca.

———. 2001. Oral history told by Louis Bird. Title: 0014. Our Voices—Guns and Bows. Bird Number: 200402. Recorder: Louis Bird (date recorded: April 20, 2001). Transcriber: Roland Bohr (date transcribed: June 2001). Our Voices website: www.ourvoices.ca.

Bishop, Charles A. 1972. Demography, Ecology and Trade among the Northern Ojibwa and Swampy Cree. *Western Canadian Journal of Anthropology* 3 (1): 58–71.

———. 1975a. Ojibwa, Cree, and the Hudson's Bay Company in Northern Ontario: Culture and Conflict in the Eighteenth Century. In *Western Canada Past and*

Present, ed. Anthony W. Rasporich, 150–62. Calgary: McClelland and Stewart West.

———. 1975b. Northern Ojibwa Cannibalism and Windigo Psychosis. In *Psychological Anthropology*, ed. Thomas R. Williams, 237–48. The Hague: Mouton.

———. 1984. The First Century: Adaptive Changes among the Western James Bay Cree between the Early Seventeenth and Early Eighteenth Centuries. In *The Subarctic Fur Trade: Native Social and Economic Adaptations*, ed. Shepard Krech III, 21–53. Vancouver: University of British Columbia Press.

———. 1998. The Politics of Property among Northern Algonquians. In *Property in Economic Context*, ed. Robert C. Hunt and Antonio Gilman, 247–67. Monographs in Economic Anthropology 14. Lanham, Md.: University Press of America.

———. 2002. Northern Ojibwa Emergence: The Migration. In *Papers of the Thirty-Third Algonquian Conference*, ed. H. C. Wolfart, 13–109. Winnipeg: University of Manitoba Press.

Bishop, Charles A., and Shepard Krech III. 1980. Matriorganization: The Basis of Aboriginal Subarctic Social Organization. *Arctic Anthropology* 17 (2): 34–45.

Black, Glenn A. 1967. *Angel Site: An Archaeological, Historical, and Ethnological Study*. 2 vols. Indianapolis: Indiana Historical Society.

Blackburn, Thomas C., ed. 1975. *December's Child: A Book of Chumash Oral Narratives*, collected by John P. Harrington. Berkeley: University of California Press.

Blakely, Robert L., and David S. Matthews. 1990. Bioarchaeological Evidence for a Spanish-Native American Conflict in the Sixteenth Century Southeast. *American Antiquity* 55:718–44.

Blakeslee, Donald J. 1994. The Archaeological Context of Human Skeletons in the Northern and Central Plains. In *Skeletal Biology in the Great Plains: Migration, Warfare, Health, and Subsistence*, ed. Douglas W. Owsley and Richard L. Jantz, 9–32. Washington, D.C.: Smithsonian Institution Press.

Blick, Jeffrey. 1988. Genocidal Warfare in Tribal Societies as a Result of European-Induced Culture Conflict. *Man* 23:654–70.

Blitz, John H. 1988. Adoption of the Bow in Prehistoric North America. *North American Archaeologist* 9:123–45.

Boas, Franz. 1966. *Kwakiutl Ethnography*, ed. Helen Codere. Chicago: University of Chicago Press.

Boas, Franz, and George Hunt. 1897. The Social Organization and the Secret Societies of the Kwakiutl Indians. In *Annual Report of the National Museum for 1895*. Washington, D.C.: Government Printing Office.

Bockstoce, John R., ed. 1988. *The Journal of Rochfort Maguire, 1852–1854: Two Years at Point Barrow, Alaska, Aboard HMS Plover in the Search for Sir John Franklin*. 2 vols. 2nd series, nos. 169 and 170. London: Hakluyt Society.

Bolscher, Marianne. 1982. *The Potlatch in Anthropological Theory: A Re-evaluation of Certain Ethnographic Data and Theoretical Approaches*. Nortorf, Germany: Volkerkundliche Arbeitsgemeinschaft.

Bolton, Herbert Eugene, ed. 1916. *Spanish Explorations in the Southwest, 1542–1706*. New York: Scribner's.

———. 1987. *The Hasinais: Southern Caddoans as Seen by the Earliest Europeans*. Norman: University of Oklahoma Press.

Borica, Diego de. 1795. Sobre una escaramuza con los gentiles. [Letter from Governor Borica to Comandante Goicoechea, Nov. 2, 1795, Monterey.] Provincial Records 4:35–36. California Archives (23:310–11), Bancroft Library, Berkeley.

———. 1796. Castigo y conversión de indios. [Letter from Governor Borica to Comandante Goicoechea.] Provincial Records 4:55–56. California Archives (23:331–32), Bancroft Library, Berkeley.

Bovee, Dana L., and Douglas W. Owsley. 1994. Evidence of Warfare at the Heerwald Site. In *Skeletal Biology in the Great Plains: Migration, Warfare, Health, and Subsistence*, ed. Douglas W. Owsley and Richard L. Jantz, 355–62. Washington, D.C.: Smithsonian Institution Press.

Bowers, Stephen. 1897. The Santa Barbara Indians. Unpublished manuscript, Southwest Museum, Los Angeles.

Boyd, Robert T. 1990. Demographic History, 1774–1874. In *Handbook of North American Indians*. Vol. 7: *Northwest Coast*, ed. Wayne Suttles, 135–48. Washington, D.C.: Smithsonian Institution.

———. 1996. *People of the Dalles, the Indians of Wascopam Mission: A Historical Ethnography Based on the Papers of the Methodist Missionaries*. Lincoln: University of Nebraska Press.

———. 1999. *The Coming of the Spirit of Pestilence*. Vancouver: UBC Press.

Bracken, Christopher. 1997. *The Potlatch Papers: A Colonial Case History*. Chicago: University of Chicago Press.

Bradley, Bruce A. 1992. Excavations at Sand Canyon Pueblo. In *The Sand Canyon Archaeological Project: A Progress Report*, ed. William D. Lipe, 79–97. Occasional Papers, no. 2. Cortez, Colo.: Crow Canyon Archaeological Center.

Brain, Jeffrey P., and Philip Phillips. 1996. *Shell Gorgets: Styles of the Late Prehistoric and Protohistoric Southeast*. Cambridge, Mass.: Peabody Museum Press.

Brandão, José António. 1997. *"Your Fyre Shall Burn No More": Iroquois Policy toward New France and Its Native Allies to 1701*. Lincoln: University of Nebraska Press.

Brehm, H. C. 1981. *The History of the Duck River Cache*. Miscellaneous Paper no. 6. Knoxville: Tennessee Anthropological Association.

Bridges, Patricia S., Keith P. Jacobi, and Mary L. Powell. 2000. Warfare-Related Trauma in the Late Prehistory of Alabama. In *Bioarchaeological Studies of Life in the Age of Agriculture: A View from the Southeast*, ed. Patricia M. Lambert, 35–62. Tuscaloosa: University of Alabama Press.

Brightman, Robert. 1993. *Grateful Prey: Rock Cree Human-Animal Relationships*. Berkeley: University of California Press.

Brooks, James F. 2002. Violence, Exchange, and Renewal in the American Southwest. *Ethnohistory* 49:205–18.

Brooks, Robert L. 1994a. Southern Plains Cultural Complexes. In *Skeletal Biology in the Great Plains: Migration, Warfare, Health, and Subsistence*, ed. Douglas W. Owsley and Richard L. Jantz, 33–50. Washington, D.C.: Smithsonian Institution Press.

———. 1994b. Women's Roles in Plains Indian Warfare. In *Skeletal Biology in the Great Plains: Migration, Warfare, Health, and Subsistence*, ed. Douglas W. Owsley and Richard L. Jantz, 317–24. Washington, D.C.: Smithsonian Institution Press.

Brower, Charles David. n.d. The Northernmost American: An Autobiography. Unpublished manuscript. Stefansson Collection. Dartmouth College Library, Hanover, N.H.

Brown, Alan K. 1967. *The Aboriginal Population of the Santa Barbara Channel*. Reports of the University of California Archaeological Survey no. 69. Berkeley.

Brown, James A. 1975. Spiro Art and Its Mortuary Contexts. In *Death and the Afterlife in Pre-Columbian America*, ed. Elizabeth P. Benson, 1–32. Washington, D.C.: Dumbarton Oaks.

———. 1985. The Mississippian Period. In *Ancient Art of the American Woodland Indians*, ed. Andrea P. A. Belloli, 93–146. New York: Harry N. Abrams.

———. 2001. Human Figures and the Southeastern Ancestor Shrine. In *Fleeting Identities: Perishable Material Culture in Archaeological Research*, ed. Penelope B. Drooker, 76–93. Center for Archaeological Investigations, Occasional Paper no. 28. Carbondale: Southern Illinois University.

Brown, James A., and Robert F. Sasso. 2001. Prelude to History on the Eastern Prairies. In *Societies in Eclipse: Archaeology of the Eastern Woodland Indians, A.D. 1400–1700*, ed. David S. Brose, C. Wesley Cowan, and Robert C. Mainfort Jr., 205–28. Washington, D.C.: Smithsonian Institution Press.

Brown, Jennifer S. H., and Robert Brightman. 1988. *"The Orders of the Dreamed": George Nelson on Cree and Northern Ojibwa Religion and Myth*. Winnipeg: University of Manitoba Press.

Bullock, Peter Y. 1998. Does the Reality of Anasazi Violence Prove the Myth of Anasazi Cannibalism? In *Deciphering Anasazi Violence*, ed. Peter Y. Bullock, 35–51. Santa Fe, N.Mex.: HRM Books.

Bunzel, Ruth L. 1932. Zuni Ritual Poetry. *47th Annual Report of the Bureau of American Ethnology, 1929–1930*, 611–835. Washington, D.C.: Government Printing Office.

Burch, Ernest S., Jr. 1974. Eskimo Warfare in Northwest Alaska. *Anthropological Papers of the University of Alaska* 16 (2): 1–14.

———. 1988. War and Trade. In *Crossroads of Continents: Cultures of Siberia and Alaska*, ed. William W. Fitzhugh and Aron Crowell, 227–40. Washington, D.C.: Smithsonian Institution.

———. 1991. From Skeptic to Believer: The Making of an Oral Historian. *Alaska History* 6 (1): 1–16.

———. 1998a. Boundaries and Borders in Early Contact North-Central Alaska. *Arctic Anthropology* 35 (2): 19–48.

———. 1998b. *The Iñupiaq Eskimo Nations of Northwest Alaska*. Fairbanks: University of Alaska Press.

———. 2003. *The Cultural and Natural Heritage of Northwest Alaska*. Vol. 6: *The Organization of National Life*. Report prepared for NANA Museum of the Arctic (Kotzebue, Ala.), and the United States National Park Service (Anchorage, Ala.).

———. 2005. *Alliance and Conflict: The World System of the Iñupiaq Eskimos*. Lincoln: University of Nebraska Press.

Burch, Ernest S., Jr., Eliza Jones, Hannah P. Loon, and Lawrence Kaplan. 1999. The Ethnogenesis of the Kuuvaum Kaṇiaġmiut. *Ethnohistory* 46(2): 291–327.

Burch, Ernest S., Jr., and Craig W. Mishler. 1995. The Di'hąįį Gwich'in: Mystery People of Northern Alaska. *Arctic Anthropology* 32 (1): 147–72.

Burger, Richard L. 1988. Unity and Heterogeneity within the Chavin Horizon. In *Peruvian Prehistory*, ed. Richard W. Keatinge, 99–144. Cambridge, U.K.: Cambridge University Press.

Cabrillo, Juan Rodríguez. [1542–43] 1929. Translation [Voyage of Cabrillo]. In *Spanish Voyages to the Northwest Coast in the Sixteenth Century*, ed. Henry R. Wagner, 79–93. San Francisco: California Historical Society.

Carman, John. 1997a. Introduction: Approaches to Violence. In *Material Harm: Archaeological Studies of War and Violence*, ed. John Carman, 1–23. Glasgow, U.K.: Cruithne Press.

———. 1997b. Giving Archaeology a Moral Voice. In *Material Harm: Archaeological Studies of War and Violence*, ed. John Carman, 220–39. Glasgow, U.K.: Cruithne Press.

Carneiro, Robert L. 1970. A Theory of the Origin of the State. *Science* 169:234–43.

———. 1981. The Chiefdom: Precursor of the State. In *The Transition to Statehood in the New World*, ed. Grant D. Jones and Robert R. Krautz, 37–79. Cambridge, U.K.: Cambridge University Press.

———. 1994. War and Peace: Alternating Realities in Human History. In *Studying War: Anthropological Perspectives*, ed. Stephen P. Reyna and R. E. Downs, 3–27. Langhorne, Penn.: Gordon and Breach.

———. 1998. What Happened at the Flashpoint? Conjectures on Chiefdom Formation at the Very Moment of Conception. In *Chiefdoms and Chieftaincy in the America*, ed. Elsa M. Redmond, 18–42. Gainesville: University Press of Florida.

Carr, Christopher. 2005. Rethinking Interregional Hopewellian "Interaction." In *Gathering Hopewell: Society, Ritual, and Ritual Interaction*, ed. Christopher Carr and D. Troy Case, 575–623. New York: Kluwer.

Castañeda, Pedro. 1966. *The Journey of Coronado*. Ann Arbor, Mich.: University Microfilms.

Chacon, Richard, Yamilette Chacon, and Angel Guandinago. 2007. Blood for the Earth: The Inti Raimi Festival among the Cotacachi and Otavalo Indians of Highland Ecuador. In *Problems in Paradise: Warfare among the Indigenous Peoples of Latin America*, ed. Richard J. Chacon and Rubén G. Mendoza. Tucson: University of Arizona Press. Forthcoming.

Chacon, Richard J., and David H. Dye. 2007. *The Taking and Displaying of Human Body Parts as Trophies by Amerindians*. New York: Springer Press. Forthcoming.

Chagnon, Napoleon A. 1988. Life Histories, Blood Revenge, and Warfare in a Tribal Population. *Science* 239:985–92.

———. 1992. *Yanomamö*. 4th ed. Fort Worth, Tex.: Harcourt Brace Jovanovich.

Chappell, Edward. 1817. *Narrative of a Voyage to Hudson's Bay in His Majesty's Ship Rosamond*. London: Printed for J. Mawman, Ludgate Street.

Chatters, James C. 1989. Pacifism and the Organization of Conflict on the Plateau of Northwestern America. In *Cultures in Conflict: Current Archaeological Perspectives*, ed. Diana Claire Tkaczuk and Brian C. Vivian, 241–52. Calgary: University of Calgary Archaeological Association.

Childress, Mitchell R., and Camille Wharey. 1996. Unit 4 Mound Excavations at the Chucalissa Site, 1960–1970. In *Mounds, Embankments, and Ceremonialism in the*

Mid-South, ed. Robert C. Mainfort and Richard Walling, 64–77. Research Series, no. 46. Fayetteville: Arkansas Archeological Survey.

Clark, Annette McFadyen. 1974. *Koyukuk River Culture*. Canadian Ethnology Service Paper, no. 18. Ottawa: National Museums of Canada.

————. 1977. Trade at the Cross Roads. In *Problems in the Prehistory of the North American Subarctic: The Athapaskan Question*, ed. J. W. Helmer, S. Van Dyke, and F. J. Kense, 130–34. Calgary: University of Calgary Archaeological Association.

Clark, Annette McFadyen, and Donald W. Clark. 1976. Koyukuk Indian–Kobuk Eskimo Interaction. In *Contributions to Anthropology: The Interior Peoples of Northern Alaska*, ed. Edwin S. Hall Jr., 193–220. Archaeological Survey of Canada Paper no. 49. Ottawa: National Museum of Man.

Clark, Brenda L. 1979. Thule Occupation of Western Hudson Bay. In *Thule Eskimo Culture: An Anthropological Perspective*, ed. Allen P. McCartney, 89–109. Mercury Series, Archaeological Survey of Canada Paper no. 88. Ottawa: National Museum of Man.

Clark, Donald W. 1981. Prehistory of the Western Subarctic. In *Handbook of North American Indians*. Vol. 6: *Subarctic*, ed. June Helm, 107–29. Washington, D.C.: Smithsonian Institution.

Clayton, Daniel W. *2000. Islands of Truth: The Imperial Fashioning of Vancouver Island*. Vancouver: UBC Press.

Codere, Helen. 1950. *Fighting with Property: A Study of Kwakiutl Potlatching and Warfare, 1792–1930*. Glückstadt, Germany: J. J. Agstin.

Cojti Cuxil, Demetrio. 1995. *Configuracion del pensamiento politico del Pueblo Maya (2da. Parte)*. Cuidad de Guatemala: Editorial Cholsamaj.

Cojti Ren, A. Vexnim. 2004. *Maya Archaeology and the Political and Cultural Identity of Contemporary Maya in Guatemala*. http://www.mayainfo.org.

Cole, Douglas, and Ira Chaikin. 1990. *An Iron Hand upon the People: The Law against the Potlatch on the Northwest Coast*. Vancouver/Toronto: Douglas and McIntyre.

Cole, Douglas, and David Darling. 1990. History of the Early Period. In *Handbook of North American Indians*. Vol. 7: *Northwest Coast*, ed. Wayne Suttles, 119–34. Washington, D.C.: Smithsonian Institution.

Cole, Sally J. 1985. Additional Information on Basketmaker Mask or Face Representations in Rock Art of Southeastern Utah. *Southwestern Lore* 51 (1): 14–18.

————. 1989. Iconography and Symbolism in Basketmaker Rock Art. In *Rock Art of the Western Canyons*, ed. Jane S. Day, Paul D. Friedman, and Marcia J. Tate, 59–85. Cultural Resources Series, no. 28. Denver: Colorado Bureau of Land Management.

Conklin, Beth. 2003. Speaking Truth to Power. *Anthropology News* 44 (7): 5.

Conrad, Lawrence A. 1989. The Southeastern Ceremonial Complex on the Northern Middle Mississippian Frontier: Late Prehistoric Politico-Religious Systems in the Central Illinois River Valley. In *The Southeastern Ceremonial Complex: Artifacts and Analysis*, ed. Patricia Galloway, 93–113. Lincoln: University of Nebraska Press.

————. 1991. The Middle Mississippian Cultures of the Central Illinois River Valley. In *Cahokia and the Hinterlands: Middle Mississippian Cultures of the Midwest*, ed. Thomas E. Emerson and R. Barry Lewis, 119–56. Urbana: University of Illinois Press.

Cook, Sherburne F. 1976. *The Conflict between the California Indian and White Civiliza-tion.* Berkeley: University of California Press.

Cook, Sherburne F., and Woodrow Borah. 1979. Mission Registers as Sources of Vital Statistics: Eight Missions of Northern California. In *Essays in Population and History: Mexico and California,* vol. 3, 177–311. Berkeley: University of California Press.

Costansó, Miguel. [1769–70] 1983. The Miguel Costansó Journal of Portolá's Expe-dition. In *Gaspar de Portolá: Explorer and Founder of California,* by F. Boneu Companys, trans. Alan K. Brown, 159–298. Lérida, Spain: Instituto de Estudios Ilerdenses.

Cota, Pablo, and José Ignacio Guevara. 1795. Interrogatorio de reos. [Report on inter-rogation of prisoners, October 26, 1795, Santa Bárbara.] Provincial State Papers 14:37. California Archives (8:38), Bancroft Library, Berkeley.

Cottier, John W., and Michael D. Southard. 1977. An Introduction to the Archaeology of Towosahgy State Archaeological Site. *Missouri Archaeologist* 38:230–71.

Coupland, Gary. 1989. Warfare and Social Complexity on the Northwest Coast. In *Cultures in Conflict: Current Archaeological Perspectives, Proceedings of the Twenti-eth Annual Conference of the Archaeological Association of the University of Calgary,* ed. Diana Claire Tkaczuk and Brian C. Vivan, 205–14. Calgary: University of Calgary Archaeological Association.

Courville, C. B. 1952. Cranial Injuries among the Early Indians of California. *Los Ange-les Neurological Society* 17 (4): 137–62.

Crespí, Juan. [1769–70] 2001. *A Description of Distant Roads: Original Journals of the First Expedition into California, 1769–1770,* ed. Alan K. Brown. San Diego, Calif.: San Diego State University Press.

Cumming, S. J. C. 1928. HBC Posts, Keewatin District: No. 11—Island Lake Post. *The Beaver; Outfit 259,* 3:16–117.

Curtis, Edward S. 1915. *The North American Indian: The Indians of the United States, the Dominion of Canada and Alaska,* vol. 10. New York: Johnson Reprint.

Cybulski, Jerome S. 1990. Human Biology. In *Handbook of North American Indians.* Vol. 7: *Northwest Coast, ed. Wayne Suttles,* 52–59. Washington, D.C.: Smithson-ian Institution.

———. 1992. *A Greenville Burial Ground: Human Remains and Mortuary Elements in British Columbia Coast Prehistory.* Mercury Series Paper, no. 146. Hill, Quebec: Archaeological Survey of Canada, Canadian Museum of Civilization.

———. 1994. Culture Change, Demographic History, and Health and Disease on the Northwest Coast. In *In the Wake of Contact: Biological Responses to Conquest,* ed. Clark Spencer Larsen and George R. Milner, 75–85. New York: Wiley-Liss.

———. 1999. Trauma and Warfare at Prince Rupert Harbour. *Midden* 31:5–7.

Dalan, Rinita A., George R. Holley, William I. Woods, Harold W. Watters Jr., and John A. Koepke. 2003. *Envisioning Cahokia: A Landscape Perspective.* DeKalb: North-ern Illinois University Press.

Darling, J. Andrew. 1998. Mass Inhumation and the Execution of Witches in the American Southwest. *American Anthropologist* 100:732–52.

Day, B. Grove. 1964. *Coronado's Quest.* Berkeley: University of California Press.

DeBoer, Warren R. 2004. Little Bighorn on the Scioto: The Rocky Mountain Connection to Ohio Hopewell. *American Antiquity* 69:85–107.

Deloria, Vine. 1969. *Custer Died for Your Sins: An Indian Manifesto*. New York: Avon.

———. 1995. *Red Earth, White Lies: Native Americans and the Myth of Scientific Fact*. New York: Scribner.

DePratter, Chester B. 1983. *Late Prehistoric and Early Historic Chiefdoms in the Southeastern United States*. Ph.D. dissertation, University of Georgia, Athens.

———. 1991. *Late Prehistoric and Early Historic Chiefdoms in the Southeastern United States*. New York: Garland.

Dice, Michael H. 1993. *Disarticulated Human Remains from Reach III of the Towaoc Canal, Ute Mountain Ute Reservation, Montezuma County, Colorado*. Four Corners Archaeological Project Report no. 22. Yellow Jacket, Colo.: Complete Archaeological Consultants.

DiPeso, Charles C. 1974. *Casas Grandes: A Fallen Trading Center of the Gran Chichimeca*. Amerind Foundation Publications, no. 9. Flagstaff, Ariz.: Northland Press.

Divale, William, 1984. *Matrilocal Residence in Pre-Literate Society*. Ann Arbor: UMI Research Press.

Donald, Leland. 1997. *Aboriginal Slavery on the Northwest Coast of North America*. Berkeley: University of California Press.

Donald, Leland, and Donald H. Mitchell. 1975. Some Correlates of Local Group Rank among the Southern Kwakiutl. *Ethnology* 14:325–46.

Dongoske, Kurt, Mark Aldenderfer, and Karen Doehner. 2000 *Working Together: Native Americans and Archaeologists*. Washington, D.C.: Society for American Archaeology.

Dongoske, Kurt E., Debra L. Martin, and T. J. Ferguson. 2000. Critique of the Claim of Cannibalism at Cowboy Wash. *American Antiquity* 65:179–90.

Dorsey, George A., and Henry R. Voth. 1901. The Oraibi Soyal Ceremony. *The Field Museum of Natural History Publications* 55, Anthropological Series 3 (1): 5–59. Chicago.

Dozier, Edward P. 1957. The Hopi and the Tewa. *Scientific American* 196:127ff.

———. 1966. *Hano: A Tewa Indian Community in Arizona*. New York: Holt, Rinehart and Winston.

Driver, Harold S. 1961. *Indians of North America*. Chicago: University of Chicago Press.

Drucker, Philip, and Robert Heizer. 1967. *To Make My Name Good: A Reexamination of the Southern Kwakiutl Potlatch*. Berkeley: University of California Press.

Duff, Wilson. 1997. *The Indian History of British Columbia: The Impact of the White Man*. Victoria: Royal British Columbia Museum.

Duggan, Marie C. 2000. *Market and Church on the Mexican Frontier: Alta California, 1769–1832*. Ph.D. dissertation, New School University.

Duncan, David. 1996. *Hernando de Soto: A Savage Quest in the Americas*. Norman: University of Oklahoma Press.

Dye, David H. 1990. Warfare in the Sixteenth-Century Southeast: The de Soto Expedition in the Interior. In *Columbian Consequences*, vol. 2, ed. David H. Thomas, 211–22. Washington, D.C.: Smithsonian Institution Press.

———. 1993. Reconstruction of the de Soto Expedition Route in Arkansas: The Mississippi Alluvial Plain. In *The Expedition of Hernando de Soto West of the Mississippi, 1541–1543: Proceedings of the de Soto Symposia, 1988 and 1990*, ed. Gloria A. Young and Michael P. Hoffman, 36–57. Fayetteville: University of Arkansas Press.

———. 1994. The Art of War in the Sixteenth-Century Central Mississippi Valley. In *Perspectives on the Southeast: Linguistics, Archaeology, and Ethnohistory*, ed. Patricia B. Kwachka, 44–60. Athens: University of Georgia Press.

———. 1995. Feasting with the Enemy: Mississippian Warfare and Prestige-Goods Circulation. In *Native American Interactions: Multiscalar Analyses and Interpretations in the Eastern Woodlands*, ed. Michael S. Nassaney and Kenneth E. Sassaman, 289–316. Knoxville: University of Tennessee Press.

———. 1996. Riverine Adaptation in the Midsouth. In *Of Caves and Shell Mounds*, ed. Kenneth C. Carstens and Patty J. Watson, 140–58. Tuscaloosa: University of Alabama Press.

———. 2002a. Warfare in the Protohistoric Southeast: 1500–1700. In *Between Contacts and Colonies: Archaeological Perspectives on the Protohistoric Southeast*, ed. Cameron B. Wesson and Mark A. Rees, 126–41. Tuscaloosa: University of Alabama Press.

———. 2002b. The 1936 University of Tennessee WPA-TVA Excavations at the Link Farm Site (40HS6), Humphreys County, Tennessee. Paper presented at the 59th Annual Meeting of the Southeastern Archaeological Conference, Biloxi.

———. 2004. Art, Ritual, and Chiefly Warfare in the Mississippian World. In *Hero, Hawk, and Open Hand*, ed. Richard F. Townsend and Robert V. Sharp, 190–205. Chicago: Art Institute of Chicago.

———. 2006. *Warfare in the Eastern Woodlands: A Cultural Evolutionary Perspective.* Walnut Creek, Calif.: AltaMira Press.

———. 2007. Scalplocks, Forearms, and Severed Hands: Late Prehistoric Trophy-Taking Behavior in the Midcontinent. *Midcontinental Journal of Archaeology.* Forthcoming.

Earle, Timothy. 1997. *How Chiefs Come to Power: The Political Economy in Prehistory.* Stanford, Calif.: Stanford University Press.

Edgerton, Robert. 1992. *Sick Societies.* New York: Free Press.

Ellis, Florence Hawley. 1951. Patterns of Aggression and the War Cult in Southwestern Pueblos. *Southwestern Journal of Anthropology* 7 (2): 177–201.

———. 1979. Isleta Pueblo. *Handbook of the North American Indians.* Vol. 9: *Southwest*, ed. Alfonso Ortiz, 351–65. Washington, D.C.: Smithsonian Institution Press.

Ellis, Henry. [1748] 1968. *An Account of a Voyage for the Discovery of a North-West Passage by Hudson's Streights, to the Western and Southern Ocean of America.* 2 vols. New York: Johnson Reprint.

Ember, Carol R. 1975. Residential Variation among Hunter-Gatherers. *Behavior Science Research* 10:199–227.

———. 1978. Myths about Hunter-Gatherers. *Ethnology* 17(4): 439–48.

Ember, Carol R., and Melvin Ember. 1992. Resource Unpredictability, Mistrust, and War. *Journal of Conflict Resolution* 36 (2): 242–62.

Ember, Melvin, and Carol R. Ember. 1994a. Cross-Cultural Studies of War and Peace: Recent Achievements and Future Possibilities. In *Studying War: Anthropologi-*

cal Perspectives, ed. Stephen P. Reyna and R. E. Downs, 185–208. Amsterdam: Gordon and Breach.

———. 1994b. War, Socialization, and Interpersonal Violence. *Journal of Conflict Resolution* 38 (4): 620–46.

———. 1997. Violence in the Ethnographic Record: Results of Cross-Cultural Research on War and Aggression. In *Troubled Times: Violence and Warfare in the Past*, ed. Debra L. Martin and David W. Frayer, 1–20. Langhorne, Penn.: Gordon and Breach.

Emerson, Thomas E. 1982. *Mississippian Stone Images in Illinois*. Circular no. 6. Urbana: Illinois Archaeological Survey.

———. 1995. *Settlement, Symbolism, and Hegemony in the Cahokian Countryside*. Ph.D. dissertation, University of Wisconsin–Madison. University Microfilms, Ann Arbor.

———. 1997. *Cahokia and the Archaeology of Power*. Tuscaloosa: University of Alabama Press.

———. 1999. The Langford Tradition and the Process of Tribalization on the Middle Mississippian Borders. *Midcontinental Journal of Archaeology* 24 (1): 3–56.

———. 2002. An Introduction to Cahokia 2002: Diversity, Complexity, and History. *Midcontinental Journal of Archaeology* 27 (2): 127–48.

Emerson, Thomas E., and James A. Brown. 1992. The Late Prehistory and Protohistory of Illinois. In *Calumet and Fleur-de-Lys: Archaeology of Indian and French Contact in the Midcontinent*, ed. John A. Walthall and Thomas E. Emerson, 77–128. Washington, D.C.: Smithsonian Institution Press.

Emerson, Thomas E., and Kristin Hedman. 1999. Langford Tradition Mortuary Patterns at the Material Services Quarry Site in the Upper Illinois River Valley. Paper presented at the 45th Midwest Archaeological Conference, East Lansing, Michigan.

Emerson, Thomas E., Randall E. Hughes, Mary R. Hynes, and Sarah U. Wisseman. 2003. The Sourcing and Interpretation of Cahokia-Style Figurines in the Trans-Mississippi South and Southeast. *American Antiquity* 68:287–313.

Emerson, Thomas E., and R. Barry Lewis, eds. 1991. *Cahokia and the Hinterlands: Middle Mississippian Cultures of the Midwest*. Urbana: University of Illinois Press.

Emerson, Thomas E., Dale L. McElrath, and Andrew C. Fortier, eds. 2000. *Late Woodland Societies: Tradition and Transformation across the Midcontinent*. Lincoln: University of Nebraska Press.

Emerson, Thomas E., and Anne Titelbaum. 2000. The Des Plaines Complex and the Late Woodland Stage in Northern Illinois. In *Late Woodland Societies: Tradition and Transformation in the Midcontinent*, ed. Thomas E. Emerson, Dale L. McElrath, and Andrew C. Fortier, 413–28. Lincoln: University of Nebraska Press.

Engelbrecht, W. E. 1987. Factors Maintaining Low Population Density among the Prehistoric New York Iroquois. *American Antiquity* 52:13–27.

Engelhardt, Zephyrin. 1932. *Mission Santa Inés*. Santa Barbara, Calif.: Mission Santa Bárbara.

Esarey, Duane, and Sharron K. Santure. 1990. The Morton Site Oneota Component and the Bold Counselor Phase. In *Archaeological Investigations at the Morton Vil-*

lage and Norris Farms 36 Cemetery, ed. Sharron K. Santure, Alan D. Harn, and Duane Esarey, 162–66. Reports of Investigations, no. 45. Springfield: Illinois State Museum.

Ewers, John. 1975. Intertribal Warfare as the Precursor of Indian-White Warfare on the Northern Great Plains. *Western Historical Quarterly* 6:397–410.

Fagan, Brian. 2000. *The Little Ice Age: How Climate Made History, 1300–1850.* New York: Basic Books.

Fages, Pedro. [1775] 1937. *A Historical, Political, and Natural Description of California*, ed. Herbert I. Priestley. Berkeley: University of California Press.

———. 1783. [Letter from Governor Fages to the Inspector General, May 15, 1783.] Provincial Records 3:98. California Archives (23:100), Bancroft Library, Berkeley.

Farmer, J. D. 1997. Iconographic Evidence of Basketmaker Warfare and Human Sacrifice: A Contextual Approach to Early Anasazi Art. *Kiva* 62 (4): 391–420.

Ferguson, R. Brian. 1984. A Reexamination of the Causes of Northwest Coast Warfare. In *Warfare, Culture, and Environment*, ed. R. Brian Ferguson, 267–328. Orlando, Fla.: Academic Press.

———, ed. 1984. *Warfare, Culture, and Environment.* Orlando, Fla.: Academic Press.

———. 1990. Explaining War. In *The Anthropology of War*, ed. Jonathan Haas, 26–55. New York: Cambridge University Press.

———. 1992. Tribal Warfare. *Scientific American* 266:108–13.

Ferguson, R. Brian, and Leslie E. Farragher. 1988. *The Anthropology of War: A Bibliography.* Occasional Papers no. 1. New York: Harry Frank Guggenheim Foundation.

Ferguson, R. Brian, and Neil Whitehead. 1992. The Violent Edge of Empire. In *War in the Tribal Zone: Expanding States and Indigenous Warfare*, ed. R. Ferguson and N. Whitehead, 1–30. Santa Fe, N.Mex.: School of American Research Press.

Fewkes, Jesse Walter. 1897. Tusayan Katcinas. *Fifteenth Annual Report of the Bureau of American Ethnology*, 245–313. Washington, D.C.: Government Printing Office.

Fienup-Riordan, Ann. 1984. Regional Groupings on the Yukon-Kuskokwim Delta. *Études/Inuit Studies* 8 (supplementary issue): 63–93.

———, ed. 1988. *The Yup'ik Eskimos, As Described in the Travel Journals and Ethnographic Accounts of John and Edith Kilbuck, Who Served with the Alaska Mission of the Moravian Church.* Kingston, Ontario: Limestone Press.

———. 1989. Eskimo War and Peace. In *Keynote Speeches from the Sixth Inuit Studies Conference, Copenhagen, October 1988*, ed. Jens Dahl, 90–107. Institute for Eskimologi 14. Copenhagen: Københavns Universitet.

———. 1990. Yup'ik Warfare and the Myth of the Peaceful Eskimo. In *Eskimo Essays: Yup'ik Lives and How We See Them*, ed. Ann Fienup-Riordan, 146–66. New Brunswick, N.J.: Rutgers University Press.

———. 1994. Eskimo War and Peace. In *Anthropology of the North Pacific Rim*, ed. William W. Fitzhugh and Valérie Chaussonnet, 321–35. Washington, D.C.: Smithsonian Institution Press.

———. n.d. The Past as Prologue: Regional Groupings and the Cultural Significance of Harvest Disruption on the Yukon-Kuskokwim Delta. Unpublished manuscript; copy in possession of the author.

Fladmark, Knut R., Kenneth M. Ames, and Patricia D. Sutherland. 1990. Prehistory of the Northern Coast of British Columbia. In *Handbook of North American Indians*. Vol. 7: *Northwest Coast*, ed. Wayne Suttles, 229–39. Washington, D.C.: Smithsonian Institution.

Forde, C. Daryll. 1931. Ethnography of the Yuma Indians. *University of California Publications in American Archaeology and Ethnology* 28 (4): 83–278.

Fossett, Renée. 2001. *In Order to Live Untroubled: Inuit of the Central Arctic, 1550 to 1940*. Winnipeg: University of Manitoba Press.

Francis, Daniel. 1979. Les Relations entre Indiens et Inuit dans L'est de la baie d'Hudson, 1700–1840. *Études/Inuit Studies* 3 (2): 73–83.

Francis, Daniel, and Toby Morantz. 1983. *Partners in Furs: A History of the Fur Trade in Eastern James Bay, 1600–1870*. Montreal: McGill-Queen's University Press.

Frazier, Kendrick. 1999. *People of Chaco: A Canyon and Its Culture*. New York: W. W. Norton.

Fritz, Gayle J. 1990. Multiple Pathways to Farming in Precontact Eastern North America. *Journal of World Prehistory* 4:387–435.

Galois, Robert. 1994. *Kwakwaka'wakw Settlements, 1775–1920: A Geographical Analysis and Gazetteer*. Vancouver: UBC Press.

Garcilaso de la Vega, the Inca. 1993. La Florida. In *The De Soto Chronicles: The Expedition of Hernando De Soto to North America in 1539–1543*, vol. 2, ed. Lawrence A. Clayton, Vernon J. Knight Jr., and Edward C. Moore, 25–576. Tuscaloosa: University of Alabama Press.

Gat, Azar. 1999. The Pattern of Fighting in Simple, Small-Scale, Prestate Societies. *Journal of Anthropological Research* 55:563–83.

Geertz, Clifford. 1999. *A Life of Learning*. American Council of Learned Societies Occasional Paper 45. New York.

General, Paul, and Gary Warrick. 2004. The Haudenosaunee (Six Nations) and Archaeology. *Society of American Archaeology* 5 (4): 29–30.

Gibson, James R. 1992. *Otter Skins, Boston Ships, and China Goods: The Maritime Fur Trade of the Northwest Coast, 1785–1841*. Montreal: McGill-Queen's University Press.

Gibson, Jon. 1974. Aboriginal Warfare in the Protohistoric Southeast: An Alternative Perspective. *American Antiquity* 39:130–33.

Gill, George W. 1994. Skeletal Injuries of Pioneers. In *Skeletal Biology in the Great Plains: Migration, Warfare, Health, and Subsistence*, ed. Douglas W. Owsley and Richard L. Jantz, 159–72. Washington, D.C.: Smithsonian Institution Press.

Given, Brian. 1978. *A Study of European Weapons Technology as a Locus of Native Trade-Dependence Prior to the Iroquois Defeat of the Huron, 1648–52*. Master's thesis, Carleton University, Ottawa, Canada.

Glassow, Michael A. 1996. *Purisimeño Chumash Prehistory: Maritime Adaptations along the Southern California Coast*. Fort Worth, Tex.: Harcourt Brace.

Goicoechea, Felipe de. 1785. [Letter from Comandante Goicoechea to Governor Fages, June 28, 1785, Santa Bárbara.] Provincial State Papers 5:157. California Archives (3:329–30), Bancroft Library, Berkeley.

———. 1786. [Letter from Comandante Goicoechea to Governor Fages, December 19,

1786, Santa Bárbara.] Provincial State Papers 6:73. California Archives (3:331), Bancroft Library, Berkeley.

———. 1787a. [Letter from Comandante Goicoechea to Governor Fages, July 20, 1787, Santa Bárbara.] Provincial State Papers 7:91–92. California Archives (4:92–93), Bancroft Library, Berkeley.

———. 1787b. [Letter from Comandante Goicoechea to Governor Fages, August 20, 1787, Santa Bárbara.] Provincial State Papers 7:76. California Archives (4:77), Bancroft Library, Berkeley.

———. [1790a] 1978. [Correspondence with Governor Fages, September 2 and October 9, 1790, and report on interrogation of prisoners, December 14, 1790, Santa Bárbara.] Unpublished translation by Maureen Campión de Necochea from the Archivo General de la Nación 46(4). Manuscript on file at Cultural Resources Section, Los Padres National Forest, Goleta.

———. 1790b. [Letter from Comandante Goicoechea to Governor Fages, September 2, 1790, Santa Bárbara.] Provincial State Papers, Benicia Military 9:6. California Archives (15:209), Bancroft Library, Berkeley.

———. 1794. Sedición de Indios. [Letter from Comandante Goicoechea to Governor Arrillaga, September 20, 1794, Santa Bárbara.] Provincial State Papers 12:100. California Archives (7:101), Bancroft Library, Berkeley.

———. 1795. Sobre diligencias practicadas. [Letter from Comandante Goicoechea to Governor Borica, November 2, 1795, Santa Bárbara.] Provincial State Papers 14:35. California Archives (8:36), Bancroft Library, Berkeley.

———. 1796. Rancherías de Gentiles. [Report by Comandante Goicoechea to Governor Borica, March 12, 1796, Santa Bárbara.] State Papers, Missions 2:94–98. California Archives (50:229–33), Bancroft Library, Berkeley.

———. 1798. [Diary of Comandante Goicoechea forwarded to Governor Borica, October 21, 1798, Santa Bárbara.] California Mission Documents MS 403. Santa Barbara Mission Archive Library.

Goldman, Irving. 1981. *The Mouth of Heaven: An Introduction to Kwakiutl Religious Thought*. Huntington, N.Y.: Robert E. Krieger.

Gough, Barry M. 1984. *Gunboat Frontier—British Maritime Authority and Northwest Coast Indians, 1846–90*. Vancouver: UBC Press.

Grady, Diane L., Kate A. Latham, and Valerie A. Andrushko. 2001. *Archaeological Investigations at CA-SCL-674, The Rubino Site, San Jose, Santa Clara County, California*. Vol. 2: *Human Skeletal Biology of CA-SCL-674*. Archives of California Prehistory no. 50. Salinas, Calif.: Coyote Press.

Graham, Andrew. 1969. *Andrew Graham's Observations on Hudson's Bay, 1767–91*, ed. Glyndwr Williams. London: Hudson's Bay Record Society.

Grant, Campbell. 1978. Interior Chumash. In *Handbook of North American Indians*. Vol. 8: *California*, ed. Robert F. Heizer, 530–34. Washington, D.C.: Smithsonian Institution.

Greene, Jerome. 1994. *Lakota and Cheyenne: Indian Views of the Great Sioux War, 1876–1877*. Norman: University of Oklahoma Press.

Griffin, James B. 1967. Eastern North American Archaeology: A Summary. *Science* 156:175–91.

Grumet, Robert Steven. 1975. Changes in Coast Tsimshian Redistributive Activities in the Fort Simpson Region of British Columbia, 1788–1862. *Ethnohistory* 22:295–318.

Guilaine, Jean, and Jean Zammit. 2005. *The Origins of War: Violence in Prehistory*. Oxford, U.K.: Blackwell.

Guldenzopf, D. B. 1986. *The Colonial Transformation of Mohawk Iroquois Society*. Doctoral dissertation, State University of New York, Albany.

Gumerman, George J., and Murray Gell-Mann. 1994. Cultural Evolution in the Prehistoric Southwest. In *Themes in Southwest Prehistory*, ed. George J. Gumerman, 11–32. Santa Fe, N.Mex.: School of American Research Press.

Haas, Jonathan. 1990. Warfare and the Evolution of Tribal Polities in the Prehistoric Southwest. In *The Anthropology of War*, ed. Jonathan Haas, 171–89. School of American Research Book. Cambridge, U.K.: Cambridge University Press.

———. 1996. War. In *Encyclopedia of Cultural Anthropology*, vol. 4, 357–61. New York: Henry Holt.

———. 1999. The Origins of War and Ethnic Violence. In *Ancient Warfare: Archaeological Perspectives*, ed. John Carman and Anthony Harding, 11–24. Stroud, U.K.: Sutton Publishing.

———. 2001. Warfare and the Evolution of Culture. In *Archaeology at the Millennium*, ed. Gary M. Feinman and T. Douglas Price, 329–50. New York: Kluwer.

———. 2003. The Archaeology of War. *Anthropology News* 44 (5): 7.

———. 2004. Archaeology of War. *Anthropology News* 45 (1): 3.

Haas, Jonathan, and Winifred Creamer, eds. 1993. *Stress and Warfare among the Kayenta Anasazi of the Thirteenth Century A.D.* Fieldiana Anthropology, n.s., no. 21. Chicago: Field Museum of Natural History.

———. 1996. The Role of Warfare in the Pueblo III Period. In *The Prehistoric Pueblo World, A.D. 1150–1350*, ed. Michael A. Adler, 205–13. Tucson: University of Arizona Press.

———. 1997. Warfare among the Pueblos: Myth, History, and Ethnography. *Ethnohistory* 44 (2): 235–61.

Habicht-Mauche, Judith Ann. 1988. *An Analysis of Southwestern-Style Utility Ceramics from the Southern Plains in the Context of Protohistoric Plains-Pueblo Interaction*. Ph.D dissertation, Department of Anthropology, Harvard University, Cambridge, Mass.

Hale, John Rigby. 1990. *Artists and Warfare in the Renaissance*. New Haven, Conn.: Yale University Press.

Hallenbeck, Cleve. 1971. *Alvar Núñez Cabeza de Vaca: The Journey en Route of the First European to Cross the Continent of North America*. Port Washington, N.Y.: Kennikat Press.

Hally, David J. 1993. The Territorial Size of Mississippian Chiefdoms. In *Archaeology of Eastern North America: Papers in Honor of Stephen Williams*, ed. James B. Stoltman, 143–68. Archaeological Report no. 25. Jacksonville: Mississippi Department of Archives and History.

Hammond, George P., and Agapito Rey. 1953. *Don Juan de Oñate: Colonizer of New Mexico, 1595–1628*. Albuquerque: University of New Mexico Press.

———. 1966. *The Rediscovery of New Mexico, 1580–1594: The Explorations of Chamuscado,*

Espejo, Castaño de Sosa, Morlete, and Leyva de Bonilla and Humaña. Albuquerque: University of New Mexico Press.

Harrington, John P. 1914. [Notes from Luisa Ygnacio, Santa Barbara, March 11, 1914]. Chumash Ethnographic Field Notes (12 reels of microfilm), Rl. 3:73. On file, Department of Anthropology, University of California, Santa Barbara.

———. [1924] 1986. Proposal to Annotate and Publish the Relation of the Voyage of Juan Rodríguez Cabrillo. In *The Papers of John P. Harrington: Southern California/ Basin.* Ethnographic Field Notes, pt. 3, Rl. 177:3–11. National Anthropological Archives, Smithsonian Institution, Washington, D.C. Microfilm edition, Millwood, N.Y.: Kraus International Publications.

———. 1986. Chumash. In *The Papers of John P. Harrington: Southern California/Basin.* Ethnographic Field Notes, pt. 3, Rls. 1–96. National Anthropological Archives, Smithsonian Institution, Washington, D.C. Microfilm edition, Millwood, N.Y.: Kraus International Publications.

Hassler, Peter. 1992. Human Sacrifice among the Aztecs? *World Press Review* (December). http://www.elcamino.edu/Faculty/suarez/Cour/H19/WpSacrfice1.htm.

Havard, J. 1987. *Stockholm Syndrome.* Sydney: Macmillan Education Australia.

HBCA (Hudson's Bay Company Archives). 1834. B.120/e/1, Report on Millbank Sound, March 15, 1834.

———. 1849–1850. B.185/a/1. Fort Rupert Journal.

———. n.d. Cited from microfilm, National Archives of Canada, Ottawa.

Hearne, Samuel. 1958. *A Journey from Prince of Wales's Fort in Hudson's Bay to the Northern Ocean in the Years 1769, 1770, 1771, 1772,* ed. Richard Glover. Toronto: Macmillan Company of Canada.

Heath, Charles. 2004. Catawba Militarism: Ethnohistorical and Archaeological Overviews. *North Carolina Archaeology* 53:80–120.

Heidenreich, Conrad E. 1978. Huron. In *Handbook of North American Indians.* Vol. 15: *Northeast,* ed. Bruce G. Trigger, 368–88. Washington, D.C.: Smithsonian Institution.

Heizer, Robert F. 1974. *The Destruction of California Indians.* Berkeley: University of California Press.

Heizer, Robert F., and Albert B. Elsasser. 1980. *The Natural World of the California Indians.* Berkeley: University of California Press.

Henning, Dale R. 1998. The Oneota Tradition. In *Archaeology on the Great Plains,* ed. W. Raymond Wood, 345–414. Lawrence: University of Kansas Press.

Hibben, Frank C. 1975. *Kiva Art of the Anasazi.* Las Vegas: KC Publications.

Hickerson, Harold. 1965. The Virginia Deer and Intertribal Buffer Zones in the Upper Mississippi Valley. In *Man, Culture, and Animals,* ed. Anthony Leeds and Andrew P. Vayda, 43–66. Publication 78. Washington, D.C.: American Association for the Advancement of Science.

Hill, W. W. 1982. *An Ethnology of Santa Clara Pueblo, New Mexico,* ed. Charles H. Lange. Albuquerque: University of New Mexico Press.

Holley, George R. 1999. Late Prehistoric Towns in the Southeast. In *Great Towns and Regional Polities in the Prehistoric American Southwest and Southeast,* ed. Jill E. Neitzel, 23–38. Albuquerque: University of New Mexico Press.

Holliman, Sandra E., and Douglas W. Owsley. 1994. Osteology of the Fay Tolton Site: Implications for Warfare during the Initial Middle Missouri Variant. In *Skeletal Biology in the Great Plains: Migration, Warfare, Health, and Subsistence*, ed. Douglas W. Owsley and Richard L. Jantz, 344–54. Washington, D.C.: Smithsonian Institution Press.

Holm, Bill. 1990. Kwakiutl: Winter Ceremonies. In *Handbook of North American Indians*. Vol. 7: *Northwest Coast*, ed. Wayne Suttles, 378–86. Washington, D.C.: Smithsonian Institution.

Honigmann, John J. 1962. *Social Networks in Great Whale River: Notes on an Eskimo, Montagnais-Naskapi, and Euro-Canadian Community*. National Museum of Canada Bulletin no. 178. Ottawa: Department of Northern Affairs and National Resources.

Horne, Stephen. 1981. *The Inland Chumash: Ethnography, Ethnohistory, and Archaeology*. Ph.D. dissertation, Department of Anthropology, University of California, Santa Barbara.

Howard, Julie, and Joel C. Janetski. 1992. Human Scalps from Eastern Utah. *Utah Archaeology* 5 (1): 125–32.

Hrdlička, Ales. 1944. *The Anthropology of Kodiak Island*. Philadelphia: Wistar Institute of Anatomy and Biology Press.

Hudson, Charles. 1976. *The Southeastern Indians*. Knoxville: University of Tennessee Press.

———. 1997. *Knights of Spain, Warriors of the Sun: Hernando de Soto and the South's Ancient Chiefdoms*. Athens: University of Georgia Press.

Hudson, Travis, Thomas Blackburn, Rosario Curletti, and Janice Timbrook, eds. 1977. *The Eye of the Flute: Chumash Traditional History and Ritual as Told by Fernando Librado Kitsepawit to John P. Harrington*. Santa Barbara, Calif.: Santa Barbara Museum of Natural History.

Hunt, George T. 1940. *The Wars of the Iroquois: A Study in Intertribal Trade Relations*. Madison: University of Wisconsin Press.

Hurst, Winston B., and Christy G. Turner II. 1993. Rediscovering the "Great Discovery": Wetherill's First Cave 7 and Its Record of Basketmaker Violence. In *Anasazi Basketmaker: Papers from the 1990 Wetherill–Grand Gulch Symposium*, ed. Victoria M. Atkins, 142–91. Cultural Resource Series, no. 24. Salt Lake City: Bureau of Land Management.

Hutchinson, Dale L. 1996. Brief Encounters: Tatham Mound and the Evidence for Spanish and Native American Confrontation. *International Journal of Osteoarchaeology* 6:51–65.

Inglis, Richard, and James C. Haggarty. 2000. Cook to Jewitt: Three Decades of Change in Nootka Sound. In *Nuu-chah-nulth/Voices Histories, Objects and Journeys*, ed. Alan L. Hoover, 92–106. Victoria, B.C.: Royal British Columbia Museum.

Isham, James. 1949. *James Isham's Observations on Hudsons Bay, 1743, and Notes and Observations on a Book Entitled A Voyage to Hudsons Bay in the Dobbs Galley, 1749*, ed. E. E. Rich. London: Hudson's Bay Record Society.

Jackman, Jarrell C. 1993. *Felipe de Goicoechea: Santa Barbara Presidio Comandante*. Santa Barbara, Calif.: Anson Luman Press.

Jackson, Donald. 1955. *Black Hawk: An Autobiography*. Urbana: University of Illinois.

Jackson, Douglas, and Mike Hargrave. 2003. The Hoxie Farm Site Fortified Village: Archaeological and Geophysical Investigations. Paper presented at the 49th Annual Meeting of the Midwest Archaeological Conference, Milwaukee, Wisc.

Jackson, Robert H. 1994. *Indian Population Decline: The Missions of Northwestern New Spain, 1687–1840*. Albuquerque: University of New Mexico Press.

Jacobsen, Johan Adrian. 1977. *Alaskan Voyage, 1881–1883*, trans. Erna Gunther. Chicago: University of Chicago Press.

Jefferies, Richard W. 1995. The Status of Archaic Period Research in the Midwestern United States. *Archaeology of Eastern North America* 23:119–45.

Jennings, Francis, William N. Fenton, and Mary A. Druke, eds. 1985. *Iroquois Indians: A Documentary History of the Diplomacy of the Six Nations and Their League: Guide to the Microfilm Collection*. Woodbridge, Conn.: Research Publications.

Jeremie, Nicolas. 1926. *Twenty Years of York Factory, 1694–1714: Jeremie's Account of Hudson Strait and Bay*, trans. Robert Douglas and J. N. Wallace. Ottawa: Thornburn and Abbott.

Johnson, Craig M. 1998. The Coalescent Tradition. In *Archaeology on the Great Plains*, ed. W. Raymond Wood, 308–44. Lawrence: University of Kansas Press.

Johnson, John R. 1978. The Trail to Kashtiq. *Journal of California Anthropology* 5:188–98.

———. 1984. Indian History in the Santa Barbara Back Country. *Los Padres Notes* (Los Padres Interpretive Association) 3:1–24.

———. 1986. The Chumash History of Mission Creek. *Noticias: Quarterly Bulletin of the Santa Barbara Historical Society* 32 (2): 21–37.

———. 1988. *Chumash Social Organization: An Ethnohistoric Perspective*. Ph.D. dissertation, University of California, Santa Barbara.

———. 1989. The Chumash and the Missions. In *Columbian Consequences: Archaeological and Historical Perspectives on the Spanish Borderlands West*, ed. David Hurst Thomas, 365–76. Washington, D.C.: Smithsonian Institution Press.

———. 1997. The Indians of Mission San Fernando. *Southern California Quarterly* 79:249–90.

———. 1999a. Chumash Population History. In *Cultural Affiliation and Lineal Descendants of Chumash Peoples*, ed. Sally McLendon and John R. Johnson, 93–130. Report prepared for the Archeology and Ethnography Program, National Park Service. Santa Barbara: Santa Barbara Museum of Natural History and New York: CUNY Hunter College.

———. 1999b. Lineal Descendants from the Santa Monica Mountains. In *Cultural Affiliation and Lineal Descendants of Chumash Peoples*, ed. Sally McLendon and John R. Johnson, 263–350. Report prepared for the Archeology and Ethnography Program, National Park Service. Santa Barbara: Santa Barbara Museum of Natural History and New York: CUNY Hunter College.

———. 2000. Social Responses to Climate Change among the Chumash Indians of South-Central California. In *The Way the Wind Blows: Climate, History and Human Action*, ed. Robert J. McIntosh, Joseph A. Tainter, and Susan Keech McIntosh, 301–27. New York: Columbia University Press.

Jopling, Carol F. 1989. *The Coppers of the Northwest Coast Indians: Their Origin, Development and Possible Antecedents.* Philadelphia: American Philosophical Society.

Jorgensen, Joseph G. 1980. *Western Indians: Comparative Environments, Languages, and Cultures of 172 Western American Indian Tribes.* San Francisco: W. H. Freeman.

Julig, Patrick J. 1982. *Human Use of the Albany River from Preceramic Times to the Late Eighteenth Century.* Master's thesis, York University, Toronto.

———. 1988. Prehistoric Site Survey in the Western James Bay Lowlands, Northern Ontario. In *Boreal Forest and Sub-Arctic Archaeology*, ed. C. S. Reid. Occasional Publications of the London Chapter of the Ontario Archaeological Society 6. London.

Jurmain, Robert D. 1991. Paleoepidemiology of Trauma in a Prehistoric Central California Population. In *Human Paleopathology: Current Syntheses and Future Options*, ed. Donald J. Ortner and Arthur C. Aufderheide, 241–48. Washington, D.C.: Smithsonian Institution Press.

———. 2001. Paleoepidemiological Patterns of Trauma in a Prehistoric Population from Central California. *American Journal of Physical Anthropology* 115:13–23.

Keeley, Lawrence H. 1996. *War before Civilization.* New York: Oxford University Press.

———. 2001. Giving War a Chance. In *Deadly Landscapes: Case Studies in Prehistoric Southwestern Warfare*, ed. Glen E. Rice and Steven A. LeBlanc, 331–42. Salt Lake City: University of Utah Press.

Kelly, Arthur R., and Lewis H. Larson Jr. 1957. Explorations at the Etowah Indian Mounds near Cartersville, Georgia: Seasons 1954, 1955, 1956. *Archaeology* 10:39–48.

Kelly, Raymond. 2000. *Warless Societies and the Origin of War.* Ann Arbor: University of Michigan Press.

Kelsey, Harry. 1986. *Juan Rodríguez Cabrillo.* San Marino, Calif.: Huntington Library.

Kennett, Douglas. 2005. *Island Chumash.* Berkeley: University of California Press.

Kennett, Douglas J., and James P. Kennett. 2000. Competitive and Cooperative Responses to Climatic Instability in Coastal Southern California. *American Antiquity* 65:379–95.

Kessel, John. 1979. *Kiva, Cross, and Crown: The Pecos Indians and New Mexico 1540–1840.* Washington, D.C.: National Park Service.

Kidder, Alfred V., and Samuel V. Guernsey. 1919. *Archaeological Explorations in Northeastern Arizona.* Bureau of American Ethnology Bulletin 65. Washington, D.C.: Government Printing Office.

King, Adam. 1996. *Tracing Organizational Change in Mississippian Chiefdoms of the Etowah River Valley, Georgia.* Ph.D. dissertation, Pennsylvania State University, University Park.

———. 1999. DeSoto's Itaba and the Nature of Sixteenth Century Paramount Chiefdoms. *Southeastern Archaeology* 18:110–23.

———. 2001. Long-Term Histories of Mississippian Centers: The Developmental Sequence of Etowah and Its Comparison to Moundville and Cahokia. *Southeastern Archaeology* 20:1–17.

———. 2003. *Etowah: The Political History of a Chiefdom Capital.* Tuscaloosa: University of Alabama Press.

King, Chester D. 1975. The Names and Locations of Historic Chumash Villages (assembled by Thomas Blackburn). *Journal of California Anthropology* 2:171–79.

———. 1976. Chumash Intervillage Economic Exchange. In *Native Californians: A Theoretical Retrospective*, ed. Lowell J. Bean and Thomas C. Blackburn, 289–318. Socorro, N.Mex.: Ballena Press.

———. 1984. Ethnohistoric Background. In *Archaeological Investigations on the San Antonio Terrace, Vandenberg Air Force Base, California*, Appendix I. Report submitted to the U.S. Army Corps of Engineers, Los Angeles District, by Chambers Consultants and Planners. Salinas, Calif.: Coyote Press.

King, Frances B. 1993. Climate, Culture, and Oneota Subsistence in Central Illinois. In *Foraging and Farming in the Eastern Woodlands*, ed. C. Margaret Scarry, 232–54. Gainesville: University Press of Florida.

King, Linda B. 1982. *Medea Creek Cemetery: Late Inland Chumash Patterns of Social Organization, Exchange and Warfare*. Ph.D. dissertation, Department of Anthropology, University of California, Los Angeles.

Klar, Kathryn, Kenneth Whistler, and Sally McLendon. 1999. The Chumash Languages: An Overview. In *Cultural Affiliation and Lineal Descendants of Chumash Peoples*, ed. Sally McLendon and John R. Johnson, 21–27. Report prepared for the Archeology and Ethnography Program, National Park Service. Santa Barbara: Santa Barbara Museum of Natural History and New York: CUNY Hunter College.

Knight, Vernon J., Jr. 1986. The Institutional Organization of Mississippian Religion. *American Antiquity* 51:675–87.

Knight, Vernon J., Jr., James A. Brown, and George E. Lankford. 2001. On the Subject Matter of Southeastern Ceremonial Complex Art. *Southeastern Archaeology* 20:129–41.

Kohler, Timothy A., and Carla Van West. 1996. The Calculus of Self-Interest in the Development of Cooperation: Sociopolitical Development and Risk among the Northern Anasazi. In *Evolving Complexity and Environmental Risk in the Prehistoric Southwest*, ed. Joseph A. Tainter and Bonnie Bagley Tainter, 169–96. Studies in the Sciences of Complexity. Santa Fe, N.Mex.: Santa Fe Institute.

Kotzebue, Otto von. [1821] 1967. *A Voyage of Discovery into the South Sea and Beering's Straits, for the Purpose of Exploring a North-East Passage, Undertaken in the Years 1815–18*. 3 vols. London: Longman, Hurst, Reese, Orme and Brown. Reprint, Amsterdam: N. Israel.

Krauss, Michael E. 1982. *Native Peoples and Languages of Alaska*, rev. ed. Fairbanks: University of Alaska, Alaska Native Language Center.

Krech, Shepard. 1999. *The Ecological Indian*. New York: W. W. Norton.

Kroeber, Alfred L. 1925. *Handbook of California Indians*. Bureau of American Ethnology Bulletin 28. Washington, D.C.: Smithsonian Institution.

———. 1939. *Cultural and Natural Areas of Native North America*. Berkeley: University of California Press.

Kroeber, Clifton B. 1980. Lower Colorado River Peoples: Hostilities and Hunger, 1850–1857. *Journal of California and Great Basin Anthropology* 2:187–98.

Kroeber, Clifton B., and Bernard L. Fontana. 1986. *Massacre on the Gila: An Account of the Last Major Battle between American Indians, with Reflections on the Origin of War.* Tucson: University of Arizona Press.

Kuckelman, Kristin A., Ricky R. Lightfoot, and Debra L. Martin. 2002. The Bioarchaeology and Taphonomy of Violence at Castle Rock and Sand Canyon Pueblos, Southwestern Colorado. *American Antiquity* 67 (3): 486–513.

Kuhn, R. D., and M. L. Sempowski. 2001. A New Approach to Dating the League of the Iroquois. *American Antiquity* 66 (2): 310–14.

Kunkel, Peter H. 1962. *Yokuts and Pomo Political Institutions: A Comparative Study.* Ph.D. dissertation, University of California, Los Angeles.

Kurtz, James. 1984. The Bow and Arrow Wars: Warfare between the Yukon and Coastal Eskimos. The Magagmyut: Warriors of the Coast. Unpublished manuscript, U.S. Bureau of Indian Affairs, ANCSA Office, Anchorage, Alaska.

Lafferty, Robert H., III, and James E. Price. 1996. Southeast Missouri. In *Prehistory of the Central Mississippi Valley*, ed. Charles H. McNutt, 1–45. Tuscaloosa: University of Alabama Press.

Lambert, Patricia M. 1993. Health in Prehistoric Populations of the Santa Barbara Channel Islands. *American Antiquity* 58:509–21.

———. 1994. *War and Peace on the Western Front: A Study of Violent Conflict and Its Correlates in Prehistoric Hunter-Gatherer Societies of Coastal California.* Ph.D. dissertation, University of California, Santa Barbara.

———. 1997a. Male Aggression in Prehistoric California: An 8,000-Year Perspective. Paper presented at the 96th Annual Meeting of the American Anthropological Association, Washington, D.C.

———. 1997b. Patterns of Violence in Prehistoric Hunter-Gatherer Societies of Coastal Southern California. In *Troubled Times: Violence and Warfare in the Past*, ed. Debra L. Martin and David W. Frayer, 77–110. Amsterdam: Gordon and Breach.

———. 1999. Human Remains. In *The Puebloan Occupation of the Ute Mountain Piedmont.* Vol. 5: *Environmental and Bioarchaeological Studies*, ed. B. R. Billman, 111–61, 203–36. Soil Systems Publications in Archaeology no. 22. Phoenix.

———. 2002. The Archaeology of War: A North American Perspective. *Journal of Archaeological Research* 10:207–41.

———. 2008. Prehistoric War and the Modern Condition: Lessons from the Ancient Chumash. Manuscript on file with the author.

Lambert, Patricia M., Brian R. Billman, and Banks L. Leonard. 2000. Explaining Variability in Mutilated Human Bone Assemblages from the American Southwest: A Case Study from the Southern Piedmont of Sleeping Ute Mountain, Colorado. *International Journal of Osteoarchaeology* 10:49–64.

Lambert, Patricia M., Banks L. Leonard, Brian R. Billman, Richard A. Marlar, Margaret E. Newman, and Karl J. Reinhard. 2000. Response to Critique of the Claim of Cannibalism at Cowboy Wash. *American Antiquity* 65:397–406.

Lambert, Patricia M., and Phillip L. Walker. 1991. The Physical Anthropological Evidence for the Evolution of Social Complexity in Coastal Southern California. *Antiquity* 65:963–73.

Landberg, Leif C. W. 1965. *The Chumash Indians of Southern California.* Southwest Museum Papers, no. 19. Los Angeles.

Lankford, George E., ed. 1987. *Native American Legends*. Little Rock, Ark.: August House.

———. 1993. Legends of the Adelantado. In *The Expedition of Hernando de Soto West of the Mississippi, 1541–1543: Proceedings of the de Soto Symposia, 1988 and 1990*, ed. Gloria A. Young and Michael P. Hoffman, 173–91. Fayetteville: University of Arkansas Press.

Larsen, Clark S. 1997. *Bioarchaeology: Interpreting Behavior from the Human Skeleton*. Cambridge, U.K.: Cambridge University Press.

Larsen, Clark S., H. P. Huynh, and B. G. McEwan. 1996. Death by Gunshot: Biocultural Implications of Trauma at Mission San Luis. *International Journal of Osteoarchaeology* 6:42–50.

Larson, Daniel O., John R. Johnson, and Joel C. Michaelsen. 1994. Missionization among the Coastal Chumash of Central California: A Study of Risk Minimization Strategies. *American Anthropologist* 96:263–99.

Larson, Daniel O., Joel C. Michaelsen, and Phillip L. Walker. 1989. Climatic Variability: A Compounding Factor Causing Culture Change among Prehistoric Coastal Populations. Paper presented at the 54th Annual Meeting of the Society for American Archaeology, Atlanta.

Larson, Lewis H., Jr. 1971. Archaeological Implications of Social Stratification at the Etowah Site, Georgia. In *Approaches to the Social Dimensions of Mortuary Practices*, ed. James A. Brown, 58–67. Society for American Archaeology, Memoir 25. Washington, D.C.

Larson, Robert. 1997. *Red Cloud: Warrior Statesmen of the Lakota Sioux*. Norman: University of Oklahoma Press.

Lasuén, Fermín Francisco de. [1785–1803] 1965. *The Writings of Fermín Francisco de Lasuén*, ed. Finbar Kenneally. 2 vols. Richmond, Va.: Academy of American Franciscan History.

Laylander, Don. 2000. *Early Ethnography of the Californias, 1533–1825*. Archives of California Prehistory no. 47. Salinas, Calif.: Coyote Press.

Leacock, Eleanor. 1978. Women's Status in Egalitarian Society: Implications for Social Evolution. *Current Anthropology* 19:247–75.

LeBlanc, Steven A. 1999. *Prehistoric Warfare in the American Southwest*. Salt Lake City: University of Utah Press.

———. 2003. Prehistory of Warfare. *Archaeology* 56 (3): 18–25.

LeBlanc, Steven A., and Glen E. Rice. 2001. Southwestern Warfare: The Value of Case Studies. In *Deadly Landscapes: Case Studies in Prehistoric Southwestern Warfare*, ed. Glen E. Rice and Steven A. LeBlanc, 1–18. Salt Lake City: University of Utah Press.

Lekson, Stephen H. 2002. War in the Southwest, War in the World. *American Antiquity* 67 (4): 607–24.

Leonard, Banks L., Patricia M. Lambert, and Richard A. Marlar. 2001. Cannibalism, Witch-Killing, Parsimony, and Empiricism. Paper presented at the 66th Annual Meeting of the Society for American Archaeology, New Orleans.

Lightfoot, Ricky R., and Kristen A. Kuckelman. 1995. Ancestral Pueblo Violence in the Northern Southwest. Paper presented at the 60th Annual Meeting of the Society for American Archaeology, Minneapolis.

———. 2001. A Case of Warfare in the Mesa Verde Region. In *Deadly Landscapes: Case Studies in Prehistoric Southwestern Warfare*, ed. Glen E. Rice and Steven A. LeBlanc, 51–64. Salt Lake City: University of Utah Press.

Littlefield, Loraine. 1987. Women Traders in the Maritime Fur Trade. In *Native Peoples, Native Lands, Canadian Indians, Inuit and Metis*, ed. Bruce Alden Cox, 173–85. Ottawa: Carleton University Press.

Loendorf, Lawrence L., and Stuart W. Conner. 1993. The Pectol Shields and the Shield-Bearing Warrior Rock Art Motif. *Journal of California and Great Basin Anthropology* 15:216–24.

Lomatuway'ma, Michael, Lorena Lomatuway'ma, and Sidney Namingha. 1993. *Hopi Ruin Legends: Kiqotutuwotsi*, ed. Ekkehart Malotki. Lincoln: University of Nebraska Press.

Longinos Martínez, José. [1792] 1961. *Journal of José Longinos Martínez: Notes and Observations of the Naturalist of the Botanical Expedition in Old and New California and the South Coast, 1791–1792*, ed. Lesley Byrd Simpson. San Francisco: John Howell.

Lorant, Stefan, ed. 1946. *The New World: The First Pictures of America*. New York: Duell, Sloan and Pearce.

———. 1965. *The New World: The First Pictures of America*. Rev. ed. New York: Duell, Sloan and Pearce.

Lord, John Keast. 1866. *The Naturalist in Vancouver Island and British Columbia*. 2 vols. London: Richard Bently.

Loud, Llewellyn L. 1924. The Stege Mounds at Richmond, California. *University of California Publications in American Archaeology and Ethnology* 17:355–72.

Lovisek, Joan A. 2007. Northwest Coast Human Trophy Taking: An Ethnohistorical Perspective. In *The Taking and Displaying of Human Body Parts as Trophies by Amerindians*, ed. Richard Chacon and David H. Dye. New York: Springer Press. Forthcoming.

Lowrey, Nathan S. 1999. An Ethnoarchaeological Inquiry into the Functional Relationship between Projectile Point and Armour Technologies of the Northwest Coast. *North American Archaeologist* 20:47–73.

Luebben, Ralph A., and Paul R. Nickens. 1982. A Mass Interment in an Early Pueblo III Kiva in Southwestern Colorado. *Journal of Intermountain Archeology* 1:66–79.

Lytwyn, Victor P. 2002a. *Muskekowuck Athinuwick: Original People of the Great Swampy Land*. Winnipeg: University of Manitoba Press.

———. 2002b. "God Was Angry with Their Country": The Smallpox Epidemic of 1782–83 among the Hudson Bay Lowland Cree. In *Papers of the 30th Algonquian Conference*, ed. David Pentland, 142–64. Winnipeg: University of Manitoba Press.

MacDonald, George F. 1989. *Kitwanga Fort Report*. Hull, Quebec: Canadian Museum of Civilization.

Mackie, Richard Somerset. 1997. *Trading beyond the Mountains: The British Fur Trade on the Pacific, 1793–1843*. Vancouver: UBC Press.

Madsen, David B. 1989. *Exploring the Fremont*. Salt Lake City: University of Utah Museum of Natural History.

Mails, Thomas. 1973. *Dog Soldier Societies of the Plains*. New York: Marlowe.

Malville, Nancy J. 1989. Two Fragmented Human Bone Assemblages from Yellow Jacket, Southwestern Colorado. *Kiva* 55:3–22.

Marlar, Jennifer E., Richard A. Marlar, Karl J. Reinhard, Banks L. Leonard, and Patricia M. Lambert. 2000. Microscopic and Molecular Evidence for the Human Origin of the Coprolite from the "Cannibalism" Site at Cowboy Wash (5MT10010). *Southwestern Lore* 66:14–22.

Marlar, Richard A., Banks L. Leonard, Brian R. Billman, Patricia M. Lambert, and Jennifer E. Marlar. 2000. Biochemical Evidence of Cannibalism at a Prehistoric Puebloan Site in Southwestern Colorado. *Nature* 407:74–78.

Martin, Debra L. 1997. Violence against Women in the La Plata River Valley (A.D. 1000–1300). In *Troubled Times: Violence and Warfare in the Past*, ed. Debra L. Martin and David W. Frayer, 45–76. Amsterdam: Gordon and Breach.

Martin, Debra, and David Frayer. 1997. *Troubled Times: Violence and Warfare in the Past*. Amsterdam: Gordon and Breach.

Maschner, Herbert D. G. 1997. The Evolution of Northwest Coast Warfare. In *Troubled Times: Violence and Warfare in the Past*, ed. Debra L. Martin and David W. Frayer, 267–302. Amsterdam: Gordon and Breach.

———. 2000. Catastrophic Change and Regional Interaction: The Southern Bering Sea in a Dynamic World System. In *Identities and Cultural Contacts in the Arctic: Proceedings from a Conference at the Danish National Museum, Copenhagen*, ed. M. Appelt, J. Berglund, and H. C. Gullov, 252–64. Copenhagen: Danish National Museum and Danish Polar Center.

Maschner, Herbert D. G., and Katherine L. Reedy-Maschner. 1998. Raid, Retreat, Defend (Repeat): The Archaeology and Ethnohistory of Warfare on the North Pacific Rim. *Journal of Anthropological Archaeology* 17:19–51.

Mason, Owen K. 1998. The Contest between the Ipiutak, Old Bering Sea and Birnirk Polities and the Origin of Whaling during the First Millennium AD along Bering Strait. *Journal of Anthropological Archaeology* 17:240–325.

———. 2000. Ipiutak/Birnirk Relationships in Northwest Alaska: Master and Slave or Partners in Trade? In *Identities and Cultural Contacts in the Arctic: Proceedings from a Conference at the Danish National Museum, Copenhagen, November 30 to December 2, 1999*, ed. Martin Appelt, Joel Berglund, and Hans Christian Gullov, 229–51. Copenhagen: Danish National Museum and Danish Polar Center.

Matson, Richard G., and Gary Coupland. 1995. *The Prehistory of the Northwest Coast*. San Diego: Academic Press.

Mauss, Marcel. 1990. *The Gift: The Form and Reason for Exchange in Archaic Societies*, trans. W. D. Halls. London: Routledge.

Mauzé, Marie. 1994. The Person, Reincarnation, the Kwakiutl. In *Amerindian Rebirth: Reincarnation Belief among North American Indians and Inuit*, ed. Antonia Mills and Richard Slobodin, 177–91. Toronto: University of Toronto Press.

MBV (Mission San Buenaventura). n.d. *Libro de Bautismos*, book 1. Copy on file, Santa Barbara Mission Archive Library, Santa Barbara.

McCorkle, Thomas. 1978. Intergroup Conflict. In *Handbook of North American Indians*. Vol. 8: *California*, ed. Robert F. Heizer, 694–700. Washington, D.C.: Smithsonian Institution.

McElrath, Dale A., Thomas E. Emerson, and Andrew C. Fortier. 2000. Social Evolution or Social Response? A Fresh Look at the "Good Gray Cultures" after Four Decades of Midwest Research. In *Late Woodland Societies: Tradition and Transformation across the Midcontinent*, ed. Thomas E. Emerson, Dale L. McElrath, and Andrew C. Fortier, 3–36. Lincoln: University of Nebraska Press.

McGhee, Robert. 1984. Thule Prehistory of Canada. In *Handbook of North American Indians*. Vol. 5: *Arctic*, ed. David Damas, 369–76. Washington, D.C.: Smithsonian Institution.

McKennan, Robert A. 1933. Ethnographic Field Notes: Chandalar River Region, Legends about War and Shamans. McKennan Collection Series 2. University of Alaska Archives, Fairbanks.

———. 1965. *The Chandalar Kutchin*. Technical Paper no. 17. Montreal: Arctic Institute of North America.

McLendon, Sally, and John R. Johnson, eds. 1999. *Cultural Affiliation and Lineal Descendants of Chumash Peoples*. Report prepared for the Archeology and Ethnography Program, National Park Service. Santa Barbara: Santa Barbara Museum of Natural History and New York: CUNY Hunter College.

Means, Russell, and Marvin J. Wolf. 1995. *Where White Men Fear to Tread: The Autobiography of Russell Means*. New York: St. Martin's Press.

Mehrer, Mark. 1995. *Cahokia's Countryside: Household Archaeology, Settlement Patterns, and Social Power*. DeKalb: Northern Illinois University Press.

Melbye, Jerry, and Scott I. Fairgrieve. 1994. A Massacre and Possible Cannibalism in the Canadian Arctic: New Evidence from the Saunaktuk Site (NgTn-1). *Arctic Anthropology* 31:57–77.

Mensforth, Robert P. 2001. Warfare and Trophy Taking in the Archaic Period. In *Archaic Transitions in Ohio and Kentucky Prehistory*, ed. Olaf H. Prufer, Sara E. Pedde, and Richard S. Meindl, 110–38. Kent, Ohio: Kent State University Press.

Michael, Henry N., ed. 1967. *Lieutenant Zagoskin's Travels in Russian America, 1842–1844*. Anthropology of the North: Translations from Russian Sources no. 7. Toronto: Arctic Institute of North America.

Milanich, Jerald T. 1995. *Florida Indians and the Invasion from Europe*. Gainesville: University Press of Florida.

Miller, Elizabeth. 1994. Evidence for Prehistoric Scalping in Northeastern Nebraska. *Plains Anthropologist* 39:211–19.

Milliken, Randall. 1995. *A Time of Little Choice: The Disintegration of Tribal Culture in the San Francisco Bay Area, 1769–1810*. Menlo Park, Calif.: Ballena Press.

Milliken, Randall, and John R. Johnson. 2005. *An Ethnogeography of Salinan and Northern Chumash Communities—1769 to 1810*. Report prepared for California Department of Transportation, District 5. Davis, Calif.: Far Western Anthropological Research Group.

Milner, George R. 1995. An Osteological Perspective on Prehistoric Warfare. In *Regional Approaches to Mortuary Analysis*, ed. Lane A. Beck, 221–44. New York: Plenum.

———. 1998. *The Cahokia Chiefdom*. Washington, D.C.: Smithsonian Institution Press.

———. 1999. Warfare in Prehistoric and Early Historic Eastern North America. *Journal of Archaeological Research* 7:105–51.

———. 2000. Palisaded Settlements in Prehistoric Eastern North America. In *City Walls: The Urban Enceinte in Global Perspective*, ed. James D. Tracy, 46–70. Cambridge, U.K.: Cambridge University Press.

———. 2004. *The Moundbuilders: Ancient Peoples of Eastern North America*. London: Thames and Hudson.

———. 2005. Nineteenth-Century Arrow Wounds and Perceptions of Prehistoric Warfare. *American Antiquity* 70 (1): 144–56.

Milner, George R., Eve Anderson, and Virginia G. Smith. 1991. Warfare in Late Prehistoric West-Central Illinois. *American Antiquity* 56:581–603.

Milner, George R., Clark S. Larsen, Dale L. Hutchinson, Matthew A. Williamson, and Dorothy A. Humpf. 2000. Conquistadors, Excavators, or Rodents: What Damaged the King Site Skeletons? *American Antiquity* 65:355–64.

Milner, George R., and Sissel Schroeder. 1999. Mississippian Sociopolitical Systems. In *Great Towns and Regional Polities in the Prehistoric American Southwest and Southeast*, ed. Jill E. Neitzel, 95–107. Albuquerque: University of New Mexico Press.

Milner, George R., and Virginia G. Smith. 1990. Oneota Human Skeletal Remains. In *Archaeological Investigations at the Morton Village and Norris Farms 36 Cemetery*, ed. Sharron K. Santure, Alan D. Harn, and Duane Esarey, 111–48. Reports of Investigations, no. 45. Springfield: Illinois State Museum.

Mitchell, Donald. 1984. Predatory Warfare, Social Status, and the North Pacific Slave Trade. *Ethnology* 23:39–48.

MLP (Mission La Purísima). n.d. *Libro de Bautismos*. Copy on file, Santa Barbara Mission Archive Library, Santa Barbara.

Montejo, Victor. 1993. In the Name of the Pot, the Sun, the Broken Spear, the Rock, the Stick, the Idol, Ad Infinitum, Ad Nauseam: An Expose of Anglo Anthropologists Obsessions with and Invention of Mayan Gods. *Wicazo SA Review* 9 (1): 12–16.

———. 1999a. Becoming Maya? Appropriation of the White Shaman. http://www2.hawaii.edu/~quetzil/uhm2001/Becoming_Maya.html.

———. 1999b. *Voices from Exile: Violence and Survival in Modern Maya History*. Norman: University of Oklahoma Press.

Montes, Catarino. 1997. Interview with John Johnson, recorded during field trip to San Emigdio Canyon, May 21, 1997.

Moore, John. 1996. *The Cheyenne*. Cambridge, U.K.: Blackwell.

Moorehead, Warren K. 1932. Description of Excavations, Mound C, First Season. In *The Etowah Papers*, ed. Warren K. Moorehead, 68–87. Andover, Mass.: Phillips Academy.

Morantz, Toby. 1982. Northern Algonquian Concepts of Status and Leadership Reviewed: A Case of the Eighteenth-century Trading Captain System. *Canadian Review of Sociology and Anthropology* 19 (4): 482–501.

Moratto, Michael J. 1984. *California Archaeology*. New York: Academic Press.

Morris, Earl H. 1925. Exploring the Canyon of Death. *National Geographic Magazine* 48 (3): 262–300.

———. 1939. *Archaeological Studies in the La Plata District: Southwestern Colorado and Northwestern New Mexico*. Washington, D.C.: Carnegie Institution of Washington.

Morris, William, ed. 1978. *The American Heritage Dictionary of the English Language.* Boston: Houghton Mifflin.

Morse, Phyllis A. 1993. The Parkin Archeological Site and Its Role in Determining the Route of the de Soto Expedition. In *The Expedition of Hernando de Soto West of the Mississippi, 1541–1543: Proceedings of the De Soto Symposia, 1988 and 1990,* ed. Gloria A. Young and Michael P. Hoffman, 58–67. Fayetteville: University of Arkansas Press.

Moss, Madonna. 1993. Shellfish, Gender, and Status on the Northwest Coast: Reconciling Archaeological, Ethnographic, and Ethnohistorical Records of the Tlingit. *American Anthropologist* 95:631–52.

Moss, Madonna L., and Jon M. Erlandson. 1992. Forts, Refuge Rocks, and Defensive Sites: The Antiquity of Warfare along the North Pacific Coast of North America. *Arctic Anthropology* 29:73–90.

Moulton, Gary E., ed. 1988. *The Journals of the Lewis and Clark Expedition: July 28–November 1, 1805,* vol. 5. Lincoln: University of Nebraska Press.

MSB (Mission Santa Bárbara). n.d. *Libro de Bautismos.* Copy on file, Santa Barbara Mission Archive Library, Santa Barbara.

MSF (Mission San Fernando). n.d. *Libro de Bautismos.* Copy on file, Archdiocese Archives of Los Angeles, Mission San Fernando, Mission Hills.

Nash, Charles H. 1972. *Chucalissa: Excavations and Burials through 1963.* Anthropological Research Center Occasional Papers, no. 6. Memphis: University of Memphis.

———. n.d. Unpublished field log. Chucalissa Museum, University of Memphis.

Nassaney, Michael S., and Kendra Pyle. 1999. The Adoption of the Bow and Arrow in Eastern North America: A View from Central Arkansas. *American Antiquity* 64 (2): 243–63.

Neiburger, E. J. 1989. A Prehistoric Scalping, 600 A.D. *Central States Archaeological Journal* 36:204–8.

Neitzel, Robert S. 1965. *Archaeology of the Fatherland Site: The Grand Village of the Natchez.* Anthropology Papers 51(1). New York: American Museum of Natural History.

Nelson, Edward William. 1899. The Eskimo about Bering Strait. In *Eighteenth Annual Report of the Bureau of American Ethnology, 1896–97,* pt. 1, 3–518. Washington, D.C.: Government Printing Office.

Neve, Felipe de. 1782. [Instructions for the Comandante of the Presidio of Santa Bárbara and for the sergeants of the guards of missions to be established along the Channel, March 6, 1782, San Gabriel.] Provincial State Papers 3:85–89. California Archives (2:86–90), Bancroft Library, Berkeley.

Nicholas, George. 1997. Archaeology, Education and the Secwepemc. *SAA Bulletin* 15 (2): 9–11.

———. 2004. What Do I Really Want from a Relationship with Native Americans? *SAA Archaeological Record* 4 (3): 29–33.

Nickens, Paul R. 1975. Prehistoric Cannibalism in the Mancos Canyon, Southwestern Colorado. *Kiva* 4:283–93.

O'Leary, Matthew. 1995. Geography and Chronology of Central Yupiit Warrior Traditions. Paper presented at the Annual Meeting of the Alaska Anthropological Association, Anchorage, Alaska. On file at the Bureau of Indian Affairs ANCSA Office, Anchorage, Alaska.

Osgood, Cornelius. 1936. *Contributions to the Ethnography of the Kutchin.* Yale University Publications in Anthropology, no. 14. New Haven, Conn.

———. 1937. *The Ethnography of the Tanaina.* Yale University Publications in Anthropology, no. 16. New Haven, Conn.

———. 1940. *Ingalik Material Culture.* Yale University Publications in Anthropology, no. 22. New Haven, Conn.

———. 1958. *Ingalik Social Culture.* Yale University Publications in Anthropology, no. 53. New Haven, Conn.

———. 1959. *Ingalik Mental Culture.* Yale University Publications in Anthropology, no. 56. New Haven, Conn.

O'Shea, John M., and Patricia S. Bridges. 1989. The Sargent Site Ossuary (25Cu28), Custer County, Nebraska. *Plains Anthropologist* 34:7–21.

Ostermann, Hother, and Erik Holtved, eds. 1952. The Alaska Eskimos, as Described in the Posthumous Notes of Dr. Knud Rasmussen. *Report of the Fifth Thule Expedition 1921–24,* vol. 10, no. 3. Copenhagen: Gyldendal.

Oswalt, Wendell H. 1967. *Alaskan Eskimos.* San Francisco: Chandler Publishing.

———. 1990. *Bashful No Longer: An Alaskan Eskimo Ethnohistory, 1778–1988.* Norman: University of Oklahoma Press.

Otterbein, Keith F. 1970. *The Evolution of War: A Cross-Cultural Study.* New Haven, Conn.: Human Relations Area File Press.

———. 1973. The Anthropology of War. In *Handbook of Social and Cultural Anthropology,* ed. John J. Honigmann, 923–58. New York: Rand McNally.

———. 1994. *Feuding and Warfare.* Amsterdam: Gordon and Breach.

———. 1997. The Origins of War. *Critical Review* 11:251–77.

———. 1999. A History of Research on Warfare in Anthropology. *American Anthropologist* 101 (4): 794–805.

———. 2000a. The Doves Have Been Heard from, Where Are the Hawks? *American Anthropologist* 102(4): 841–44.

———. 2000b. Killing of Captured Enemies: A Cross-cultural Study. *Current Anthropology* 41:439–42.

———. 2003. The Archaeology of War: An Alternative View. *Anthropology News* 44 (9): 9.

———. 2004. *How War Began.* College Station: Texas A&M University Press.

Owsley, Douglas W. 1994. Warfare in Coalescent Tradition Populations of the Northern Plains. In *Skeletal Biology in the Great Plains: Migration, Warfare, Health, and Subsistence,* ed. Douglas W. Owsley and Richard L. Jantz, 333–44. Washington, D.C.: Smithsonian Institution Press.

Owsley, Douglas W., and H. E. Berryman. 1975. Ethnographic and Archaeological Evidence of Scalping in the Southeastern United States. *Tennessee Archaeologist* 31:41–58.

Owsley, Douglas W., H. E. Berryman, and W. M. Bass. 1977. Demographic and Osteological Evidence for Warfare at the Larson Site, South Dakota. *Plains Anthropologist Memoir* 13:119–31.

Owsley, Douglas W., and Richard L. Jantz, eds. 1994. *Skeletal Biology in the Great Plains: Migration, Warfare, Health, and Subsistence.* Washington, D.C.: Smithsonian Institution Press.

Owsley, Douglas W., M. K. Marks, and M. H. Manhein. 1999. Southern Plains. In *Bioarcheology of the South Central United States,* ed. J. C. Rose, 153–83. Arkansas Archaeological Survey Research Series 55. Fayetteville.

Owsley, Douglas W., S. Novak, L. Jantz, and C. Clark. 1998. Examination of the Utah State Antiquity Skeletal Collection. Report on file, Utah Division of State History, Antiquities Section, Salt Lake City.

Parsons, Elsie Clews. 1932. Isleta, New Mexico. *Forty-Seventh Annual Report of the Bureau of American Ethnology, 1929–1930,* 193–466. Washington, D.C.: Government Printing Office.

———. 1939. *Pueblo Indian Religion.* 2 vols. Chicago: University of Chicago Press.

Pauketat, Timothy R. 1994. *The Ascent of Chiefs: Cahokia and Mississippian Politics in Native North America.* Tuscaloosa: University of Alabama Press.

———. 1999. America's Ancient Warriors. *MHQ: The Quarterly Journal of Military History* 11 (4): 50–55.

———. 2003. Resettled Farmers and the Making of a Mississippian Polity. *American Antiquity* 68:39–66.

———. 2004. *Ancient Cahokia and the Mississippians.* Cambridge, U.K.: Cambridge University Press.

Pauketat, Timothy R., and Susan M. Alt. 2004. The Making and Meaning of a Mississippian Ax Head Cache. *Antiquity* 78 (302): 779–97.

Pauketat, Timothy R., and Thomas E. Emerson, eds. 1997. *Cahokia: Domination and Ideology in the Mississippian World.* Lincoln: University of Nebraska Press.

———. 1999. The Representation of Hegemony as Community at Cahokia. In *Material Symbols: Culture and Economy in Prehistory,* ed. John E. Robb, 302–17. Occasional Paper no. 26. Carbondale: Southern Illinois University.

Payne, Claudine. 1994. *Mississippian Capitals: An Archaeological Investigation of Pre-Columbian Political Structure.* Ph.D. dissertation, University of Florida, Gainesville.

Petersen, James, and John Crock. 2007. Handsome Death: The Taking, Veneration, and Consumption of Human Remains in the Insular Caribbean and Greater Amazonia. In *The Taking and Displaying of Human Body Parts as Trophies by Amerindians,* ed. Richard Chacon and David H. Dye. New York: Springer Press. Forthcoming.

Pico, Juan Estevan. [1884] 1999. List of Towns Remembered and Recorded by Juan Estevan Pico about 1884. In *Cultural Affiliation and Lineal Descendants of Chumash Peoples,* ed. Sally McLendon and John R. Johnson, Appendix IV. Report prepared for the Archeology and Ethnography Program, National Park Service. Santa Barbara: Santa Barbara Museum of Natural History and New York: CUNY Hunter College.

Pilon, Jean-Luc. 1987. *Washahoe Inninou Dahtsuounoaou: Ecological and Cultural Adaptation along the Severn River in the Hudson Bay Lowlands of Ontario.* Conservation Archaeology Report, Northwestern Region, no. 10. Kenora: Ontario Ministry of Citizenship and Culture.

Plog, Stephen, and Julie Solometo. 1997. The Never-Changing and Ever-Changing: The Evolution of Western Pueblo Ritual. *Cambridge Archaeological Journal* 7 (2): 161–82.

Polhemus, Richard R. 1987. *The Toqua Site: A Late Mississippian Dallas Phase Town.* 2 vols. University of Tennessee, Department of Anthropology, Report of Investigations 41. Knoxville.

Portolá, Gaspar de. [1769–70] 1983. Gaspar de Portolá's Expedition Journal. In *Gaspar de Portolá: Explorer and Founder of California,* by F. Boneu Companys, translated and revised by Alan K. Brown, 367–89. Lérida, Spain: Instituto de Estudios Ilerdenses.

Potter, Stephen R. 1993. *Commoners, Tribute, and Chiefs: The Development of Algonquian Culture in the Potomac Valley.* Charlottesville: University Press of Virginia.

Pratt, Kenneth L. 1984a. Classification of Eskimo Groupings in the Yukon-Kuskokwim Region: A Critical Analysis. *Études/Inuit Studies* 8 (supplementary issue): 45–61.

———. 1984b. *Yukon-Kuskokwim Eskimos, Western Alaska: Inconsistencies in Group Identification.* M.A. thesis, Western Washington University.

Preston, D. 1997. A Reporter at Large: The Lost Man. *New Yorker,* June 16.

Price, James E., and Gregory L. Fox. 1990. Recent Investigations at Towosahgy State Historic Park. *Missouri Archaeologist* 1:1–71.

Prince, Paul. 2001. Artifact Distributions at the Kitwanga Hill Fort: Protohistoric Competition and Trade on the Upper Skeena. In *Perspectives on Northern Northwest Coast Prehistory,* ed. Jerome C. Cybulski, *249–68.* Archaeological Survey of Canada Mercury Series Paper 160. Hull, Quebec: Canadian Museum of Civilization.

Provincial Archives of British Columbia. 1836–41. McNeill's Fur Trade Report, A/B/20.5/B38.

———. 1850. Fort Rupert Journal, B.185/a/1, April 13, 1850.

———. 1857. Fort Rupert Letterbooks.

———. n.d. Wilson Duff Papers, Kwakiutl Social Organization Notes from Mungo Martin, TSI-F, File 121.

Raab, L. Mark, and Daniel O. Larson. 1997. Medieval Climatic Anomaly and Punctuated Cultural Evolution in Coastal Southern California. *American Antiquity* 62:319–36.

Rabasa, José. 1997. The Representation of Violence in the Soto Narratives. In *The Hernando de Soto Expedition: History, Historiography, and "Discovery" in the Southeast,* ed. Patricia Galloway, 380–409. Lincoln: University of Nebraska Press.

Rackerby, Frank. 1967. The Archaeological Salvage of Two San Francisco Bay Shellmounds. *Contributions to the Archaeology of Southern San Francisco Bay.* Occasional Papers in Anthropology, no. 3. San Francisco: Department of Anthropology, San Francisco State College.

Radcliffe-Brown, Alfred Reginald. 1952. *Structure and Function in Primitive Society.* London: Cohen and West.

Rasmussen, Knud Johan Victor. 1933. *Across Arctic America: Narrative of the Fifth Thule Expedition.* New York: G. P. Putnam's Sons.

Rawls, James J. 1984. *The Indians of California: The Changing Image*. Norman: University of Oklahoma Press.

Ray, Arthur J., and Donald Freeman. 1978. *"Give Us Good Measure": An Economic Analysis of Relations between the Indians and the Hudson's Bay Company before 1763*. Toronto: University of Toronto Press.

Ray, Dorothy Jean. 1967. Land Tenure and Polity of the Bering Strait Eskimos. *Journal of the West* 6 (3): 371–94.

Reagan, A. B. 1933. Anciently Inhabited Caves of the Vernal (Utah) District, with Some Additional Notes on Nine Mile Canyon, Northeast Utah. *Transactions of the Kansas Academy of Science* 36:41–70.

Redmond, Elsa M. 1998. The Dynamics of Chieftaincy and the Development of Chiefdoms. In *Chiefdoms and Chieftaincy in the Americas*, ed. Elsa M. Redmond, 1–17. Gainesville: University Press of Florida.

———, ed. 1998. *Chiefdoms and Chieftaincy in the Americas*. Gainesville: University Press of Florida.

Reyna, Stephen P. 1994a. A Mode of Domination Approach to Organized Violence. In *Studying War: Anthropological Perspectives*, ed. Stephen P. Reyna and R. E. Downs, 29–65. Langhorne, Penn.: Gordon and Breach.

———. 1994b. Preface: Studying War, an Unfinished Project of the Enlightenment. In *Studying War: Anthropological Perspectives*, ed. Stephen P. Reyna and R. E. Downs, ix–xxiii. Langhorne, Penn.: Gordon and Breach.

Reyna, Stephen P., and R. E. Downs, eds. 1994. *Studying War: Anthropological Perspectives*. Langhorne, Penn.: Gordon and Breach.

Rhodes, Richard A., and Evelyn M. Todd. 1981. Subarctic Algonquian Languages. In *Handbook of North American Indians*. Vol. 6: *Subarctic*, ed. June Helm, 52–66. Washington, D.C.: Smithsonian Institution.

Rice, Glen E., and Steven A. LeBlanc, eds. 2001. *Deadly Landscapes: Case Studies in Prehistoric Southwestern Warfare*. Salt Lake City: University of Utah Press.

Rich, E. E. 1949. Introduction. In *Isham's Observations and Notes, 1743–1749*, ed. E. E. Rich, xlii–cv. London: Hudson's Bay Record Society.

Riches, David. 1979. Ecological Variation on the Northwest Coast: Models for the Generation of Cognatic and Matrilineal Descent. In *Social and Ecological Systems*, ed. P. C. Burnham and R. F. Ellen, 145–66. New York: Academic Press.

Riley, Carroll L. 1989. Warfare in the Protohistoric Southwest: An Overview. In *Cultures in Conflict: Current Archaeological Perspectives*, ed. Diana Claire Tkaczuk and Brian C. Vivian, 138–46. Proceedings of the Twentieth Annual Chacmool Conference, Archaeological Association of the University of Calgary.

Ringel, Gail. 1979. The Kwakiutl Potlatch: History, Economics and Symbols. *Ethnohistory* 26:347–62.

Rivera, Fernando de. [1774–77] 1967. Diario del Capitán Comandante Fernando de Rivera y Moncada, edited by Ernest J. Burrus. *Colección Chimalistac de libros y documentos acerca de la Nueva España 24 and 25*. Madrid: Ediciones José Turanzas.

Robson, Joseph. [1752] 1965. *An Account of Six Years Residence in Hudson's Bay, from 1733 to 1736 and 1744 to 1747*. Toronto: S. R. Publishers. Johnson Reprint.

Rohn, Arthur. 1989. Warfare and Violence among the Southwestern Pueblos. In *Cul-*

tures in Conflict: Current Archaeological Perspectives, ed. Diana Tkaczuk and Brian Vivian, 147–52. Calgary: University of Calgary Archaeology Association.

Rood, Ronald J. 2001. Archaeological Investigations at the Hysell Site, 42Sv2443. Report on file. Utah Division of State History, Antiquities Section, Salt Lake City.

Roper, Marilyn K. 1969. A Survey of the Evidence for Intrahuman Killing in the Pleistocene. *Current Anthropology* 10:427–59.

———. 2003. Prehistoric War. (Letters) *Archaeology* 56 (4): 9.

Rosman, Abraham, and Paula G. Rubel. 1971. *Feasting with Mine Enemy: Rank and Exchange among Northwest Coast Societies*. New York: Columbia University Press.

Roth, Christopher F. 2002. Goods, Names, and Selves: Rethinking the Tsimshian Potlatch. *American Ethnologist* 29:123–50.

Rothstein, Edward. 2004. Who Should Tell History: The Tribes or the Museums? *New York Times*, Critics Notebook, December 21, 2004:1–3.

Rountree, Helen C. 1989. *The Powhatan Indians of Virginia*. Norman: University of Oklahoma Press.

Rountree, Helen C., and E. Randolph Turner III. 1998. The Evolution of the Powhatan Paramount Chiefdom in Virginia. In *Chiefdoms and Chieftaincy in the Americas*, ed. Elsa M. Redmond, 265–96. Gainesville: University Press of Florida.

Sabo, George, III. 1993. Indians and Spaniards in Arkansas: Symbolic Action in the Sixteenth Century. In *The Expedition of Hernando de Soto West of the Mississippi, 1541–1543: Proceedings of the De Soto Symposia 1988 and 1990*, ed. Gloria A. Young and Michael P. Hoffman, 192–209. Fayetteville: University of Arkansas Press.

Sale, Kirkpatrick. 1991. *The Conquest of Paradise*. New York: Plume.

Sapir, Edward. 1966. The Social Organization of the West Coast Tribes. In *Indians of the North Pacific Coast*, ed. Tom McFeat, 28–48. Toronto: McClelland and Stewart.

Schaafsma, Polly. 1992. Imagery and Magic: Petroglyphs at Comanche Gap, Galisteo Basin, New Mexico. In *Archaeology, Art, and Anthropology: Papers in Honor of J. J. Brody*, ed. Meliha S. Duran and David T. Kirkpatrick, 157–74. Archaeological Society of New Mexico 18. Albuquerque.

———. 1999. Tlalocs, Kachinas, Sacred Bundles, and Related Symbolism in the Southwest and Mesoamerica. In *The Casas Grandes World*, ed. Curtis F. Schaafsma and Carroll L. Riley, 164–92. Salt Lake City: University of Utah Press.

———. 2000. *Warrior, Shield, and Star: Imagery and Ideology of Pueblo Warfare*. Santa Fe, N.Mex.: Western Edge Press.

———. 2007. Head Trophies and Scalping: Images in Southwest Rock Art. In *The Taking and Displaying of Human Trophies by Amerindians*, ed. Richard J. Chacon and David H. Dye. New York: Springer Press. Forthcoming.

Schaafsma, Polly, and Karl A. Taube. 2006. Bringing the Rain: An Ideology of Rainmaking in the Pueblo Southwest and Mesoamerica. In *The Pre-Columbian World: Searching for a Unitary Vision of Ancient America*, ed. Jeffrey Quilter and Mary Miller, 231–85. Washington, D.C.: Dumbarton Oaks.

Scheffel, David, Z. 2000. The Post-Anthropological Indian: Canada's New Images of Aboriginality in the Age of Repossession. *Anthropologica* 42:175–88.

Schenck, W. E. 1926. The Emeryville Shellmound Final Report. *The University of California Publications in American Archaeology and Ethnology* 23:147–282.

Schroeder, Sissel. 2003a. Leadership in a Contested Land. Paper presented at the 20th Annual Visiting Scholar Conference, Southern Illinois University, Carbondale.

———. 2003b. Burning Down the House: The Significance of Dating a Conflagration at Jonathan Creek. Paper presented at the 60th Annual Meeting of the Southeastern Archaeological Conference, Charlotte.

Seeman, Mark F. 1988. Ohio Hopewell Trophy-Skull Artifacts as Evidence for Competition in Middle Woodland Societies circa 50 B.C.–A.D. 350. *American Antiquity* 53:565–77.

Señán, José. [1804] 1962. Father José Señán to Governor José Joaquín de Arrillaga of California. In *The Letters of José Señán, O.F.M.: Mission San Buenaventura, 1796–1823*, ed. Leslie B. Simpson, 10–16. San Francisco: John Howell.

———. [1815] 1976. Reply to Question 27: "Cruelty and Punishments," Mission San Buenaventura. In *As the Padres Saw Them: California Indian Life and Customs as Reported by Franciscan Missionaries, 1813–1815*, ed. Maynard Geiger and Clement Meighan, 113–14. Santa Barbara, Calif.: Santa Barbara Mission Archive-Library.

Service, Elman. 1975. *Origins of the State and Civilization: The Process of Cultural Evolution*. New York: W. W. Norton.

Shaw, Robert D. 1998. An Archaeology of the Central Yupik: A Regional Overview for the Yukon-Kuskokwim Delta, Northern Bristol Bay, and Nunivak Island. *Arctic Anthropology* 35 (1): 234–46.

Sheehan, Glenn W. 1995. Whaling Surplus, Trade, War, and the Integration of Prehistoric Northern and Northwestern Alaskan Economies, A.D. 1200–1826. In *Hunting the Largest Animals: Native Whaling in the Western Arctic and Subarctic*, ed. Allen P. McCartney, 185–206. Studies in Whaling, no. 3; Occasional Publication no. 36. Edmonton: Canadian Circumpolar Institute, University of Alberta.

———. 1997. *In the Belly of the Whale: Trade and War in Eskimo Society*. Aurora Monograph Series, no. 6. Anchorage: Alaska Anthropological Association.

Sillitoe, Paul. 1985. War, Primitive. In *The Social Science Encyclopedia*, ed. Adam Kuper and Jessica Kuper, 890–91. London: Routledge and Kegan Paul.

Simon, James J. K., and Amy F. Steffian. 1994. Cannibalism or Complex Mortuary Behavior? An Analysis of Patterned Variability in the Treatment of Human Remains from the Kachemak Tradition of Kodiak Island. In *Reckoning with the Dead: The Larsen Bay Repatriation and the Smithsonian Institution*, ed. Tamara L. Bray and Thomas W. Killion, 75–100. Washington, D.C.: Smithsonian Institution Press.

Simpson, John. 1852–54. Point Barrow journal, 1852–1854. John Simpson Papers, Rare Book, Manuscript, and Special Collections Library, Duke University. Box 5, Accounts of voyages; oversized; 1851–1854.

Skinner, Alanson. 1911. *Notes on Eastern Cree and Northern Saulteaux*. Anthropological Papers of the American Museum of Natural History 9(1). New York.

Slayman, Andrew L. 1997. A Battle over Bones. *Archaeology* (January/February 1997): 16–23.

Slobodin, Richard. 1960. Eastern Kutchin Warfare. *Anthropologica*, n.s. 2 (1): 76–94.

Smiley, Francis E., and Michael R. Robbins. 1997. *Early Farmers in the Northern Southwest: Papers on Chronometry, Social Dynamics, and Ecology*. Animas–La Plata Archaeological Project Research Paper no. 7. Bureau of Reclamation, Upper Colorado Region. Flagstaff: Northern Arizona University.

Smith, Bruce D. 1986. The Archaeology of the Southeastern United States: From Dalton to de Soto 10,500–500 B.P. *Advances in World Archaeology* 5:1–92.

———. 1989. Origins of Agriculture in Eastern North America. *Science* 246:1566–71.

———. 1992. *Rivers of Change: Essays on Early Agriculture in Eastern North America*. Washington, D.C.: Smithsonian Institution Press.

———. 1995. *The Emergence of Agriculture*. New York: Scientific American Library.

Smith, Bruce D., and C. Wesley Cowan. 2003. Domesticated Crop Plants and the Evolution of Food Production Economies in Eastern North America. In *People and Plants in Ancient Eastern North America*, ed. Paul W. Minnis, 105–25. Washington, D.C.: Smithsonian Institution Press.

Smith, Maria O. 1996. Biocultural Inquiry into Archaic Period Populations of the Southeast: Trauma and Occupational Stress. In *Archaeology of the Mid-Holocene Southeast*, ed. Kenneth E. Sassaman and David G. Anderson, 134–54. Gainesville: University Press of Florida.

———. 1997. Osteological Indications of Warfare in the Archaic Period of the Western Tennessee Valley. In *Troubled Times: Violence and Warfare in the Past*, ed. Debra L. Martin and David W. Frayer, 241–65. Amsterdam: Gordon and Breach.

———. 2003. Beyond Palisades: The Nature and Frequency of Late Prehistoric Deliberate Violent Trauma in the Chickamauga Reservoir of East Tennessee. *American Journal of Physical Anthropology* 121:303–18.

Smith, Watson. 1952. *Kiva Mural Decorations at Awatovi and Kawaika-a*. Papers of the Peabody Museum of American Archaeology and Ethnology, vol. 37. Cambridge, Mass.: Harvard University.

Snow, Dean R. 1994. *The Iroquois*. The Peoples of America. Oxford: Blackwell.

———. 1995. *Mohawk Valley Archaeology: The Sites*. Occasional Papers in Anthropology, no. 23. University Park: Matson Museum of Anthropology.

Snow, Dean R., Charles T. Gehring, and William A. Starna, eds. 1996. *In Mohawk Country: Early Narratives about a Native People*. Syracuse: Syracuse University Press.

Southerlin, Bobby G. 1993. *Mississippian Settlement Patterns in the Etowah River Valley near Cartersville, Bartow County, Georgia*. Master's thesis, University of Georgia, Athens.

Spencer, Herbert. [1886] 1975. *The Principles of Sociology*. Westport, Conn.: Greenwood.

Spencer, Page, Gregory Nowacki, Michael Fleming, Terry Brock, and Torre Jorgenson. 2002. Home Is Where the Habitat Is: An Ecosystem Foundation for Wildlife Distribution and Behavior. *Arctic Journal of the United States* 16 (fall/winter): 6–17.

Steadman, Dawnie W. 1998. The Population Shuffle in the Central Illinois Valley: A Diachronic Model of Mississippian Biocultural Interactions. *World Archaeology* 30:306–26.

Stearman, Allyn. 1994. Only Slaves Climb Trees: Revisiting the Myth of the Ecologically Noble Savage in Amazonia. *Human Nature* 5 (4): 339–56.

Steinen, Karl T. 1992. Ambushes, Raids, and Palisades: Mississippian Warfare in the Interior Southeast. *Southeastern Archaeology* 11:132–39.

Stephen, Alexander M. 1936. *Hopi Journal of Alexander M. Stephen*, ed. Elsie Clews Parsons. 2 vols. Columbia University Contributions to Anthropology 23. New York.

Stevenson, Matilda Coxe. 1904. *The Zuñi Indians*. Twenty-third Annual Report of the Bureau of American Ethnology, 1901–02. Washington, D.C.: Government Printing Office.

Stewart, K. M. 1947. Mohave Warfare. *Southwestern Journal of Anthropology* 3:257–78.

Stewart, R. Michael. 1995. The Status of Woodland Prehistory in the Middle Atlantic Region. *Archaeology of Eastern North America* 23:177–206.

Stine, Scott. 1994. Extreme and Persistent Drought in California and Patagonia during Mediaeval Time. *Nature* 369:546–49.

Stuart, David E. 2000. *Anasazi America*. Albuquerque: University of New Mexico Press.

Sutherland, Patricia D. 2001. Revisiting an Old Concept: The North Coast Interaction Sphere. In *Perspectives on Northern Northwest Coast Prehistory, ed.* Jerome C. Cybulski, *49–59.* Archaeological Survey of Canada Mercury Series Paper 160. Hull, Quebec: Canadian Museum of Civilization.

Suttles, Wayne. 1954. Post-Contact Culture Change among the Lummi Indians. *British Columbia Historical Quarterly* 18:29–102.

———. 1991. Streams of Property, Armor of Wealth: The Traditional Kwakiutl Potlatch. In *Chiefly Feasts: The Enduring Kwakiutl Potlatch*, ed. Aldona Jonaitis, 71–134. Vancouver, B.C.: Douglas and McIntyre.

———. 2000. The Ethnographic Significance of the Fort Langley Journals. In *The Fort Langley Journals, 1827–30*, ed. Morag Maclachlan, 163–262. Vancouver: UBC Press.

Swanton, John R. 1911. *Indian Tribes of the Lower Mississippi Valley and Adjacent Coast of the Gulf of Mexico*. Bureau of American Ethnology Bulletin no. 43. Washington, D.C.: Smithsonian Institution.

———. 1946. *The Indians of the Southeastern United States*. Bureau of American Ethnology Bulletin no. 137. Washington, D.C.: Smithsonian Institution.

Swidler, Nina, Kurt Dongoske, Roger Ayon, and Allan Downer. 1997. *Native Americans and Archaeologists: Stepping Stones to Common Ground*. Walnut Creek, Calif.: AltaMira Press.

Tapis, Estevan. 1803. [Letter to Governor Arrillaga, June 30, 1803, Santa Bárbara.] California Mission Documents MS 437. Santa Barbara Mission Archive Library.

Taylor, Colin. 1975. *The Warriors of the Plains*. New York: Arco Publishing.

Tenney, J. Asa. 1986. Trauma among Early Californian Populations. *American Journal of Physical Anthropology* 69:271.

Tiffany, J. A., S. J. Schermer, J. L. Theler, D. W. Owsley, D. C. Anderson, E. A. Bettis III, and D. M. Thompson. 1988. The Hanging Valley Site (13HR28): A Stratified Woodland Burial Locale in Western Iowa. *Plains Anthropologist* 33:219–59.

Timbrook, Jan. 1987. Virtuous Herbs: Plants in Chumash Medicine. *Journal of Ethnobiology* 7:171–80.

Titiev, Mischa. 1944. *Old Oraibi: A Study of the Hopi Indians of Third Mesa*. Papers of the Peabody Museum of American Archaeology and Ethnology, vol. 22(1). Cambridge, Mass.: Harvard University.

Tlapoyawa, Kurly. 2003. Did "Mexika Human Sacrifice" Exist? Mexika Eagle Society website. http://www.mexika.org/TlapoSac.htm.

Tolmie, William F. 1963. *The Journals of William Fraser Tolmie: Physician and Fur Trader*. Vancouver, B.C.: Mitchell Press.

Topic, John. 1989. The Ostra Site: The Earliest Fortified Site in the New World? In *Cultures in Conflict: Current Archaeological Perspectives*, ed. Diana Tkaczuk and Brian Vivian, 215–28. Calgary: University of Calgary Archaeology Association.

Townsend, Joan. 1979. Indian or Eskimo? Interaction and Identity in Southern Alaska. *Arctic Anthropology* 16 (2): 160–82.

Trigger, Bruce. 1976. *The Children of Aataentsic: A History of the Huron People to 1660*. 2 vols. Montreal: McGill-Queen's University Press.

Trubitt, Mary Beth D. 2003. Mississippian Period Warfare and Palisade Construction at Cahokia. In *Theory, Method, and Practice in Modern Archaeology*, ed. Robert J. Jeske and Douglas K. Charles, 148–62. Westport, Conn.: Praeger.

Turner, Christy G., II, and Jacqueline A. Turner. 1990. Perimortem Damage to Human Skeletal Remains from Wupatki National Monument. *Kiva* 55 (3): 187–212.

———. 1999. *Man Corn: Cannibalism and Violence in the Prehistoric American Southwest*. Salt Lake City: University of Utah Press.

Turney-High, Harry H. 1949. *Primitive War*. Columbia: University of South Carolina Press.

Tyrrell, J. B., ed. 1931. *Documents Relating to the Early History of Hudson Bay*. Toronto: Champlain Society.

Tyson, R. A. 1977. Historical Accounts as Aids to Physical Anthropology: Examples of Head Injury in Baja California. *Pacific Coast Archaeological Society Quarterly* 13:52–58.

Urcid, J. 1994. Cannibalism and Curated Skulls: Bone Ritualism on Kodiak Island. In *Reckoning with the Dead: The Larsen Bay Repatriation and the Smithsonian Institution*, ed. Tamara L. Bray and Thomas W. Killion, 101–21. Washington, D.C.: Smithsonian Institution Press.

Vancouver, George. 1801. *A Voyage of Discovery to the North Pacific Ocean, and Round the World: In Which the Coast of North-West America has been Carefully Examined and Accurately Surveyed: Undertaken by His Majesty's Command, Principally with a View to Ascertain the Existence of Any Navigable Communication between the North Pacific and North Atlantic Oceans; And Performed in the Years 1790, 1791, 1792, 1793, 1794 and 1795, in the Discovery Sloop of War, and Armed Tender Chatham, under the Command of Captain George Vancouver*. London: John Stockdale.

VanStone, James W. 1967. *Eskimos of the Nushagak River: An Ethnographic History*. Seattle: University of Washington Press.

———, ed. 1973. *V. S. Khromchenko's Coastal Explorations in Southwestern Alaska, 1822*, trans. David H. Kraus. Fieldiana Anthropology vol. 64. Chicago: Field Museum of Natural History.

————, ed. 1977. *A. F. Kashevarov's Coastal Explorations in Northwest Alaska, 1838*, trans. David H. Kraus. Fieldiana Anthropology vol. 69. Chicago: Field Museum of Natural History.

————, ed. 1978. *E. W. Nelson's Notes on the Indians of the Yukon and Innoko Rivers, Alaska*. Fieldiana Anthropology vol. 70. Chicago: Field Museum of Natural History.

————. 1979a. Athapaskan-Eskimo Relations in West-Central Alaska: An Ethnohistorical Perspective. *Arctic Anthropology* 16 (2): 152–59.

————. 1979b. *Ingalik Contact Ecology: An Ethnohistory of the Lower–Middle Yukon, 1790–1935*. Fieldiana Anthropology vol. 71. Chicago: Field Museum of Natural History.

————, ed. 1988. *Russian Exploration in Southwest Alaska: The Travel Journals of Petr Korsakovskiy (1818) and Ivan Ya. Vasilev (1829)*, trans. David H. Kraus. Rasmuson Library Historical Translation Series no. 4. Fairbanks: University of Alaska Press.

VanStone, James W., and Ives Goddard. 1981. Territorial Groups of West-Central Alaska before 1898. In *Handbook of North American Indians*. Vol. 6: *Subarctic*, ed. June Helm, 556–61. Washington, D.C.: Smithsonian Institution Press.

Vargas-Cetina, Gabriela. 2003. Representations of Indigenousness. *Anthropology News* 44 (5): 11–12.

Varien, M. S., W. D. Lipe, M. A. Adler, I. M. Thompson, and B. A. Bradley. 1996. Southwest Colorado and Southeast Utah Settlement Patterns, A.D. 1100–1300. In *The Prehistoric Pueblo World, A.D. 1150–1350*, ed. Michael A. Adler, 86–113. Tucson: University of Arizona Press.

Varner, John G., and Jeannette J. Varner, trans. and eds. 1951. *The Florida of the Inca*. Austin: University of Texas Press.

Vayda, Andrew P. 1974. Warfare in Ecological Perspective. *Annual Review of Ecology and Systematics* 5:183–93.

Wagner, Henry R. 1929. *Spanish Voyages to the Northwest Coast in the Sixteenth Century*. San Francisco: California Historical Society.

Walens, Stanley. 1981. *Feasting with Cannibals: An Essay on Kwakiutl Cosmology*. Princeton, N.J.: Princeton University Press.

Walker, Phillip L. 1989. Cranial Injuries as Evidence of Violence in Prehistoric Southern California. *American Journal of Physical Anthropology* 80:313–23.

————. 1990. Tool Marks on Skeletal Remains from Saunaktuk (NgTn-1). In *Archaeological Investigations at Saunaktuk*, ed. C. D. Arnold, 114–23. Yellowknife: Prince of Wales Northern Heritage Center, Department of Culture and Communications, Government of the Northwest Territories.

————. 2000. Bioarchaeological Ethics: A Historical Perspective on the Value of Human Remains. In *Biological Anthropology of the Human Skeleton*, ed. M. Anne Katzenberg and Shelley R. Saunders, 3–39. New York: Wiley-Liss.

Walker, Phillip L., and John R. Johnson. 1992. Effects of Contact on the Chumash Indians. In *Disease and Demography in the Americas*, ed. John W. Verano and Douglas H. Ubelaker, 127–39. Washington, D.C.: Smithsonian Institution.

————. 1994. The Decline of the Chumash Indian Population. In *In the Wake of Contact: Biological Responses to Contact*, ed. Clark S. Larsen and George R. Milner, 109–20. New York: Wiley-Liss.

———. 2003. For Everything There Is a Season: Chumash Indian Births, Marriages, and Deaths at the Alta California Missions. In *Human Biologists in the Archives: Demography, Health, Nutrition, and Genetics in Historical Populations*, ed. D. Ann Herring and Alan C. Swedlund, 53–77. Cambridge, U.K.: Cambridge University Press.

Walker, Phillip L., and Patricia M. Lambert. 1989. Skeletal Evidence for Stress during a Period of Cultural Change in Prehistoric California. In *Advances in Paleopathology*. Journal of Paleopathology: Monographic Publication 1. Chieti, Italy: Marino Solfanelli.

Wallis, Wilson D., and Micha Titiev. 1945. Hopi Notes from Chimopavi. In *Papers of the Michigan Academy of Science, Arts, and Letters* 30, 523–55. Ann Arbor: University of Michigan Press.

Walthall, John A. 1980. *Prehistoric Indians of the Southeast.* Tuscaloosa: University of Alabama Press.

Waring, Antonio J., Jr. 1968. The Southern Cult and Muskhogean Ceremonial. In *The Waring Papers: The Collected Works of Antonio J. Waring, Jr.*, ed. Stephen Williams, 30–69. Papers of the Peabody Museum of American Archaeology and Ethnology, vol. 58. Cambridge, Mass.: Harvard University.

Watson, Patty J. 1989. Early Plant Cultivation in the Eastern Woodlands of North America. In *Foraging and Farming*, ed. David R. Harris and G. C. Hillman, 555–71. London: Unwin Hyman.

Webb, William S., and David L. DeJarnette. 1942. *An Archeological Survey of the Pickwick Basin in the Adjacent Portions of the States of Alabama, Mississippi and Tennessee.* Bureau of American Ethnology Bulletin 129. Washington, D.C.: Smithsonian Institution.

Webster, David. 1999. Ancient Maya Warfare. In *War and Society in the Ancient and Medieval Worlds*, ed. Kurt Raaflaub and Nathan Rosenstein, 333–60. Cambridge, Mass.: Center for Hellenic Studies, Harvard University.

Wedel, Waldo. 1941. Archaeological Investigations at Buena Vista Lake, Kern County, California. *Bureau of American Ethnology Bulletin* 130:1–171. Washington, D.C.: Smithsonian Institution.

White, Chris. 1974. Lower Colorado River Area Aboriginal Warfare and Alliance Dynamics. In *'Antap: California Indian Political and Economic Organization*, ed. Lowell John Bean and Thomas F. King, 113–35. Ramona, Calif.: Ballena Press.

White, Leslie A. 1932. The Acoma Indians. In *Forty-Seventh Annual Report of the Bureau of American Ethnology, 1929–1930*, 17–192. Washington, D.C.: Government Printing Office.

———. 1935. *The Pueblo of Santo Domingo, New Mexico.* Memoirs of the American Anthropological Association 43. Menasha, Wisc.

White, Timothy D. 1992. *Prehistoric Cannibalism at Mancos 5MTUMR-2346.* Princeton, N.J.: Princeton University Press.

Wiberg, Randy S. 1988. *The Santa Rita Village Mortuary Complex (CA-ALA-413): Evidence and Implications of a Meganos Intrusion.* Archives of California Prehistory no. 18. Salinas, Calif.: Coyote Press.

Wike, Joyce A. 1951. *The Effect of the Maritime Fur Trade on Northwest Coast Indian Society.* Ph.D. dissertation in political science, Colombia University.

———. 1958. Problems in Fur Trade Analysis: The Northwest Coast. *American Anthropologist* 60:1086–1101.

Wilcox, David R., and Jonathan Haas. 1994. The Scream of the Butterfly: Competition and Conflict in the Prehistoric Southwest. In *Themes in Southwest Prehistory*, ed. George J. Gumerman, 211–38. Santa Fe, N.Mex.: School of American Research Press.

Wilcox, David R., Gerald Robertson Jr., and J. Scott Wood. 2001. Antecedents to Perry Mesa: Early Pueblo III Defensive Refuge Systems in West-Central Arizona. In *Deadly Landscapes: Case Studies in Prehistoric Southwestern Warfare*, ed. Glen E. Rice and Steven A. LeBlanc, 109–40. Salt Lake City: University of Utah Press.

Willey, Patrick S. 1990. *Prehistoric Warfare on the Great Plains*. New York: Garland.

Willey, Patrick, and W. M. Bass. 1978. A Scalped Skull from Pawnee County. *Kansas Anthropological Association Newsletter* 24.

Willey, Patrick, and Thomas E. Emerson. 1993. The Osteology and Archaeology of the Crow Creek Massacre. In *Prehistory and Human Ecology of the Western Prairies and Northern Plains*, ed. Joseph A. Tiffany, 227–69. Plains Anthropologist 38 (no. 145, Memoir 27): 27–69.

Williams, Glyndwr. 1969. Introduction. In *Andrew Graham's Observation on Hudson's Bay, 1767–1791*, ed. Glyndwr Williams, xiii–lxxii. London: Hudson's Bay Record Society.

Williams, John A. 1991. Evidence of Scalping from a Woodland Cemetery on the Northern Plains. *American Journal of Physical Anthropology* (supplement) 12:184.

———. 1994. Disease Profiles of Archaic and Woodland Populations in the Northern Plains. In *Skeletal Biology in the Great Plains: Migration, Warfare, Health, and Subsistence*, ed. Douglas W. Owsley and Richard L. Jantz, 91–108. Washington, D.C.: Smithsonian Institution Press.

Williamson, Matthew A., Cheryl A. Johnston, Steven A. Symes, and John J. Schultz. 2003. Interpersonal Violence between 18th Century Native Americans and Europeans in Ohio. In *American Journal of Physical Anthropology* 122:113–22.

Wilson, Richard. 1991. Machine Guns and Mountain Spirits. *Critique of Anthropology* 11 (1): 33–61.

Winham, R. Peter, and F. A. Calabrese. 1998. The Middle Missouri Tradition. In *Archaeology on the Great Plains*, ed. W. Raymond Wood, 269–307. Lawrence: University of Kansas Press.

Winship, George Parker. 1896. *The Coronado Expedition, 1540–1542*. 14th Annual Report of the Bureau of American Ethnology. Washington, D.C.: Government Printing Office.

Woodbury, Anthony C. 1984. Eskimo and Aleut Languages. In *Handbook of North American Indians*. Vol. 5: *Arctic*, ed. David Damas, 49–63. Washington, D.C.: Smithsonian Institution.

Work, John. 1945. *The Journal of John Work*. Introduction and notes by Henry Drummond Dee. Victoria, B.C.: C. F. Banfield.

Worth, John. 1998. *Timucuan Chiefdoms of Spanish Florida*. 2 vols. Gainesville: University Press of Florida.

Wright, Barton. 1973. *Kachinas: A Hopi Artist's Documentary*. Flagstaff, Ariz: Northland Publishing, with the Heard Museum.

Wright, Henry T. 1984. Prestate Political Formations. In *On the Evolution of Complex Societies: Essays in Honor of Harry Hoijer, 1982*, ed. Timothy K. Earle, 41–77. Malibu, Calif.: Undena Publications.

Yates, Lorenzo G. 1887. Transcript of interviews with Justo Gonzales, January 1887. J. P. Harrington Collection, Santa Barbara Museum of Natural History.

————. 1891. Fragments of the History of a Lost Tribe. *American Anthropologist* (o.s.) 4:373–76. Washington, D.C.: Anthropological Society of Washington.

Young, M. Jane. 1992. Morning Star, Evening Star: Zuni Traditional Stories. In *Earth and Sky: Visions of the Cosmos in Native American Folklore*, ed. Ray A. Williamson and Claire R. Farrer, 75–109. Albuquerque: University of New Mexico Press.

Zimmerman, Larry J., and Lawrence E. Bradley. 1993. The Crow Creek Massacre: Initial Coalescent Warfare and Speculations about the Genesis of Extended Coalescent. *Plains Anthropologist* 38:215–26.

ABOUT THE CONTRIBUTORS

CHARLES A. BISHOP is a research professor in anthropology at Union College, Schenectady, New York. He has conducted ethnohistorical research among northern Algonquian-speaking Ojibwa and Cree and the Athapaskan-speaking Carrier through the use of historical records, especially of those of the Hudson's Bay Company on the fur trade.

ERNEST S. BURCH JR. is a research associate of the Arctic Studies Center, Smithsonian Institution. He has conducted ethnographic fieldwork in northwestern Alaska and the central Canadian subarctic. His primary research interest in recent years has been the early-contact-period social organization of Eskimo and northern Athapaskan peoples.

RICHARD J. CHACON is an assistant professor of anthropology at Winthrop University, South Carolina. He has conducted ethnographic fieldwork in Amazonia among the Yanomamö of Venezuela, the Yora of Peru, and the Achuar (Shiwiar) of Ecuador, and he has also worked in the Andes with the Otavalo and Cotacachi Indians of highland Ecuador. His research interests include optimal foraging theory, indigenous subsistence strategies, warfare, belief systems, ethnohistory, and the effects of globalization.

DAVID H. DYE is an associate professor of earth sciences at the University of Memphis in Tennessee. He has conduced archaeological research throughout the southeastern United States. His research interests include the archaeology and ethnohistory of the Mid-South. He has had a long-term interest in late prehistoric warfare, ritual, and iconography in the Eastern Woodlands.

THOMAS E. EMERSON is an adjunct professor of anthropology and director of the Transportation Archaeological Research Program at the University of Illinois, Urbana. He has conducted archaeological excavations throughout eastern and central North America. His research interests include the archaeology and ethnohistory of North America as well as theoretical aspects of the ideology, religions, and political economy of complex societies.

JOHN R. JOHNSON is the curator of anthropology at the Santa Barbara Museum of Natural History in California. His research interests include the culture and history of the Chumash Indians and their neighbors in south-central California through the study of archaeology, archival records, and interviews with contemporary Native Americans.

ADAM KING is an anthropologist at the South Carolina Institute of Archaeology and Anthropology in Columbia, South Carolina. He has conducted archaeological excavations throughout North America. His research interests include the archaeology, ethnology, and ethnohistory of the Southeast.

PATRICIA M. LAMBERT is an associate professor of anthropology at Utah State University. She has conducted bioarchaeological research in several regions of North America and in northern coastal Peru. Her research interests include New World bioarchaeology, prehistoric warfare, and paleopathology.

JOAN A. LOVISEK is a consulting research anthropologist specializing in ethnohistory; she heads Lovisek Research, which provides treaty and aboriginal rights research and is based in British Columbia, Canada. Her research interests include the First Nations of Canada.

VICTOR P. LYTWYN is the head of Historical and Geographical Consulting Services (in Orangeville, Ontario), a company that specializes in aboriginal and treaty rights in Canada. His research interests include the Hudson Bay Lowland Cree and the Council of Three Fires (Ojibwa, Ottawa, and Potawatomi) of the Great Lakes region.

RUBÉN G. MENDOZA is an archaeologist and professor of social and behavioral sciences at California State University–Monterey Bay. He has conducted archaeological excavations in California, Colorado, and Arizona and in Guanajuato and Puebla, Mexico. His research interests include Mesoamerican and South American civilizations and Hispanic, Native American, and mestizo traditional technologies and material cultures of the U.S. Southwest. He currently serves as the director for the California State University–Monterey Bay's Institute for Archaeological Science, Technology, and Visualization.

GEORGE R. MILNER is a professor of anthropology at Pennsylvania State University. He has directed numerous excavations of prehistoric villages and cemeteries in eastern North America. His research interests include human osteology, especially the life experience of past peoples, which has involved studies of skeletons from North America, Europe, Egypt, and Oceania.

POLLY SCHAAFSMA is an archaeologist at the Museum of Indian Arts and Culture/Laboratory of Anthropology of the Museum of New Mexico. She has conducted excavations and surveys throughout southwestern North America. Her research interests include rock art and belief systems along with documenting the presence of Mesoamerican influence in the Southwest.

DEAN R. SNOW is a professor and head of anthropology at Pennsylvania State University. His research interests include the archaeology and ethnohistory of the Northeast, with an emphasis on the Iroquois.

INDEX

Acoma, 127
Adair, James, 225
Aglurmiut (Yup'ik), 28
Algonquian, 33
Ames, Kenneth, 62
Anasazi, 116–117
Anderson, David, 164–165
Angel (site), 187
Anileo, 169
Apaches, 126
Athapaskan/Athabaskan, 14, 18–29, 219
Aztalan, 137

Barbareño language, 105
Barí, 152
Battle Cave, 209, 220

battles, open, 18, 23–25, 98, 102–103
Beale, Anthony, 44, 51
Bella Coola (Heiltsuk), 66, 70
Benedict, Ruth, 114, 158
Bird, Louis, 36–38, 42–43
Bishop, Charles A., 6
Blackburn, Thomas, 98
Black Hawk, 228
Boas, Franz, 58, 72
Boyd, Robert, 65
Brain, Jeffrey, 174, 180
Brandão, José António, 157
Brant, Joseph, 158
Brower, Charles, 17
Brown, Alan, 88
Brown, James, 172

Buisson de Sainte-Cosme, Jean-François, 166
Bunzel, Ruth, 123
Burch, Ernest S., Jr., 6, 29
Burger, Richard, 118

Cabeza de Vaca, Alvar Núñez, 225, 229
Cabrillo, Juan Rodríguez, 79–80, 111
Cahokia, 8, 133–148
Cahuilla, 78
cannibalism, 37, 52, 56, 70, 117, 203, 210–212, 218–219; ritual cannibalism, 41, 55, 57
Carneiro, Robert, 131, 146–147, 197
Casas Grandes, 211–213, 220
Casqui, 168–170
Castle Rock, 211, 220
Catlin, George, 225
Cayuga, 150
Chaco Canyon, 210
Chacon, Richard, 9
Champlain, Samuel de, 225
Chappell, Edward, 49–50
Cheyenne, 228
chiefdom, 8–9, 133, 145–147, 165–166, 185, 187, 190, 196–197
chieftaincies, 144–146
Chipewyan, 43, 57
Chucalissa, 178–180
Chumash, 7, 74–113
Coats, William, 37, 50
Cochimí, 78
Codere, Helen, 6, 58–59, 62–73
Cofaqui, 166–167
Cofitachequi, 166–167, 169
Cojti Ren, A. Vexnim, 223, 229
Conklin, Beth, 226–227
Cook, Sherburne, 111
Coronado, Francisco Vasquez de, 225, 229
Coupland, Gary, 64
Cowboy Wash, 10
Creamer, Winifred, 114
Cree, 6
Crespí, Juan, 83–86
Crouseo (Crusoe), Robinson, 44, 57

Crow Creek massacre, 130, 136, 138, 140, 213–214, 220
Cupeño, 78
Cybulski, Jerome, 62, 217–218

de Añasco, Juan, 166
de la Potherie, Bacqueville, 39
de la Vega, Garcilaso, 166–170, 229
Deloria, Vine, 223, 226
DePratter, Chester, 165
desecration, 8, 160–181, 189
de Soto, Hernando, 161, 166–170, 190, 224–225, 229
Dos Pueblos, 87–89, 102, 109
Duck River cache, 172
Duff, Wilson, 65
Duggan, Marie C., 113
Dye, David, 8

Eastern Woodlands, 8–9, 150, 162, 183–200, 215, 218, 220
Edwards, Fred, 135
"El Buchón," 84–86, 109
Ellis, Henry, 39, 43, 49
Ember, Carol and Melvin, 19, 32, 50–51, 82
Emerson, Thomas E., 7–8
Engelhardt, Zephyrin, 88–89
epidemics, 8, 46, 58, 66–68, 70–71, 102, 104–105, 111, 152–154
Eries, 150, 153–154
Eskimo: Alaskan, 6, 14–29; Hudson/James Bay, see Inuit, Hudson/James Bay
Etowah, 173–176, 180

Fages, Pedro, 80, 82, 91
Fay Tolten, 213, 220
Ferguson, R. Brian, 118, 231
Fewkes, Jesse Walter, 122
Fienup-Riordan, Ann, 28
firearms. See guns
fortifications, 7, 17–18, 62–64, 72, 116–117, 129–130, 135–137, 146, 162, 164, 172–174, 177, 184–191, 196–197, 211, 215
Francis, Daniel, 46
Francisco de Lasuén, Fermín, 90

Freeman, Donald, 57
Fremont population, 116, 211–212

Gabrielino, 78
Garcés, Francisco, 225
Geertz, Clifford, 127
Given, Brian, 41
Goicoechea, 91–92, 95, 112
Gonzales, Justo, 102–104
Graham, Andrew, 34, 39–42, 50, 54, 56
Great Plains, 203, 212–215, 220
Guachoyas, 168–169
Guldenzopf, D. B, 158
guns, 8, 41–43, 49, 51, 55, 65–66, 138, 153, 216

Haas, Jonathan, 114
Habicht-Mauche, Judith, 126
Haida, 62, 64
Harrington, John, 100, 110
Hasinai Caddo, 160–161
Hassler, Peter, 223
health, precontact, 140
Heizer, Robert, 223
Hobbes, Thomas, 131, 200
Hodgson, John, 48
Hopewell, 195
Hopi, 120, 122–123, 125, 127
Horne, Stephen, 89, 111
Hoxie Farm, 137
Hudson's Bay Company (HBC), 33–57,
    67–68
human trophies, 6–8, 58–59, 64, 66, 70, 72,
    116, 151, 163, 179, 203–205, 208–209,
    211, 213, 220; taken by British, 47
Hunt, George T., 58, 157–158
hunter-gatherers, 9, 16, 31–33, 60, 80,
    108, 117, 133, 143, 146, 185, 187,
    191–192, 205
Hurons, 150, 153–154, 159, 189
Hurst, Winston, 116
Hutchins, Thomas, 47
Hymahi, 166–167

iconography: See under Iroquois;
    Mississippian; Pueblo cosmology

Ineseño language, 105
Inuit, 219; Alaska, 17–18, 27; Hudson/
    James Bay, 6, 32–57
Iroquois, 8, 33, 50, 149–158, 189, 197;
    iconography, 152–153
Isbister, Joseph, 49, 57
Isham, James, 34

James, Edward, 46
Jarvis, Edward, 52
Jeremie, Nicholas, 37, 39
Johnson, John R., 7
Jonathan Creek site, 173, 180
Jorgenson, Joseph, 75–77
José María, 90

kachinas, 118–119, 125
Keeley, Lawrence, 77, 130, 139, 183
Kelly, Raymond, 32
Kennett, Douglas, 206
"Kennewick Man," 217
King, Adam, 8, 174
Kino, Eusebio Francisco, 225
Kitanemuk, 110, 112
Knight, James, 34, 36–39, 56–57
Koger's Island, 215
Koyukon, 22
Kroeber, Alfred, 102, 110, 200
Kwakiutl, 58–60, 64–73

Lafiteau, Joseph, 225
Lambert, Patricia, 9, 63
Langford Tradition, 146
Larson site, 220
League of the Iroquois. See Iroquois
LeBlanc, Steven, 115–116, 209–210
Librado, Fernando Kitsepawit, 100
"Little Ice Age," 9, 29, 36, 197, 220
Longinos Martínez, José, 80, 82
Lovisek, Joan A., 6–7, 232
Lowland Cree, 32–57
Lowrey, Nathan, 63
Luiseño language, 78
Lytwyn, Victor, 6

magic. *See* sorcery
Marquette, Jacques, 225
Marten, Humphrey, 46–47
Maschner, Herbert, 63
Material Service Quarry, 138
Mauss, Marcel, 59
McCorkle, Thomas, 75–77
Means, Russell, 6, 224
Mendoza, Ruben G., 9
Milner, George R., 8–9, 139
Mississippian, 7–8, 129–148, 162–181, 184,
        216; iconography, 140–142, 170
Mohave, 75
Mohawks, 150, 153–154, 158
Monks Mound, 134, 137
Montagnais. *See* Cree
Montejo, Victor, 223, 224
Montes, Catarino, 102
Morantz, Toby, 46
Munk, Jens, 34
Myatt, Joseph, 44–45

Nash, Charles, 178
Navajos, 126
neutrals, 150, 153–154
Neve, Felipe de, 80, 88, 91
nomads, Plains, 126, 228–229
Nootka (Nuu-chah-nulth), 65
Norris Farms cemetery, 130, 136, 138–
        140, 198, 200, 216
Nottaway. *See* Iroquois

Ocute, 166
Ojibwa, 44
Oldmixon, John, 37
Omahas, 228
Omushkegok, 36–38
Oneidas, 150
Oneotas, 137, 198, 216
Onondagas, 150
open battles, 18, 23–25, 98, 102–103
Ottawas, 50
Otterbein, Keith, 30–31, 149–150, 226

Pacaha, 168–169

Paiutes, 126
Parsons, Elsie Clews, 123
Patofa, 166–167
Pauketat, Timothy, 133
Pecos, 229
Petuns, 150, 154
Phillips, Philip, 174
Pico, Juan Estevan, 100
Pinson Cave, 215, 220
Piro, 122, 126
Plains nomads, 126, 228–229
Plog, Stephen, 125
Polhemus, Richard, 172–173
Pomoan, 75
population changes, 9, 25, 27, 55, 58,
        62–68, 71, 73, 104–105, 117, 130,
        191–200, 206–207, 220
Portolá, Gaspar de, 83–95
potlatch, 6, 58–59, 67–73
Potts, John, 44
Potts, Richard, 47–48
Powhatan, 166
prestige, 8, 50, 63–64, 67, 130, 143–
        144, 150–151, 157–159, 163,
        180, 228
Pueblo 7, 114–128, 158, 208–212, 229;
        cosmology, 119–125, 127
Purisimeño language, 105

Quechan (Yuma), 75

Radisson, Pierre, 153
Ray, Arthur, 57
Redmond, Elsa, 145
Reedy-Maschner, K. L., 63
*Report of the Royal Commission on
        Aboriginal Peoples*, 59
revenge, 7, 19, 27–28, 32, 48–51, 66–67,
        77, 82–83, 107, 126, 151, 153, 159,
        163, 167, 183
Reyna, Stephen, 31
Riches, David, 63–64
Rivera y Moncada, Fernando, 87–88
Robson, Joseph, 34, 42
Rosman, Abraham, 68

Rousseau, Jean-Jacques, 130, 200
Rubel, Paula, 68

Sabo, George, 169–170
Salish, 62, 64–66
Sand Canyon Pueblo, 211, 220
Saquot, 48, 52
Sauk, 228
Saunaktuk, 219–220
scalping, 39–40, 44, 50, 56–57, 87, 101, 111,
    115–116, 119, 122–123, 128, 139,
    167, 196, 211, 214–217, 223, 228
scalps as fetish, 123, 128
Schaarfsma, Polly, 7
Senan, Jose, 82–83, 86
Senecas, 150, 154
Serrano, 78
shield magic, 116–120
Shoshone, 199
Sillitoe, Paul, 56
Sioux, 228
slaves, 7, 38, 46, 48, 59, 62–73, 229
Smith, Bruce, 193
Smith, Maria, 199
Snow, Dean R., 8
Solometo, Julie, 125
sorcery, 6–7, 18, 32, 48–51, 55, 77, 108,
    126, 151, 184. See also scalps as
    fetish; shield magic
Spence, George, 57
Spencer, Herbert, 131
Susquehannocks, 150

Takic, 78
Tataviam, 78
Taylor, Alexander, 89–90
Temple, Robert, 44
territorial acquisition, 6, 19, 49, 53, 74
terrorist forays, 18–20, 25
Tiwa, 122, 126–127
Tlingit, 62, 64, 67
Toqua, 172–173, 180
Towosahgy, 177–180
tribes, 60, 186–187

Trigger, Bruce, 42
Troyes, Pierre de, 38
Tsimshian, 67
Turner, Christy, 116, 210
Turner, Jacqueline, 210
Turney-High, Harry, 183

Utes, 126
Uto-Aztecan languages, 78, 110

Vancouver, George, 64
Ventureño language, 105, 109–110

Wakashan, 67
Walens, Stanley, 70–71
Waorani, 152
war, definition of, 4, 131–132, 183–184
Warden, Matthew, 47
Wausakeeshick, 48
weapons descriptions, 18, 24–25, 42, 56,
    63, 65, 98, 118, 130, 137–138, 184,
    195–196, 205–207, 209, 214, 218,
    220. See also guns
Wenros, 150
Wetherill's Cave, 209, 220
White, Leslie, 127
Whitehead, Neil, 231
Willey, Pat, 139–140
Winter Ceremonial, 6–7, 69–73
Witchcraft. See sorcery
Wolf, Marvin, 6, 224
Wright, 148

Yanomamö, 205–206
Yates, Lorenzo, 104
Ygnacio, Luisa, 100–101
Yojuanes, 160–161
Yokuts, 7, 75, 91, 94, 100, 102
Yuman, 75, 78, 107–109
Yup'ik, 28
Yurok, 75

Zuni, 120, 123

CPSIA information can be obtained at www.ICGtesting.com
Printed in the USA
LVOW060404180112

264342LV00002B/3/P